Mentoring-Coaching

A guide for education professionals

Mentoring-Coaching

A guide for education professionals

Roger Pask and Barrie Joy

Open University Press

Open University Press
McGraw-Hill Education
McGraw-Hill House
Shoppenhangers Road
Maidenhead
Berkshire
England
SL6 2QL

email: enquiries@openup.co.uk
world wide web: www.openup.co.uk

and Two Penn Plaza, New York, NY 10121-2289, USA

First published 2007

A catalogue record of this book is available from the British Library

ISBN-13 978 0 335 22538 5 (pb) 978 0 335 22539 2 (hb)
ISBN-10 335 22538 1 (pb) 0 335 22539 X (hb)

Library of Congress Cataloging-in-Publication Data
CIP data applied for

Typeset by RefineCatch Limited, Bungay, Suffolk
Printed in the UK by Bell and Bain Ltd, Glasgow

The *McGraw·Hill* Companies

Contents

Acknowledgements

The insights that have led to the writing of this book have been generated in a number of ways that the writers wish to acknowledge. They have come from two main sources. The first is the stream of thinking developed by writers and researchers over a period of more than a hundred years. The second main source is comprised of colleagues with whom the writers have worked and who have been willing to share their thinking and practice in a spirit of generosity that has made working in this field extremely rewarding.

The research and writing upon which the contents of this book have drawn divide broadly into three main streams, two of which have merged in recent times. These two have been concerned mainly with the field of education – in particular with the fascinating subject of human learning – and the linked issues of leadership and management. A full list of all the texts on both subjects from which this writing has drawn is included in the references. It is important however to give prominence in these acknowledgements to the writing of David Kolb, and to the writing and personal influence of Chris Watkins at the Institute of Education, London University. For a while Chris was doctoral supervisor for one of the authors and over a longer period has been an influential colleague for both writers. He has been a mentor-coach in the true sense of posing questions that have made us think – including the seminal question of what is meant by the word 'learning'.

Equally influential on the subject of leadership has been the extensive writing of Michael Fullan.

The third stream may have begun with the theses of Sigmund Freud who probed beneath the surface of human consciousness. He not only developed the discipline of psychoanalysis practically from scratch but also began a trail of thinking that led via Carl Rogers and others through the emergence of psychotherapy and counselling to the work of Gerard Egan. This book owes a debt to Egan and to the whole concept of 'the helper' articulated in depth and considerable detail in *The Skilled Helper* (2002). The London Leadership Centre was introduced to the work of Egan by Ann Dering from the Centre for Educational Leadership in Manchester. It was Ann who showed how relevant Egan's work could be in the field of educational leadership, and upon whose applications this book has considerably expanded.

Many other strands of thinking flowed from Freud's work that have threaded their way into this book. They include the work of David McClelland and of Daniel Goleman, whose work on social motives and emotional intelligence competencies has been applied to the process of mentoring-coaching. Lastly, in this web of writing is the seminal research by Umberto Maturana and Francisco Varela, and the highly readable thesis of Antonio Damasio. Both these works explore the foundations of human consciousness and supplement the thinking of Carl Rogers on what it might mean to be truly human.

There is a further substantial group of people to whom this book owes a debt. It includes all those people – numbering around two or three thousand – who have participated in learning about mentoring-coaching on courses that have been offered by the London Centre for Leadership in Learning and elsewhere around the country. Their active participation in the process of thinking through what it might mean to enter a mentoring-coaching relationship has been part of the extensive research process that has helped shape what is written in the pages that follow. Similarly, people with whom members of the Centre's team have worked as mentor-coaches have caused us to think deeply about the uniqueness of each new such relationship. Sometimes this has provided a high level of emotional, social and intellectual challenge. Most importantly it has also generated deep affirmation of the power and value of the process.

The book also owes a considerable debt to all those colleagues – numbering around twenty at the Centre and many more through the National College for School Leadership – with whom we have worked as co-facilitators on courses in mentor-coaching or the closely related courses on client-centred or process consultancy. A particular contribution has been made by Kay Bedford, Head of Swiss Cottage Special School in London. Kay has contributed a great deal of thinking to the course. She has also exemplified some of the critical skills involved in mentoring-coaching and, perhaps most importantly, has demonstrated on a day-to-day basis in her school at all levels, including work by her staff among pupils with acute special needs – how a culture of mentoring-coaching can be developed in an organization, and how, in such a culture, highly effective leadership and management can impact to amazingly positive effect within an organization. Her paper setting out the process of developing this culture – a continuing story – is included as a case study in Chapter 16.

All those who have co-facilitated these courses have brought their own ideas and their own skills as leaders of learning and these have often been woven into the fabric of the programmes that have been delivered in order to respond to the learning needs of particular groups of participants. Pat Clark and Howard Kennedy – senior staff at the London Leadership Centre – made major contributions to the early form of the course programme. Four facilitators, who have made a significant impact upon the shape of courses since then and upon the thinking of this book, are Julia Harper, Carol Raphael, Janet Wallace and Simon Williams. Carol's work in reading drafts of this book, in questioning parts of the meaning in order to generate greater readability and greater clarity and in helping to uncover deeper levels of thinking, has been especially valuable.

Finally, most of the work that has led to the development of the thinking that informs this book was undertaken under the auspices of the London Leadership Centre – now the London Centre for Leadership in Learning, Institute of Education, London University. The administrative team supporting that work have patiently accepted the need to collect and collate research and to reprocess many new versions of the materials used on courses in mentoring-coaching. They have given form to the expression of the thinking as it has evolved. None of that work would have been possible without the approval and support of the Founding Director of the London Leadership Centre, Dame Patricia Collarbone and her successor, Strategic Director of the London Centre for Leadership in Learning and Pro-Director of the Institute of Education, Leisha Fullick.

Throughout the development of the course and the evolution of the model we have drawn extensively on the patience and commitment of three successive administrators at LCLL – Jackie Barry, Erin Downey and Ruth Daglish. None of what has been achieved in the field and in this book would have been possible without them. As the book has neared publication the authors have been very conscious of the patient and effective support of staff of McGraw-Hill/Open University Press, and in particular the guidance and help of Fiona Richman – without whose support this book would not have been published.

As with all projects like serious writing there are personal partners and families to whom a debt is owed – of patience, encouragement and support. Attention due to them has had to be sacrificed to give time to the research and drafting that has led to the completion of this text. Without such encouragement and active support this book would not have been written.

PART 1
Mentoring-coaching: About this Book

This book is about mentoring-coaching. It shows how mentoring and coaching are so inseparably linked that they are best viewed as a single process. Hence the hyphen.

Research has indicated that there is much for organizations to gain by building mentoring-coaching into the daily practice of leaders and managers at all levels and in all kinds of organization. In work undertaken by Hay McBer and by Daniel Goleman et al. (2002), coaching styles of leadership have been shown to correlate significantly with high levels of performance – output and profits in the private sector, and sustained high standards in public service organizations. The link with sports coaching is highly appealing to many and it might be seen as 'sexy' to have a regular coach regardless of the field of work. In some contexts – for example public service organizations – staff at all levels of responsibility have a contractual duty to coach other staff. It is not uncommon even for people to have a 'life coach'. Coaching is in vogue, but what exactly is it?

Mentoring, a much older and broader concept, has waned somewhat in popularity with the advent of coaching and in some respects is undergoing an identity crisis. Linked variously and unevenly with induction, longer-term training and supervision, career grooming and even patronage in some quarters, it also has traditional associations with individual pastoral support and personal development. More recently it has seen a resurgence in some fields – education, for instance, where 'learning mentors' feature increasingly in many schools. But what exactly is mentoring? Is it the same as coaching, merely another name for the same process? Though they are inseparably linked, this book will show that they are distinct processes, or rather distinctive parts of a single process: mentoring-coaching.

The book explains the nature of the process and its two main parts, and sets out a proven model that is holistic and practical. It aims to help busy professionals to chart their way through a process that can seem complex and time consuming but which is in fact easy to follow and highly cost-effective.

This is a practitioners' book. It is not just *about* mentoring, coaching or even mentoring-coaching. It aims to show *how to* mentor-coach – to present a memorable model and a stage-by-stage guide on how to proceed, including some sample ways of exercising the essential skills, especially listening and questioning. It also aims to show how a client can get the best from the process, as an equal partner.

It is written for three main audiences. The first is the growing group of professionals who have taken part in the courses that have been offered by the London Centre for Leadership in Learning at the Institute of Education, University of London. The number of people from a wide range of backgrounds who have taken part in this programme runs into thousands. The standard course is of three days duration, at the end of which most participants can begin to implement the model and develop the essential skills through thoughtful and self-analytical practice. The book is intended to serve as an aid to memory for such participants and an anchor for some of the disciplines required to become a highly skilled mentor-coach. These disciplines – though not hard to identify and begin to practise – are frighteningly easy to default from. The book aims to help resist that tendency and to provide a way to deepen the learning.

The second audience is that group of people, especially though not exclusively in education, who have heard that coaching is a very important leadership/managerial skill/practice and want to know more about how to build it into their working style without having to read extensively or obtain formal qualifications.

The third, and in some ways most important group, is made up of people who can gain clarity of thinking and clear paths to action through the role of client in the mentoring-coaching process.

Over time the three audiences may well, to some degree, merge.

The busy practitioner wanting to get started on a new way of working and for whom the philosophy and methodology of mentoring-coaching are appealing, will be able to make a start drawing on the support of just the first half of this book. So also will the person who has participated in one of the courses run by the Institute of Education. All audiences will find the first nine chapters intensely practical. The format of Chapters 3 to 9 aims to facilitate reading in 'bits' – on the tube or bus, for example. Each of the chapters provides practical help in formulating appropriate questions at the end, followed by questions to stimulate further thinking.

The need for this book also arises from the confusion generated by casual use of fine-sounding terms. As suggested earlier, the words *mentor* and *coach* have a positive ring to them. People are pleased with the thought that their activity can be labelled positively and so describe certain relationships with colleagues using words like mentor or coach without paying any particular attention to their behaviour – to what precisely it is that they do.

> Terms travel well; concepts do not. (Fullan, 2005)

It is important to distinguish mentoring and coaching from other kinds of behaviour, such as advising, telling, guiding, instructing and so on. This is not simply a matter of semantics. Each such term conveys a particular set of behaviours and each differs from the others in certain identifiable ways. Similarly, mentoring and coaching are terms that convey a distinctive set of behaviours that differ both from each other and from the sets of behaviours summarized in the other terms listed in this paragraph.

Readers need to be able to identify the distinct behaviour sets – in summary, the concepts which need to travel with these terms if their use is to have clear value, meaning and purpose.

> Calling oneself a mentor or coach does not make one so, any more than calling oneself a genius. It is behaviour that distinguishes. (Pask, 2005)

This is a book about behaviour.

The purpose of it is then to explore a particular view of the interlinked terms 'mentoring' and 'coaching' with a degree of rigour. It aims to help readers who wish to develop their own thinking about how to apply them. It is based on a passionate commitment to respect for all other human beings as a right. Readers are encouraged to apply these concepts and behaviours in a respectful and structured manner.

On a cautionary note, this is not an instruction manual. The model and the values underpinning it demand that the mentor-coach and the partner in this process engage in serious thinking. It would be disrespectful and manipulative to ask professional people, or indeed any other human being, to engage in this kind of process in a rigid procedural way. The book also eschews instrumental thinking. It is not about how to gain compliance from others. To distort the terms mentoring and coaching and the associated concepts into practices designed to manipulate people in their work or in their private lives can be both disempowering and abusive.

Yet the book promotes 'alignment'. Mentoring-coaching is seen as a tool and a set of processes aimed at helping people make their very best contribution to their personal and professional contexts *and at the same time* gain profound fulfilment and a sense of becoming more of a *person* (Rogers, 1961) – in other words, becoming more truly human.

In the first chapter a very clear definition of the two linked terms is offered and some of their origins explored. This section also explores how the uniqueness of every person can be paid full respect through these linked processes.

Also introduced is the notion of a process that can be represented by a model or framework that is relatively easy to remember and that can be used as a tool to guide anyone through the potentially complex territory to be travelled.

It will be important for the reader to be alert to the fact that each person who takes on the role of mentor-coach is unique – as is each person who is being helped by this process. No formula is offered, simply a framework or scaffold, a *process* within which every practitioner and every client can work effectively by committing to build a unique response to a unique situation. There is no notion of conformity or compliance. The generic model aims to enrich individuals, situations, relationships (whether personal or professional) and communities, by identifying the need and wish to change, and thus make them all stronger.

The next seven chapters of the book deal with the start of the relationship and the six separate (and linked) stages of the model and process. Each section explains the nature and purpose of the stage in question. It relates it to other stages of the model and offers a rationale for that particular stage. It examines some of the critical skills needed to operate effectively at each point, and some of the potential pitfalls that may be encountered. It also discusses why some of what are referred to as skills may well be *competencies*, as defined by David McClelland (1973), that can be acquired and developed over time.

Other published work that an interested reader may want to study is referred to, both in the text and in the references. The references offer rich pickings to the student of this subject who wishes to probe its depths. The aim is to provide a manageable text for busy practitioners. The work on which this book draws is the subject of continuing evaluation and research. This research has had a sustained impact on the shape of the model and upon the training courses offered to prospective mentor-coaches. Chapters 3 to 8 of the book offer practical guidance based on sound theory rather than extensive theoretical exposition *per se*. Chapter 9 addresses the requirement for mentor-coach and client to attend closely to evidence generated in the process.

It is anticipated that most readers will benefit practically from reading the first part of the book and then setting it aside for a while, in order to find time to try out the model in practice, perhaps a few times, and some of the key skills in everyday work relationships. This will give them the feel of what is being considered and will also generate a number of issues/questions about the experience of working with the model. Part Two of the book aims to address a number of those issues, for example, why is it harder to work as a mentor-coach in some circumstances than others? It does not contain a compendium of such questions. Rather it looks at ideas and frameworks that have either evolved from the work undertaken by the Institute of Education or by people in similar fields. Some of the work drawn upon goes back over a hundred years, to some degree from a theoretical point of view (though 'theory' – sometimes seen as an off-putting term – consists merely of generalizations from practice that have been systematically tested and re-presented as frameworks for thinking). It is also hoped that Part Two will encourage deeper thinking by readers about their role as mentor-coach or client, and help them reflect about themselves and their own behaviours.

More of what is contained in Part Two is summarized in the introduction to that part after Chapter 9. It is important to note that Parts One and Two of the book are not respectively about the two parts of the model.

The concepts of mentoring and coaching are linked in a very special way, particularly in the model advocated, and the final chapter of the book explains how practitioners can consciously associate them as they work with their clients. The aspiration is effectively to promote the journey of a deeply respectful concept in human relationships, to the benefit not only of both parties to this process but also of those with whom they, in their turn, also relate and work.

There is a small issue of terminology to be clarified. It is the question as to what the participants in the mentoring-coaching relationship should be called. The terms 'mentor' and 'coach' are in relatively common usage. The other party to the process can be called 'client' or 'mentee-coachee', but the authors are aware of the clumsy sound of such terms, especially when linked by a hyphen. More significantly the suffix '-ee' suggests someone to whom something is done, a passive person in some ways. This is emphatically not how we perceive the mentoring-coaching relationship. The word 'client' is preferable, even though it has many other overtones, including some that are commercial. Strictly speaking, if the word 'mentor' can be extended to mean what we define it as in this book, the same could be said for the word 'client'. It means literally 'one whose cause an advocate pleads'. By extension it could equally be taken to mean 'one whose cause an advocate helps him/her plead', or 'one who is helped to plead/manage his/her own cause'. We have used the terms 'mentor-coach' and 'client' throughout.

"The choice between use of personal pronouns 'she' or 'he' has been managed by a number of devices using either randomly; using 's/he'; and by using 'he/she' and vice versa."

The book is presented as a work for people involved in education, particularly in the light of extended contractual responsibilities that many now have as 'coaches', but what is offered could equally well apply to people from *any* employment context or from none. It is 'educational' in a wide sense, though it draws some – but not all – of its genesis from education in the formal sense. Those who have been trained in the use of the model advocated frequently claim a profound impact from it upon all kinds of relationships, both professional and personal. In this sense it is truly generic. It can help readers to regain some of that ground of our humanity that has been occupied in recent times by those who seek to control the lives of others. The point behind the writing is that it unlocks the door to that elusive but highly attractive notion of 'transformation'.

1 The term 'mentoring-coaching' and the model

Common usage

Understanding terms and concepts can most readily begin with a short dictionary search. The *Shorter Oxford English Dictionary* (OED) defines a mentor as 'an experienced and trusted counsellor' and the word 'counsel' as 'an interchange of opinions'. It goes on to offer the notion of 'advice' as a further development of the meaning of 'counsel', but then suggests that 'advice' is 'the way a matter is looked at'. Further exploration of this trail may become unhelpfully esoteric. But one can see a term travelling in a way that begins to separate it from its original concept, so that it is easy for one to equate the idea of a mentor with a person who gives advice in the sense of *telling someone what to do*. The dictionary does not support that conclusion and neither does this book.

Nevertheless, the idea of a wise person who tells another what to do, gives them advice, and acts as a role model and patron is part of the substance of the way in which people think about the concept of mentor-coach. The model advocated in this book starts from a different perspective.

Roots in Greek mythology

Some people may find it helpful to refer back to the story of Ulysses and his son Telemachus who, when Ulysses was on his travels, was guided by a friend of the family named Mentor (to whom the *Shorter OED* refers in its introduction to the definition quoted earlier). Because of common usage, Mentor is envisaged as telling Telemachus how to go about becoming a wise leader of the city-state in ancient Greece. Homer's *Odyssey* supports this idea to a considerable degree. It does not, however, expound Mentor's methodology in this role. This is left to the reader to imagine.

Some later interpreters of Homer's writing suggest that the 'advice' Telemachus received from Mentor was of variable quality. This was perhaps due in part to the idea that from time to time Mentor's persona was in fact that of Athene, the goddess of wisdom and of war. She took to inhabiting him (as Greek gods were occasionally inclined to do to humans!) in order to ensure that actions were taken in the interests of the common good. When it was really Athene speaking the advice was good but when it was Mentor on his own it often didn't come out quite right. It's an enchanting story, but in the absence of modern goddesses it may take us only part of the way to a definition of the critical term – a definition already signposted clearly for us by the *OED*.

A working definition

Further search into the origin of the word may hold a more fruitful key. The word *mentor* comes from the Latin/Greek word '*mens* – a mind', and its derivative 'mentor – a thinker'. (Compare the slightly colloquial term 'minder'!) So literally a mentor is a thinker and, in the relationship to be considered in this book, helps another person also to think. This chain of thought leads to the following definition:

> A mentor is a person who helps another to think things through. (Pask, 2004)

This is a notion entirely consistent with the terms discovered in the search of the dictionary set out earlier. It is also a highly respectful notion in that it can guard against the development of a relationship and culture of dependency. It is an enriching concept. It is also enabling and empowering.

The focus of mentoring

It is necessary however to explore a little more what exactly the *things* (in this definition) are that a mentor-coach helps his/her client to think through. This is a generic model not limited only to the sphere of our working lives. It can apply to social and personal contexts and situations at a variety of levels – family, club, organization, community and so on. It will be helpful, however, if the frame or scaffold has a little more structure to it. The following model highlights the *things* that might need to be thought through by *the client*:

- Who I am.
- My role.
- Moral purpose.
- My situation.
- The issues I face.

In this book the role, issues and so on are illustrated from the context of education. However, the principles on which it is based and their application extend beyond it.

Attending to the person

The model is a personal one, in which – as will be explained in more detail later – the effective mentor-coach *attends to the person* of the client in a sustained and disciplined way. This is an essential part of what is meant by referring to the definition, concept and process as 'respectful'. It is based on a recognition that not only is each mentor-coach unique, but also that each client is. In addition, each separate encounter between the two is unique – not least because these two unique beings will each be growing and developing in the time between their meetings. Thus, attention to how a person sees herself/ himself and her/his persona and personal and/or professional history (literally 'his story') need to be a key part of the process of mentor-coaching.

Role and purpose

An essential part of this story is how the client sees her role and how she thinks about it. It is important to stress again that the context for mentor-coaching may be personal, family, community or professional – thus my role may be as a member of my peer group, as father/mother/brother/sister/aunt, neighbour, or team member/leader at work. It may be as a particular professional – a class or subject teacher, a department leader, senior staff member, head teacher, adviser, consultant, inspector, director and so on (though doctor, teacher, solicitor, estate agent, salesperson, for example, would be equally relevant roles). It's not just a question of defining the role either. It is equally about the *felt experience* of that role.

No one can think rigorously about their role without thinking also about purpose and, in particular, moral purpose. If the moral part is left out, it becomes merely 'function', and one returns then to the many dangers that come from models that try merely to generate compliance and conformity. The 'moral' part holds the process firmly in the field of people making themselves stronger (empowerment) and enhancing what it means to be *a person*. It also attends to the human context in another way, in that it invites the client to think some more about the other people to whom s/he is relating. Perhaps most importantly of all, the moral purpose under discussion stems from the values a person holds.

Context and issues

The fourth feature of this part of the process is helping the client think through her particular situation. To add to the uniqueness factor (each mentor-coach, client and their encounters are all unique) is the fact that everyone's situation is also unique. Many school/family/social/personal/work/community situations have similarities with each other, but no two are ever exactly the same. No two schools, no two classrooms are ever the same. How could they be?

So the situations each of us faces in the roles we have in our lives and in our educational contexts (and we all occupy several roles) will also be unique. In the mentor-coaching process it is the situations she faces that the client often wants to talk but the thinking process may go nowhere if these other matters are not addressed also – and preferably first. By 'situations' we do not necessarily mean 'problems'. They may be new issues yet to be addressed or issues where some success is being achieved and the client wants to understand better the processes by which that success has been brought about in order to be able to extend or replicate it.

Who needs a mentor?

Everyone needs a mentor. (Clutterbuck, 1985 cited in references as 2001)

This is in no sense a deficit model. The philosophy on which the model advanced here is based rests firmly on the belief that everyone needs a mentor-coach to help ensure success and to build upon it. Having made that clear, however, this is a model that can help a person think through problematic issues as well as new opportunities, and move forward, taking action to address them. Thus effective mentor-coaching should lead to autonomy – to the client being able, paradoxically, to do without even a mentor-coach.

Coaching: from thinking to action

Mentor-coaching is the overarching generic concept in thinking about these matters in this book. But thinking does not stop when the action phase begins, so when you address the matter of 'coaching' you are still thinking things through, only this time thinking about how to take action and indeed what action to take. Building on the notion that a coach (origin *Kocsi*, a village in Hungary where the first coach was constructed in the middle ages – see *OED*) is a means of travelling from one place to another. So the definition of a coach offered here is as follows:

> A coach is a person who helps me to think through how to get from where I am to where I need or want to be. (Joy and Pask, 2004)

My mentor-coach doesn't decide these things for me, nor tells me what to do and how to do it. That would be disrespectful – in the ways argued earlier – and would generate dependency. The client must do the thinking. The mentor-coach *helps and encourages* that process in ways described later.

Needs or wants?

The reader will have noticed that the definition refers to where I 'need *or* want to be'. There is no intention here to argue in depth about needs and wants, but some emphasis has already been placed on the concept of alignment. The mentoring-coaching process is occurring at a point in someone's history that involves other people and relationships with them. Education is critically about relationships. Its focus is intensely personal. In all relational contexts there are other human beings who have wants and needs too.

The client may have wants but there are also expectations by others. These may even include contracts of an informal and formal kind. So to focus, for example, on the work/professional situation and (to aid thinking) on a specific role as an example, a subject leader in a school is contracted to carry out certain duties in exchange for which she receives remuneration. There may be issues that present a challenge in performing those duties that may appear intractable. Equally – because they appear difficult – the client might *want* them to disappear or might *want* someone else to deal with them. Yet her reality is that she is the person who is paid to deal with the issue in question as part of her contractual responsibilities. It is important, therefore, to think – especially, though not exclusively, in the professional context – in terms of 'where I *need* to be' on account of my contractual responsibilities or because of 'public' expectations, as distinct from 'where I personally would *like* to be'.

Becoming my own person

The profoundly interesting question arises as to the extent to which you can ever genuinely be yourself if you were to devote full attention to meeting the expectations of others. As this book is primarily about the professional educational context this question is not argued here. If it were, it is likely you would contend that no individual can be truly human without devoting *some attention* to the expectations of others. Equally 'becoming a person' involves *being your own person too*. In many people's experience there are tensions between these two points. It should be sufficient to remind readers that this discussion of contractual requirements and the expectations others have of us is placed firmly in the context of clear thinking about *our role and moral purpose* as described earlier. This originates from the consideration of *how I see myself.*

> Without knowing what I am and why I am here, life is impossible.
> (Tolstoy, 1894)

Clarity in the matters addressed in the process described as mentor-coaching usually brings about the effect that once I know where I *need* to be, somehow I find myself *wanting to be there* too – or, if not, I may need to consider whether I ought to change my context. (One outcome of some mentor-coaching is that the client finds other work, or a place in another school, for example.) Clarity – the product of clear thinking – generates the motivation. But, if I am the client, it has to be *my* clarity not someone else's.

It will by now be clear that thinking things through is the activity that pervades this whole process. Thus it is argued that mentoring is the over-arching process. This predominates in the first half of the model set out below – the model that is explored in most of the rest of this book. It may be correct to call this 'pure mentoring', but it is of limited use unless it generates change – change by way of development that is for the better. Such change can only be brought about by action on the part of the client.

An easy to remember model

Mentoring-coaching may by now seem quite a challenging process in which to engage. Indeed it is. But, as is discussed later, it is a process that can be learnt and improved over time through practice. The point here is that a model – particularly one characterized in a manner that is not too difficult to hold in one's head after a short period of familiarization – can be extremely helpful. There are a number of authorities on this issue who have produced models to aid processes of this kind. The model on which this book is focused is intentionally slightly simpler than some and is produced with colour for training purposes to aid memory and convey some of the significance of each of its stages (Figure 1.1). It will form the focus for our exposition in sections that follow.

It is important to stress that this is *a* model. No claim is being made here that no other model will do the job in mind. It is a model based on one that has been developed through research and practice at what was the

London Leadership Centre and now is the London Centre for Leadership in Learning – a part of the Institute of Education, University of London.

Participants on training/development programmes are supplied with a copy of the model in which each stage is colour coded to signal its force and

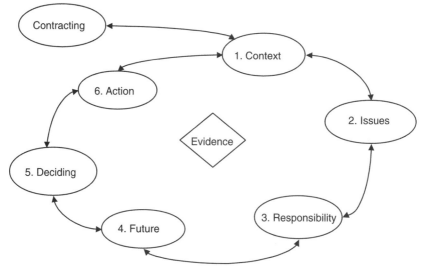

Figure 1.1   Model of mentoring-coaching.

spirit. The contracting phase and the evidence symbol are neutral in colour as they are relevant to all parts of the process. Stage 1 (Context) is green – literally green for 'Go'. Stage 2 (Issues) is amber/yellow since, as the reader will see, caution is required as the stage proceeds. Stage 3 is red and is literally a place to stop – until there is clear evidence that the client is actively wanting change and to take responsibility for whatever might happen next. Stage 4 (Future) offers an opportunity for 'blue skies thinking' – hence the colour blue. Stage 5 (Deciding) is also blue, to indicate that it is the choice generated by the thinking in the previous page. Stage 6 (Action) is purple – the 'purple patch' that begins with the feeling of taking control.

A learning-centred generic model

This is fundamentally a model for *learning* – learning both by the mentor-coach and the client. It is thoroughly, but not exclusively, applicable to matters connected with leadership, at all levels and in all contexts, not just education. This model has been applied in other service sectors, and in both public and private fields – profit-making and not-for-profit contexts. It is not just about leadership, however, neither is it exclusively about work contexts. As has already been implied, the process has been found very useful in personal, social, family and community contexts. The most extensive research carried out into the use of this model has been in the field of public education where it works extremely effectively as a key strategy in building capacity and generating sustainable improvement. It does this, among other things, by helping generate motivation and moral purpose. (Many people are not aware of moral purpose, especially their own, until they have the opportunity to talk about it.)

Although no structured research has been carried out so far into its applicability in, for example, personal, social and family contexts, there is a deal of anecdotal evidence from people who have tried to apply the model and especially the associated skills in such contexts. Many testify that the model works in a variety of situations. Even more claim that the skills associated with practice in the model have had a helpful impact on a range of relational matters – personal and private as well as social and public. The main focus here is on its value in the educational context.

Many people are sceptical about the value of things like 'models' in this kind of field, preferring a small number of simple principles. Others rely very heavily on models. Readers will have their own preferences. In this book a model is seen merely as a sketch map that aids memory and helps the practitioner chart the way through a process that could become complex. The model is most definitely not the territory itself.

Helping skills

It is not a counselling model *per se* and readers are urged to think very carefully about the limitations for its application. Many of the skills are those in which trained counsellors have extensive professional development. For those who see some potential confusion between mentoring-coaching on the one hand and counselling on the other, it may be important to make two critical points. The first may best be made by referring to the title of a world-famous book on this kind of process by Gerard Egan that has run into many editions and sold in many countries. He calls his book *The Skilled Helper* (2002). His model can appear slightly more complex than the one illustrated earlier, but his book is essentially about *how to help people* solve problems and develop opportunities in their lives. This model too is about how to *help each other – with a particular focus on thinking things through*. Counselling in a professional sense would be how to help people whose issues are obstructed by more profound personal difficulties of a kind that makes thinking especially hard. Do not use this model where specialist counselling is needed. Refer such clients to an appropriate specialist – generally via their family doctor.

The second point concerns the audience for whom this text is primarily, though not exclusively, intended. Though this model can be used effectively in many professions and in a personal context, the focus in this book is mainly upon education. That is the field where it is likely that most readers are working or at least interested in.

The need for training

This book has been written to enable people engaging in mentoring-coaching to do so competently and confidently. Beyond that, however, thoughtful use of this text will enable readers to evolve a high degree of skill in the use of the model. One way of ensuring this will be to intersperse practice and experience with reflection focused on what is written here. This is particularly important in parts of the model, like Stage 4 (Future), that offer significant challenges for the mentor-coach. The second half of the book takes such development further. After the initial read, and while reflecting on the experience of mentoring-coaching, practitioners will light upon a number of the deeper issues that arise in their work that Part Two of the book explores systematically. Thus the learning journey for practitioners in this field can be undertaken by the thorough and thoughtful exploration of this text.

Engaging in training with other practitioners can add a good deal of value to this learning process. Readers will want to consider seriously opportunities to engage in such training.

> Learning (at its most serious level) involves creating and sharing knowledge by doing things together with others. (Watkins, 2005)

Further information

Training in the use of this model can be accessed via the writers: Roger Pask can be contacted at rogerpask@btinternet.com and Barrie Joy at barriekjoy@yahoo.co.uk.

The London Centre for Leadership in Learning, Institute of Education, University of London, 20 Bedford Way, London WC1H 0AL also provides training in non-directive coaching.

Questions for the reader

- How has your understanding of the two terms – mentoring and coaching – developed as a result of reading this chapter?

- What does the hyphen signify? To what extent do you think can coaching occur without first engaging in mentoring?
- To what degree does it seem to you that coaching is actually a subset or part of mentoring?
- What feeling are you developing for the notion of 'attending to the person'? Is this more about a feeling than a rational definition?
- What do you think about the relationship between the concepts 'need' and 'want'? Can you think of a situation or circumstances in which, for you personally, needs might contrast with wants? And one where a clearly perceived need has changed into a committed want?
- In what sense can the process of mentoring-coaching help someone to become more 'their own person'? Could this apply as much to the mentor-coach as to the client?
- Can you remember the model easily without turning back the page?
- How helpful do you find having a model – or mental picture – of processes of this kind? Is there another way of charting your way through this kind of thinking that suits your learning habits better?
- What difference do you perceive between mentoring-coaching and counselling?
- What might be the benefits for you from engaging in mentoring-coaching training?
- What impact in the workplace might come from your increased clarity about this process?
- Are there any similar potential benefits for other parts of your life?

2 Getting started

In this model we have called this activity 'contracting'.

Who should be a mentor-coach?

The previous chapter began with the suggestion by the *Shorter OED*, that a mentor is an 'experienced and trusted counsellor' (counselling, in its literal sense, being 'an interchange of opinions'). 'Experienced in what?', you might ask, and 'how to generate that trust?'

These are important questions. Many people assume that the experience referred to will be in the same field as the field in which the client is operating, and that because of that (usually more extensive) experience the trust by the client will be automatic. Trust does *not* automatically develop under such circumstances. Much writing in this field and much of the experience on which this book is based suggest that there is a great deal that is fortuitous with regard to trust when this view of a mentor is taken.

Who needs one?

The common assumption that mentoring is mainly needed by inexperienced practitioners is bemusing. For example, it was for a time the case in England that newly qualified teachers and newly appointed head teachers were the only two groups of professionals in the education sector believed to need a mentor. The belief, particularly by those impatient for sector wide 'reform', that a coach is someone needed by those who currently perform poorly, or 'underperform' (whatever that may mean) is equally bemusing – and potentially damaging.

It may be worth taking another look at what is meant by the word 'experienced'. There can clearly be numerous benefits for a newly qualified teacher (or doctor, solicitor, company executive, nurse and so on) having a mentor who is experienced in the same things. There is, however, a significant danger that such a view of the 'experience' in question may lead to a relationship where the kind of 'advice' dispensed is through *telling* rather than by thinking things through. The result of this is usually that a dependency climate characterizes the relationship.

Relevant experience

There is a case for seeing the 'experience' in the dictionary definition in two other ways: experience of life in general, and experience in thinking things through. All three kinds of 'experience' may be of great value in a mentor-coach, though it may be helpful to stay close to the *Shorter OED* definition of experience as 'the action of putting something to the test'. A mentor-coach who is working in a professional context, a person with substantial experience in the same professional field as the client, who also had sound experience of the skills and processes of helping others to think things through would be very useful. Reflected experience of life in general would be an added bonus.

Implied in this contention is the clear possibility that an experienced mentor-coach may have little or no direct experience of the field or professional discipline in which the client is working. This is hard for many professionals to accept. Fundamentally, however, only a person who can help another to think through in a rigorous and structured way could operate effectively as a mentor-coach. Even so, such a person has to be or become 'trusted'.

Trust and accountability

It is generally recommended that line mangers do not mentor-coach colleagues whom they directly line manage. This is not an absolute. However, issues of accountability and vested interests can get in the way of the kind of open and honest dialogue that needs to occur in many circumstances for things to be properly thought through. Sometimes there is an issue between a client and his/her line manager. This can seriously inhibit the process if the line manager is also the mentor-coach. These are what could be called 'noises in the system'. They can be managed effectively with the necessary level of mutual awareness, but they increase the level of challenge for both parties and are therefore better avoided, especially in the period in which the mentor-coach is establishing his/her practical skills.

A voluntary and equal relationship

Equally, trust is something that cannot develop easily in a climate of compulsion. Organizations that have a policy giving an entitlement to mentor-coaching (whether for some or all members/employees) are making a sound investment in their future. Some of them undermine the potential benefit, however, by imposing the system and entitlement on each person, together with a mentor-coach selected by the management. It works best if the relationship is voluntary – if the client has some scope for choosing her own mentor-coach, and has some choice as to whether or not to participate in the system at all.

This need not be a one time choice. Sometimes what looks in prospect to be a potentially very fruitful mentor-coach/client pairing turns out not to be so. Flexibility is therefore important and it should be understood by all concerned that a change in mentor-coach is not to be deprecated. Compatibility is really important. It should mainly be the client who has the option to end a particular pairing, though in extreme cases the mentor-coach might want to signal that the partnership might come to an end if there is entrenched resistance by the client or other serious obstruction to the smooth progress of the process.

The relationship must feel and be equal. What is sometimes called 'peer mentor-coaching' can be very positive in its impact, but it can also become collusive and 'pally'. Both of the dangers of peer mentor-coaching can be averted by careful structuring and sound training, with some supervision. Equality does not, however, require peer mentor-coaching. What is essential is that *in the mentoring-coaching relationship* there is an authentic sense that two people are working together as partners on the same task, with different roles *drawn exclusively from the fact of that relationship.*

> Prerequisites of genuine dialogue: equality and the absence of coercive influences . . . (Yankelovich, 1999)

It is necessary to stress repeatedly that even a slight hint that someone needs a mentor-coach because s/he is somehow underperforming makes the business of getting started immensely difficult because it is manifestly unequal and militates against a relationship of trust and confidence. If short-term 'rescue' is what is required, something other than mentoring-coaching should be employed (see below).

Personal behaviours by the mentor-coach that help to get started

Unconditional positive regard . . . (Rogers, 1961)

The personal disposition of the mentor-coach at the beginning can do a huge amount to generate trust and confidence, even when there is already a degree of what has been referred to as 'noise in the system'. By personal disposition we mean things like warmth of tone, the way of greeting the client (even in the initial telephone contact), a smile, and general friendliness. Genuineness – something most people spot very readily (especially if it isn't there) – is another way of putting it. What must be conveyed from the very beginning and throughout the relationship is what Rogers (1961) labelled 'unconditional positive regard' and what we call 'respect for the other human being as of right'.

The centrality of confidence and trust

The main aim to be fulfilled at the start of the process is to begin a relationship of confidence and trust. Confidence is needed both by the mentor-coach and the client. It is inextricably linked to trust (and therefore to confidentiality). Without these two qualities at the very heart of the relationship the process will be at best of little use, at worst abusive and damaging.

An entirely independent process – not a deficit model

Confidence and trust will be extremely difficult to establish if there is any hint of coercion in the arrangement. It will be even more difficult if an organization or part of a system is wanting to impose a mentor-coaching arrangement on a putative client believed to be failing in some significant way.

Worse still would be a situation where it was made clear to the client that this arrangement was a plan of last resort, whereby a capability procedure is threatened if the mentor-coach cannot bring about a big improvement in the performance of the client. In this last instance the degree of resentment may well be insurmountable. Mentoring-coaching is inappropriate in such circumstances. A highly skilled and experienced mentor-coach might be able to overcome this much 'noise in the system' but it would not be easy.

Under no circumstances should mentor-coaching be undertaken at the same time as a capability procedure is in operation, and no mentor-coach should ever agree to report back from sessions anything that could be used in such a procedure.

Confidentiality

This leads naturally on to the issue of confidentiality. A relationship of trust and confidence will be much more likely to develop if a guarantee of total confidentiality can be given by the mentor-coach. (This is subject, of course, to legal limitations. For example, no mentor-coach could hold in confidence knowledge of any criminal behaviour divulged by a client. Thankfully, this hardly ever arises.) The point at general issue here is that this is a relationship in which the client is encouraged to think out loud. For many people it is not until they shape their thoughts into words that they even know what it is that they think. When they have begun to do so, however, they can begin to build on and develop their thinking. So they need to be able to voice, without hindrance, some of their inner thoughts and their feelings. In addition, there needs to be confidence that whatever is said by the client will not be taken to be a final word on any matter. Rather, anything said must be treated as part of a continuing thinking process.

We referred earlier to 'felt experience'. People who work in similar contexts to each other often have experiences that are *similar*. For example, a teacher may have a difficult class and experience an ongoing struggle for control. The facts of each such experience always differ to some degree and, more importantly, so also do the feelings engendered by the experience, sometimes markedly. Feelings are often very important in this process. It is vital that they can be expressed without fear of being reported to a third party.

Confidentiality therefore needs to be made an explicit rule at the beginning.

Some professionals, for example, LEA staff visiting a school, who are attracted by the model developed through thinking outlined in this book, feel unable to use it properly because the mentor-coach's line managers require them to keep something like a 'record of visit' that is then stored on a shared hard drive. Negotiation on this issue may be necessary at the start of the process. The range of detail that might need to feature in such negotiation is huge and cannot be explored here but two key points must be observed: (1) nothing must be promised that will not be delivered; (2) complete openness by the client will not be forthcoming without an assurance of confidentiality.

Taking notes

Confidentiality is sometimes linked in people's minds to the question of whether notes should be taken, particularly by the mentor-coach. The link with confidentiality sparks concern about what kind of notes would be taken; what they might be used for; whether both parties have access to them; and who else would see them. These are some of the concerns that lead us to suggest that notes should not be taken.

If there is genuine concern that memories might lapse between sessions, a brief *aide-mémoire* might be jotted down at the end of or after the session. Generally, it is recommended that notes are not taken at all *during* the session. The main reason for this has to do with the need for the mentor-coach to be totally attentive to the person of the client throughout the encounter – to their words, facial expression, tone, body language and so on. While eye contact does not have to be maintained throughout, the mentor-coach must make it available throughout the session.

55% of all face-to-face communication is through body language, facial expression etc. (Osbourne and Harris, 1999)

A further point in question about note taking is that no assumption should be made that a second session will begin exactly where the first one finished. Things and people may move on between sessions. A practice that has considerable benefits is for the mentor-coach to begin a second or subsequent session by inviting the client to sum up where they think the process got to previously and to follow this up by asking whether anything has changed since then.

Length and frequency of meetings

There are a number of very practical points about the arrangements for mentoring-coaching. The first is the need for a period (minimum 30 minutes, preferably one hour) when there will be no external interruptions – phone, knocks on the door and so on, other than for real emergencies. This has implications for the venue. For example, an office shared with another person is an unsuitable venue. Phones should be unplugged and/or switched off or calls intercepted. It should not be possible for someone to peer into the room from outside. The venue should, in other words, provide genuine privacy.

More than one meeting may be necessary. Frequency, length and number of meetings should be the subject of some initial discussion. Prospective mentor-coaches should be aware that this is a potentially exhausting activity – physically as well as intellectually and emotionally – for mentor-coach *and* for client. In general, a session should last for a maximum of 50 to 60 minutes, and a judgement may need to be made as to an appropriate point in the encounter to break. The stage reached in the model may sometimes provide a useful guide.

Layout of the room

The furniture layout should also be given some thought. This is not always at the disposal of the mentor-coach, particularly if the meeting occurs at the client's place of work. Most experienced practitioners try to ensure that mentor-coach and client are not separated by furniture such as a desk, though a small coffee table may be acceptable. There should however be a reasonable space between the two – to give 'personal space' to the client – and the two chairs should not be exactly facing each other, but rather angled towards each other (sometimes referred to as 'ten-to-two') to make eye contact easy but not totally unavoidable. This may sound like nit-picking. Facility in communication hinges crucially on matters of this kind – as is argued further – so it is important to try to get this right, especially in the early stages.

Clarifying expectations

Finally, in getting started there is the question of what the client is expecting to happen. This can be the cause of considerable anxiety, which could easily be allayed. One important way of allaying this might be for the mentor-coach to explain very briefly the fact that he/she will be using a model to help structure the conversation. This need not go into much detail, unless the client wants to know more about the model, in which case a very brief exposition might suffice.

Some clients assume that they are going to be given advice on issues, or that the mentor-coach is going to solve problems for them. As neither of these things is a part of this process, it is important that if these expectations are stated, they are managed constructively. By this is meant that they should not be directly negated but that some formulation should be offered that might sound something like, 'By the end of our meeting(s) I hope to have helped you come up with a good way forward on some of the things that currently bug you'. (NB: This is not a mantra! Each mentor-coach must decide the appropriate words with which to respond to the unique context.)

Client's concerns

Before proceeding to the first full stage of the model the mentor-coach should check with her client whether there are any other issues or questions that need to be addressed. This section has covered the main ground, but it is not possible to construct a compendium of all the things *any* client could possibly want to clarify, so there should be an explicit invitation to raise any other questions. This contracting phase took a long time to write about but rarely takes more than five minutes to facilitate!

To conclude, the personal disposition of the mentor-coach at the beginning can do a huge amount to generate trust and confidence, even when there is already a degree of what we have called 'noise in the system'. This means things like warmth of tone and the way of greeting the client as described earlier. Genuineness and authenticity are the crucial characteristics. They must not be forced but must come naturally from a profound belief that respect is due as of right to every human being. Without that belief it would be difficult to develop such warmth and, as a result, difficult to be an effective mentor-coach. The warmth referred to is not possessive warmth; that might lead to dependency. It is about unconditional positive regard and empathy (a quality crucially distinct from sympathy).

> Non-possessive warmth. (Rogers, 1961)

Issues the reader may want to reflect on

- Who do you know who might mentor-coach you? How have you identified that person? If not, how would you go about choosing such a person?
- What aspects of your 'experience' (as discussed earlier) might qualify you to begin to be a mentor-coach?
- How would someone need to behave to begin to gain your confidence and trust?
- What do the phrases 'unconditional positive regard' and 'non-possessive warmth' signify to you?
- Why is it important to keep mentoring-coaching separate from other processes and procedures?
- How might the issue of note taking need to be managed in your context? Would it be an issue at all for you (as mentor-coach or as client)?

- Try to practise mentally identifying body language in others, particularly in communication with work colleagues.
- Try to develop explicit awareness of your own body language in a variety of communication contexts.
- In your work context what would be the precise limitations on what, as a mentor-coach, you could keep in confidence? (This is an important question for each person to answer in their own professional context.)
- What are the concerns you would have as a client that your mentor-coach (assuming you had one) would need to allay? What would s/he need to do in order to allay them?

3 Stage 1: context

The introductory matters have been dealt with and the real business of mentoring-coaching can now begin. The first symbol in the model would have a green (for 'Go') background in the training sessions.

The client's 'story'

This is an opportunity for the client to talk about themselves in a work context, assuming it is work that is the subject of the encounter. An invitation like, 'Tell me about yourself and your school (and department) and what you do here' will usually get things started. Mentor-coaches need to be alert to the fact that we are helping the client to think about who they are, their role, moral purpose and so on. These are not questions to be asked directly, of course, but that agenda in the mind of the mentor-coach can be helpful as a framework for storing some of the things that might emerge.

Being listened to properly: an unusual experience

This is the first part of the process itself and the response to that initial invitation to talk will provide a key indicator as to how verbally communicative the client is likely to be through all the stages. The possible range is huge. Some clients seize the opportunity to talk very readily, and have a great deal they want to say.

Being listened to for an extended period of time is a far less common occurrence than we might like to think. Because it is much less common than it ought to be, when it presents itself, it is frequently grasped with both hands, so to speak (for people often talk in an animated way using gestures and a range of other body language). Once such people get going they are sometimes hard to stop!

What often passes for listening is little more than staying quiet for just as long as it takes for the 'listener' to find an opportunity, or excuse, to butt in and say what they want to say. Similarly, people are often so absorbed in their own pressures and preoccupied with their own issues that being quiet while another person talks could mean almost anything other than genuine listening. Talkers quickly sense whether or not they are really being listened to. They usually welcome being genuinely listened to and respond very readily.

The 'quiet' client

At the other extreme are people who, for a variety of reasons, say very little and need quite a lot of sensitive and careful prompting. The prompting needs to be sensitive so that there is no sense of pressure to talk, and careful because the mentor-coach must not try to put words into the mouth of the client.

The mentor-coach must not make assumptions about the reasons for the client's unwillingness to say much. It may be a time when the relationship is still being formed and confidence and trust may not yet be established. It may be that no one has seriously listened to this person for a long time and he/she is out of the habit of this kind of serious communication. It has also to be recognized that some people just don't need or like to use lots of words, and yet are quite comfortable in their personal world.

Unwillingness to talk

Unwillingness to talk can signal potential distress, possibly deep, about the work situation. Where there are clear signals of intense distress – especially if there is reason to believe that the causes of the distress may be in their personal life – it is important to recognize and act upon the need that the client may have for any specific professional help. (A client may, for example, be experiencing marital difficulties, sleeplessness through fierce anxiety, alcohol dependency, clinical depression and so on) As previously indicated, the general medical practitioner may be the best route for obtaining such help and the client should be gently and firmly encouraged to seek it by that or other appropriate means.

The reader can be assured, however, that in mentoring-coaching these are unusual experiences. The range of willingness to communicate is from general volubility to initial reticence that eases as confidence and trust grow.

Managing silence

This is a good point at which to raise the issue of silence. Most people (especially teachers!) find it very easy to fill even the shortest of silences. In fact, silences often seem a lot longer than they actually are. A silence of ten seconds can seem very long. Yet most of us need a bit of silence in which to do some of our thinking, though, of course, especially in mentoring-coaching, quite a lot of thinking is done out loud.

An effective mentor-coach needs to be able to hold the silence and to exude comfort in doing so.

There is a very small danger that a silence can be unproductive and, if protracted, even damaging. One may need to be alert to such a possibility. This is uncommon, however. Most people break silence long before that happens.

Distress at work

What is, sadly, more common than one might expect, is general distress about work situations, including a significant degree of bullying in the workplace. These are matters over which the client could be helped greatly by support in thinking things through. Once trust and confidence are established – which may take a little longer in such circumstances – the client will usually be really pleased to have the ear of someone capable of achieving empathy towards them.

Dealing with stress

It is also the case that many people believe themselves to be under stress from work to a degree that is unhelpful – something less acute than *dis*tress but likely to gnaw away at their morale and sense of self-worth. Effective mentoring-coaching helps a person to think through the causes and circumstances of work-related stress and to decide upon action to alleviate at least some of them. The first stage of this process is the sheer privilege of having someone really listen to the story of events within which stress is generated. This is where all effective mentoring-coaching begins.

A grandiose claim?

It may sound grandiose to claim that mentoring-coaching can help cure stress and distress but that is the claim that this book makes. It is not, of course, a cure that the mentor-coach dispenses – that would be preposterous, and any attempt to work in that way would be immensely counter-productive. What is being claimed (logically and rationally) is that the process described in this book helps a person to *own* issues. It also empowers and enables them in contexts where they would otherwise be in danger of accepting the role of victim. Feeling empowered and enabled are critical weapons against stress.

The place of feelings

Some people are not at ease talking about feelings. A mentor-coach needs to be comfortable when feelings are the focus of the dialogue. Two further important points need to be made.

The first is that no client should feel compelled to talk about his feelings. This does not prohibit the mentor-coach from forming a hypothesis about the feelings the client has – and every client will have feelings about the things they talk about, whether or not they recognize that fact. It is likely that a small minority of clients will want to suppress/deny them, or at least hide them until sufficient rapport has been established for it to feel safe to talk about them. Even then, there may be some resistance to focusing on feelings.

Usually a client in this state will claim to have a strongly rational focus. What is interesting is that because humans are a mixture of the rational and emotional, anyone working with other human beings, especially in the field of education, will need to be aware of the emotional side of things and to respond constructively to emotions in the work place. It may, for example, transpire later that issues/problems in the workplace may stem from unrecognized and unaddressed feelings by some colleagues.

The second point follows from this, namely that at some point emotions are almost certainly going to have to feature in the dialogue. One way of getting round the declared avoidance of the client's emotions is to ask them to *think* about how the other person or people involved might *feel* about the issue under discussion. This is likely to be possible at this stage of the model, but, if not, will become more possible in Stage 2 (Issues).

Finally, on this point, it is often the feelings associated with a particular situation that make the matter in focus unique. Even if all the details of a set of circumstances appear to be the same as one encountered before by the mentor-coach (and this is rare), it is the feelings of the people involved (including the client) that might make it unique.

Key skills in this stage: helping the story unfold

The critical task of the mentor-coach in this stage is to help the client tell her story. So active listening is critical along with a degree of questioning and prompting as required by the individual circumstance.

Active listening

> One way of listening actively is attending – attending fully to the other person.
> (Ash and Quarry, 1995)

Active listening includes *listening for intention*. It's not just a matter of hearing the words but of ensuring that both mentor-coach and client understand what it is she is trying to say. So clarifying, reflecting back, paraphrasing, summarizing may well all be useful practices by the mentor-coach. They help the mentor-coach grasp the story and *its meaning for the client*. They also help the client clarify and deepen their understanding too. With practice the mentor-coach will judge fairly easily when it is appropriate to do these things. A simple point of principle in the early stages of mentoring-coaching would be to try to avoid disrupting the flow of the story.

It is worth considering in turn each of these four skills in more detail.

Clarifying

This is about checking the meaning of what is being said. The client may be trying to explore meaning herself and may need someone to ask about a word or phrase she has used. The instance of this may begin with the mentor-coach stating, 'The sense I am getting of what you are saying is . . .' or 'You used the word . . .'. Such phrases form not only the start of an opportunity to clarify, but also an invitation to say more. Sometimes the explicit invitation, 'Say some more about that' may be appropriate. It might also be helpful in particular circumstances to invite the client to give an example of some general point she is trying to make.

Note, however, that at this stage it is not appropriate to use these phrases to challenge the client. That may be necessary later, but not in the early part of the process. The general principle at stake here is that mentoring-coaching is aimed at generating clarity about all the things listed in the previous chapter – who I am, my role and purpose and so on – and about the precise nature of what is being experienced at present. So clarifying is a vital subskill for the mentor-coach to develop.

Reflecting back

This is useful as a means of clarifying. Sometimes the mentor-coach needs only to repeat a word the client has used. At other times it might be important to rehearse the whole of a section of the context or story being told, using some of the same words the client has used. This can be supportive in helping the client develop both their story and their understanding of a situation, including what they are *feeling* about it.

A real struggle might occur here for the mentor-coach. This is not about what the mentor-coach felt when something similar happened to him, or what the mentor-coach might feel if it were to happen to him in the future. It is exclusively about both parties trying to grasp what the *client* is feeling. Reflecting back can be part of the catalyst for consciousness of feeling.

Reflecting back is also a way of demonstrating how totally focused on listening the mentor-coach is, and the commitment to getting the story absolutely straight in the mentor-coach's head. It's quite important to do this in a relatively tentative way, as you might not have got it straight and the client will need to feel that it is ok to correct what the mentor-coach says. So rather than saying, 'What you said just now is . . .' the mentor-coach could say, 'You seem to be saying . . .' or 'What I think I'm hearing you say is . . .'.

Readers new to mentoring-coaching should not worry too much about reflecting back inaccurately. Of course one must do one's best, but even very experienced mentor-coaches sometimes get hold of the wrong end of the stick – because they're human! What matters is that the reflecting back is done in such a way that inaccuracies do not damage confidence and trust from the client. So if the client says something like, 'That's not quite what I meant' and goes on to explain further, reflecting back has done its work and greater clarity will emerge.

Paraphrasing

In the context of clarifying and reflecting back, paraphrasing is important because it puts what the client has said into the words of the mentor-coach. It too can be a powerful signal that the mentor-coach is listening very carefully and has grasped what has been communicated.

The points about tentativeness also apply here. It can be used beyond the reflecting back context and can begin with 'Do you mean . . .?' or even '. . . sort of . . .?' The critical point is that it is not being done to supply a better word or by way of correction. It is the *client's* story we are considering in this stage and if what the mentor-coach is hearing doesn't somehow seem right, for whatever reason, a respectful and tentative question is appropriate, not any kind of correction by the mentor-coach. The client may as a result of a gentle question correct him or herself and that is fine; a very positive indication that the mentoring-coaching is working in fact, though this is not something for the mentor-coach to strive for too consciously.

The main point about paraphrasing is that it demonstrates for both parties that the mentor-coach has understood and can put into her own words what the client has said.

Summarizing

This serves a similar purpose to reflecting back and paraphrasing, and also helps the mentor-coach collect together the parts of what could be a fairly complex story and remember it. Putting it in words allows the client to hear their story so far in a more detached and possibly more coherent way. It also places it more firmly in the mind of the mentor-coach, helping the mentor-coach to 'own' the story mentally. Actually putting the summary into words helps it 'travel' in the mind of the mentor-coach – in the sense of the quote earlier from Fullan (2005) – and maybe marks out a neural pathway.

It is easy to get some of this wrong. Generally, it does not greatly matter if the mentor-coach paraphrases or summarizes slightly inaccurately – but please note the 'slightly'. Getting it very wrong can undermine confidence and suggests that the mentor-coach hasn't really been listening. But even in well-established, very good relationships minor misunderstandings occur. The quality of the relationship will make it easy to rectify and it is an important mark of respect for the client that the mentor-coach is keen to ensure that she has grasped and understood what has been said. So even a slightly inaccurate summary will serve a positive purpose.

Summarizing is also a very useful skill/tool for testing out whether the client is ready to move on to the next stage of the process as represented by the model. It is OK for the mentor-coach to think that the story has been told and get ready to move on, while the client thinks there is more to tell. The summary should always end with a question that would invite both confirmation of accuracy and further information, in case the story is not quite complete.

Eye contact

Throughout this whole process, and especially in this stage, maintaining eye contact is of high importance. This is not about staring or even a fixed look. Eyes are a very expressive part of the face and a 'window on the mind'. Through contact with the eye of the mentor-coach the client will discern genuineness, attentiveness, interest and engagement and, over time, empathy. That contact must be there for the client whenever she seeks it.

This means that the mentor-coach must make it available virtually all the time. The client may look away (perhaps typically upwards) while thinking about what s/he wants to say and how to say it. S/he may also even look down, possibly signalling a troubled mind. When s/he looks up again, the eyes of the mentor-coach must be there waiting and attending to him/her as a person, ready to receive what s/he might want to say next. If they are not, she may decide that the mentor-coach has in some way lost interest, and this could turn out to be a crucial moment. Trust and confidence would then be undermined.

Similarly, the eyes of the client will reveal things like unease, relief, anxiety, pleasure (at being understood) and so on.

Listening for intention

Many inexperienced mentor-coaches focus too much on the exact words being used. They are important, but Osbourn and Harris (1975) in their book, *Assertiveness Training for Women*, quote research indicating that in the average person's communication only 7 per cent of the meaning is conveyed in the actual words used. They point out that 38 per cent of meaning is conveyed through tone, volume, inflexion, speed of speech and so on, and that as much as 55 per cent is conveyed through facial expression, eye movement and many other aspects of body language. So observing and drawing upon these non-verbal aspects of communication by the client are utterly critical features of active listening. Equally important is the fact that the mentor-coach will also be communicating by these means, which are vital parts of the process of developing trust and confidence.

It might be helpful to consider an example. A client might be talking in a rational and relatively calm way about a work situation that is actually generating quite a degree of stress for her. The words might be moderate as well as rational but a subdued tone might gradually be accompanied by a tautness of facial muscles, gradually turning to a fairly grim expression paralleled by clenching of the hands and so on. She might continue to say that she is not really stressed or worried but the tone and body language indicate that she may be saying she is not worried/stressed because it is important to her to put a brave face on it.

This is an illustration of what was meant earlier. The reader should not jump to conclusions here about how to handle that circumstance. The principle of tentativeness must govern the nature of the mentor-coach's response, but beyond that – until the mentor-coach is confident of how to read people and situations of this kind (what Egan, 1992 refers to as empathic highlights) – the mentor-coach should proceed with caution.

Some authorities on issues to do with body language expound the arguments for 'mirroring'. This is where a mentor-coach might adopt posture, gestures or expressions that mirror those displayed by the client. This subject is not explored in any depth in this book. The view taken here is that when empathy is evident it can often show itself through unconscious or semiconscious mirroring behaviours. An alert mentor-coach might gradually become conscious that some of her behaviours are mirroring those of the client. This is fine, but calculated and deliberate mirroring can seem false and manipulative and should mostly be avoided.

Questioning

This is a critical and generic skill throughout the whole process of mentoring-coaching and is an important skill in this stage. It helps bring out the story. It also helps both parties make connections and highlight facts that may be significant. In this stage of the process questions to elicit information may be predominant, but understanding will also need to be generated at this stage.

Some writers like to place emphasis on the importance of open questions. Open and closed questions both have their place in effective mentoring-coaching. What is very important here is that questions are not asked that will close the story (or part of it) down too early or cement any particular meaning that is still evolving. The other relevant point is that *prompting* questions can be helpful here. But care should be taken not to lead the client.

That is not to exclude *probing* questions. So, for example, someone may say something like, 'No one in our department ever talks to me'. In reply the mentor-coach might say, 'No one?' or 'Ever?' by way of probing for precision. Some probing questions may be needed to help clarify aspects of the story, but that kind of question is more commonly helpful in the next stage of the model/process.

Trainee mentor-coaches often ask if there is a compendium of appropriate questions. There isn't! The reader can take some comfort from the fact that if the mentor-coach is attending fully to the person of the client, the questions will come fairly naturally. Even if not everything emerges at this stage, it is quite acceptable to go back later to ask respectfully about something that has been missed at Stage 1. In addition, there will be more on the subject of questioning in all stages of the model and further chapters in this book.

Challenge

> Mentor-coaches must earn the right to challenge through demonstration of empathy. The degree of challenge must be proportionate to the level of empathy generated. (Pask, 2004)

As rapport, trust and confidence grow it may be appropriate to introduce a gradually increasing amount of challenge. Challenge is best delivered through questions and it *may* have some place in this stage of the process. In telling her story the client may, for example, use generalizations – sometimes sweeping – about herself and her behaviours, feelings and attitudes, or about those of another person involved in the story. 'Always?' or 'Never?' said interrogatively but with as *neutral* a tone as possible may be all that needs to be said in such an instance. It won't necessarily feel like much of a challenge, but it is in fact inviting the client to moderate the statement she has made, and may open up the fact that there is a reality that the client has not described and maybe hasn't as yet perceived.

At this stage in the process anything stronger than that level of challenge could undermine the trust and confidence that is just beginning to flourish.

Blind spots

One of the tasks of the mentor-coach in this stage is to open up for the client any possible blind spots they may have. We all have them about all sorts of things. Challenge through questions can help throw light on them. If the challenge is too strong it can further obscure them. An example of the line of questioning that might expose a blind spot might be focused on feelings, particularly the feelings of other people involved in the story besides the client. When we are involved in a challenging situation, it is often the case that our own feelings become predominant making it hard for us to see that the feelings of others might be very relevant.

> Dysfunctional ways of thinking are called blind spots. People fail to see how some of the realities they construct for themselves are self-limiting. (Egan, 1992)

Minimal intervention by the mentor-coach

From the example of challenge given earlier can be deduced a certain amount of virtue in *short* interventions – whether questions or general prompts.

Across the whole of the process the distribution of the talk should be approximately 80 per cent by the client and 20 per cent by the mentor-coach. In this stage of the model the mentor-coach should aim to talk less than that. Summaries, clarifications, paraphrases and questions should only be used to aid the flow of the story and should be as succinct as possible. So the repetition of a single word or short phrase used by the client – allowing for further focus on it, if the client is willing – or the insertion of a very short (one word even) question is a skill really worth cultivating.

Sometimes a mentor-coach may need to do no more than make an invitational gesture or expression that seems to say, 'So ...?' but with no word spoken. Clients say it feels really good to be mentor-coached by a person who can help the process along to such great effect with so little verbal intervention. Some such extremely effective mentor-coaches have mastered the art of minimal interventions to a significant degree, even to the point where they talk in total for around 5 per cent of the whole time. When this happens, the client is in no doubt as to who owns the whole process and the progress it generates.

So, to encapsulate this thinking in a short but penetrating concept, in the role of mentor-coach *less is more*.

Attending to the person

This phrase has been used several times so far in the book and it will come up again. It is the critical disposition for the mentor-coach. Rather than worrying too much about what questions should be asked, or about getting the summarizing, clarifying, paraphrasing slightly wrong, the mentor-coach should focus as fully as possible on the other human being in the room. The mentor-coach should be trying to build on his/her respect for this other human being as of right, trying to get a sense of what it might be like to be that person in that situation. In this focus the mentor-coach will be searching for the distinctive nature of the other person and the uniqueness of their situation.

Non-judgemental?

Sometimes the biggest barriers to this are the evident similarities between the client's story and the situations encountered previously by the mentor-coach, either personally or through other clients. The critical disposition here is one of total openness and suspension of judgement of any kind. One cannot be entirely non-judgemental but one can and must, as a mentor-coach, be able to suspend judgement while hearing the story the client is telling.

Sometimes the mentor-coach may actually not feel that he/she likes the client as a person or may, as the story unfolds, hear things being talked about in ways he/she would disapprove of. It is respect, rather than liking for the client, that is required – what we have called unconditional positive regard. If the apparent values of the client don't match up to those of the mentor-coach, he/she must at this stage listen, suspend judgement and seek to understand where the other is coming from.

Immediacy

One important point is worthy of mention here. During mentoring-coaching – at almost any stage and frequently in exploring context – a client may signal by some means or other that there is an issue that is interfering, or is likely to interfere, with the process of thinking things through in this way.

The signal may not be overt – indeed, it can easily appear to be fortuitous. It can be in something as simple as the venue for the meeting – so that if it is taking place in the client's office and s/he has agreed to take a call during it, the flow of the whole process is interrupted. This is a very obvious example.

So, too, would be a raging cold that the client was suffering that inhibited their focus on the process.

Less obvious would be a growing sense that the client is preoccupied with something that is extraneous but is not making that explicit. It could be that the mentor-coach senses that the client needs to talk about a particular thing but is studiously trying to avoid doing so. The issue that isn't being talked about might even be generating distress for the client. This has come to be called in some circles, 'the elephant in the room', but in mentoring-coaching that does not mean that it is easy to deal with. The mentor-coach will have to find a gentle but determined way to help the client articulate it, so that it can be addressed and the obstacle to thinking things through can be either briefly addressed and/or possibly put to one side for the time being.

There is much more that could be written about this stage but it is enough to reiterate that Stage 1 is about helping the client to tell their story. For the mentor-coach it is about trying to discern the *felt experience* of the client and is a vital part of the genuine struggle to develop empathy towards them.

Questions a mentor-coach might ask in this stage of the model

- 'Tell me about yourself and your school/department etc. and what you do there'.
- 'Talk to me about yourself and your work and how it's been going'.
- 'Tell me about the people you work with'.
- 'You said a moment ago . . . Say a little more about that'.
- 'You haven't said anything (or much) about . . .'.
- 'I'm sensing . . . (a degree of frustration, irritation, some stress etc.) about . . .'.
- 'Have you sought anyone else's help/advice about this?' where a serious personal problem arises or where more information about a particular difficulty has surfaced.
- 'When you say . . . do you mean . . .?' when paraphrasing or clarifying.
- 'How does that make you feel?'
- 'How do you think s/he (another person or group of people) feel(s) about this?'
- 'I think what I'm hearing you say is . . .'.
- 'Correct me if I'm wrong, but are you saying . . .?'
- 'Always?', 'Never?'
- 'Unhappy?' when the client has used that or another word and a bit more insight would be helpful.

These are specific examples of some possible questions a mentor-coach might ask to aid the telling of the client's story. It is not and could not be a complete list. It would be helpful to a serious reader to try to imagine a possible or, better still, actual mentoring-coaching encounter and work through the substance of this chapter and try to note some other possible questions that could be asked – bearing in mind some of the points of principle set out in the chapter – about challenge, tentativeness or feelings, for instance.

Issues to reflect upon

- What comes to mind when you think about who *you* are, *your* role, moral purpose, context and the issues you face in your work and as a possible mentor-coach?
- Think of a time when you felt really listened to, or of someone you regard as a good listener. What is it that the person does that makes you confident you are really being listened to? Make a list (as long as possible) of the actual behaviours of the listener. Make another list of things that not so good listeners often do, but that the good listener avoids.
- How well do you manage silence?
- What do you see as the pros and cons of keeping eye contact?
- How do you manage the symptoms of the other person's distress when it arises in one-to-one conversations?
- How 'at home' are you with feelings – your own and those of others – and with talking about them?
- What obstacles can you think of to identifying the *intention* in a person's communication?
- How good would you say you are at keeping a neutral tone when asking probing questions or when challenging? Think about what might be potential blind spots in life/at work for you? Where might blind spots come from?
- How hard is it for you constructively to challenge another person?
- How disciplined are you at 'less is more'? Can you for example formulate succinct questions on the spot?
- What – from previous thought and as a result of reading this chapter – have the terms 'immediacy' and 'attending to the person' come to mean to you?

A personal learning agenda

After considering the content of the above points for reflection it may have become clear that there is a personal learning agenda emerging for you. That is not necessarily to suggest some further reading of an academic or theoretical nature, but some possible new or adapted behaviours you might want to think about.

You may already know about self-directed change and have come across some models that help you think about it (see, for example, Goleman et al., 2002). Either way it is important to stress that practice (which does not make perfect, but does help improve!) is the means by which the neural pathways governing our behavioural habits are developed. It is also important to reflect on the practice with the help of another person whom you trust to give you honest, fair and constructive feedback.

If you have not by now thought of it yourself, you might want to begin to write down some of the things that you need to develop (for instance, managing silence), if you are to become a more effective mentor-coach. Lots of people find a learning journal helpful on the kind of journey you may be embarking upon – one that you may discover to be lifelong.

4   Stage 2: Issues

Problem? What problem?

This is the point at which several models we have encountered actually begin, often with a question that is something like, 'What exactly is the problem?' This approach has a number of possible flaws.

The first potential flaw is that there may not be a problem. If the relationship is positively based, for example, in a context where 'everyone needs a mentor-coach', there may simply be opportunities to choose from for future development – building upon previous success – and a need for a bit of help to explore the options. The second very real flaw is that many people who welcome the support of a mentor-coach do not know whether there is a problem and even when they think there is one, do not exactly know what it is. They may, as previously indicated, have a blind spot and might well identify a minor issue, or even a symptom rather than the one that they most need to address.

Most people are in any case reluctant to talk about problems they encounter to someone with whom they have not clearly established the beginnings of a relationship of trust and confidence. Although we all have or encounter problems of one kind or another, to talk about them too readily is seen by many as a confession of weakness or failure. So to begin here would not necessarily draw forth an honest response.

> You don't have to be sick to get better. (Josephson, 2001)

Not a deficit model

Finally among the flaws is the assumption that to need a mentor-coach you must have a problem – a deficit. We contend that 'you don't need to be sick to get better'. If there is a problem, it and its nature are likely to become apparent to both the mentor-coach and client as a natural part of the careful and thorough exploration of the context.

In this model a more neutral stance is suggested – hence the word 'issues'. As the mentor-coach helps the client to think through the context and the client formulates words to represent their thinking and feeling, they will begin to crystalize expressions of any problem that may exist, but equally there may well be successes on which to build further.

A critical point to note is that there may be a number of possible issues and the client may well not know of them all until the opportunity to explore the context thoroughly has occurred – and even then may need help in deciding which one to talk about first in some depth.

Fundamentally, this model helps the client highlight issues to be addressed and directions to be considered that stem from their description(s) of the context. Hence issues come as the second main stage of the process.

What is the issue?

Clients sometimes come with a clear idea of the issue(s) they want to talk about. Often that is what the greater part of the session is about. On occasions, however, even when they have a clear idea to begin with, they change their minds as a result of having an all too rare opportunity to talk in a structured and rigorous way through the context. The mentor-coach has to help the client be alert to this possibility and to what the real issue is.

It is not an obviously easy task, but plenty of signals relating to this will emerge in the first main stage, though it may be that a client will simply talk him/herself out of an issue by coming to realize that what they thought they needed to talk about is actually going along fine, but without necessarily seeing at first that there is something else that needs to be surfaced or what it is.

Forming and testing hypotheses

In this stage, therefore, there may need to be some probing (testing out) of hypotheses around signals that the client has given the mentor-coach. The formulation of hypotheses is an important part of the mental capability of the skilled mentor-coach. Indeed, the skill level required here is high. In addition to formulating and holding in her head a hypothesis – or indeed two or three hypotheses at the same time – the mentor-coach will need to continue to listen to and observe carefully her client. At the same time she will need to be able tentatively to come up with ways of testing out the hypothesis without disrupting the flow of her client's thinking and talking.

It is important for the mentor-coach to strive rigorously for integrity here. She must be open to her hypothesis being confirmed or disconfirmed. All too often researchers (for that is what a mentor-coach is helping to do at this point in the process, research) form a hypothesis and become so attached to it that the mindset is one of needing to confirm the hunch, rather than be willing seriously to test it and, in this context, to help the client to test it. It is confirmation or disconfirmation by the client, directly or indirectly, that will signal the way forward. The rightness or wrongness of the hunch by the mentor-coach is a secondary issue.

A cynical/sceptical frame of mind

A client may come with a cynical view of the value of mentoring-coaching. Her mentor-coach may want to encourage scepticism and draw it out into the open. While many clients come with a definite thought in their minds about the issue to be addressed, at the opposite extreme there are two further possibilities for the mentor-coach. The first is that a client may come in a relatively dissatisfied, demotivated, demoralized or even cynical frame of mind and may have little idea as to where or how to begin. (This will very often be the case if the arrangement has been foisted upon a client by a line manager or system of some kind.) The exploration of the context should help both parties to gain some idea of what the *possible* issues might be. There are ways of stimulating this if they don't come reasonably naturally.

One way is to ask the client a question like, 'What aspects of your work in the last year have you been most pleased with?' The opportunity this kind of question presents for a focus on the positive is of considerable emotional/psychological importance. In particular, it signals the positive emphasis to be placed upon the whole process. It also offers great potential for later stages of the process, where in the mentoring-coaching part of the model an approach described as an 'Appreciative Inquiry' can be very powerful. (See the sections on Stages 4 and 5 – Future and Deciding – and Chapter 19 in Part Two of this book.)

> Appreciative inquiry is the co-operative co-evolutionary search for the best in people, their organisations and the world around them. It involves discovering what gives 'life'. . . . (Cooperrider and Whitney, 2005)

From a practical point of view, the question about what has pleased the client in recent months can provide an opportunity for her to select a success on which to build – if that is her dominant disposition in the meeting. If it is not her dominant disposition, it will help to redress a possible imbalance.

What is least pleasing?

Conversely, it can be important to ask a question about what has pleased the client least in recent months, or about 'what has not gone so well'. In both cases there may be a wealth of responses. The reader should note the careful wording of the question. It is not about what has *displeased* the client, for that might swing too easily back to something negative. Balance and measured thinking are both required here.

The main task of the mentor-coach, then, is to listen very carefully, to summarize/list the responses and to reflect them back to the client. At the same time the mentor-coach must look and listen for the signals that might indicate the part of the response that the client is exhibiting most feeling about – positive or otherwise. Examples would be enthusiasm, pleasure, confidence on one hand, or anxiety, uncertainty, disappointment, discomfort on the other.

Reflecting back the feelings

If such feelings are indicated, it is crucial that they be reflected back to the client as part of the process of testing out whether the matter that is generating those feelings is the one that she would like to address in order to bring about change. This bit of Stage 2 could be brought to a head with an appropriate closed question such as 'Is that the issue that you would most like to talk further about?', 'Is that the issue on which you would like to be coached?'

Summarizing the issues

In some cases the sort of signal referred to in the previous paragraph is not at all clear. In this event the mentor-coach may need to take particular care to summarize the possible issues for the client (giving her an opportunity to ensure that the list is complete – for even skilled mentor-coaches sometimes have memory lapses!) and then to ask the client to identify the most urgent issue with a question like, 'Of the things that we have just listed, which would be most helpful to you to talk about first?'

The choice must be real for the client. The mentor-coach does not decide the issue, either directly or by manipulation. It is worth commenting here that manipulation of the content of the meeting by the mentor-coach would conflict head-on with the values on which this whole model rests. The mentor-coach manages the process, not the content.

A managed silence

Clients often become silent for a while after such a question has been asked. The mentor-coach must resist the temptation to fill the silence, and should never suggest the answer. If the silence becomes inordinately long, the mentor-coach may want to comment on the fact that the question has clearly presented difficulty, so that the client is not left paralysed, but most silences in conversation are much shorter than we imagine, and what might seem like a long silence can be extremely productive.

Risk the silence becoming too long rather than fill it!

Given a fair opportunity, most people at this stage will have a view as to the most pressing issue, some will need a moment to be sure, may need a few seconds to gather the courage to say it and/or a little thought as to exactly how to phrase it (for it may not be exactly as the mentor-coach has summarized it). There is also the possibility that some preliminary discussion of two or three issues may need to take place before the client can decide in which issue it would be most helpful to be coached. (Note that coaching in this model may be in an issue as much as – if not more than – in a skill. More of that later.)

What if it's the 'wrong' issue?

The mentor-coach may believe that another issue that has been referred to should be tackled before the one chosen by the client. The order in which issues need to be addressed may well emerge at a later stage (e.g. Stage 5 – Deciding), but it is vital that the client be allowed to find that out, even though when Stage 5 arrives it may be necessary to track back to the end of Stage 2 (Issues). Skilled probing questions at this stage can help to avoid having to track back later, but occasionally moving forwards and backwards – as needed by the client – is perfectly in order.

In any event this is an iterative cycle, so other issues may be addressed at future meetings. It may not be until one or two issues have been addressed through more than one iteration that the client feels a real difference is being made in the work.

Tracking back

The reader may have noticed that the stages of the model are linked by two-way arrows (see Figure 1.1 on p. 13). There is some sense in which this is a linear model: Stage 1 (Context) should be followed by Stage 2 (Issues) and so on, and progress through the model should be stage by stage. The mentor-coach should not allow the client to leap forward through the stages – skipping some of them – but it is acceptable and sometimes very necessary to track back.

In the second stage the mentor-coach may get the feeling that there is a piece missing. This is often because there is! Going back to collect the piece that will help the picture or story make more sense may be absolutely necessary. (Over time one is aiming for the client to grasp the process in such a way that s/he could apply it without the immediate help of a mentor-coach, so the amount of moving forwards and backwards should be limited. Otherwise, the flow of the process will seem confused and disjointed and its clarity will be clouded.)

It may not quite make sense

The mentor-coach needs to be on the alert for things in this stage that don't quite make sense. The client may, for example, start to focus on an issue that seems to the mentor-coach to be relatively peripheral to the story that has been told so far. In this event it may be necessary to say something like, 'Take me back over that part of the story . . .'. Equally it is perfectly reasonable by this time for the mentor-coach to admit to the client that he/she doesn't quite understand. There are lots of ways of putting this. 'Tell me again (or a bit more) about that'. It may sometimes be necessary to do this to resolve what may appear to be conflicting aspects of the story – possible contradictions.

Challenge in Stage 2

It is a fine line that must be trodden here if the issue that it would be most helpful to the client to talk about is to be identified. The decision is the client's. Yet the mentor-coach has a significant responsibility to ensure that, if necessary, the decision is thoroughly tested.

As coherence in the process develops through later iterations of the cycle, clients become more confident about what they would like to be mentor-coached in next. In the first cycle this confidence may conceivably be false. Experienced mentor-coaches will develop the ability to intuit this.

At first, however, one may have just a slight suspicion that a decoy has been offered up, not deliberately, but one that is suggested because there is potential threat or unease about the issue that might be most pertinent. The 'decoy' is usually a contiguous issue and the client may not realize what he/she is doing.

Probing questions

Probing questions will be appropriate here but still delivered tentatively. Sometimes it begins with reminding the client of the possible issues that have been summarized and checking the thinking behind choosing the one we have labelled a 'decoy'. 'Tell me what the main benefits are that you hope would come from making progress on the issue you have chosen' might be a way of probing. The most important thing to note is that in this particular situation feelings – hidden or overt – are at work, so the mentor-coach needs to be aware and sensitive to how what happens next helps the client to manage or possibly dispel the anxiety that is influencing them.

Urgent or important?

It may be valuable to ask the client to rank all the possible issues that have been summarized in order of urgency/importance. The most urgent is not always the most important. We often make the mistake of neglecting the important in favour of the urgent. This can lead on to a discussion that highlights which is which and why.

Evidence

Another feature of the model (the visual representation of the process) is the square in the centre labelled 'evidence'. This is the first stage where the link with evidence is represented. (There is more on this 'bubble' in Chapter 9.) In Stage 1 the mentor-coach is in an acceptant mode, listening carefully and largely accepting – subject to clarification – what the client says.

In Stage 2 the mentor-coach has to make a judgement call. The judgement is about whether the client has accurately identified the issue that it would be most helpful at this point in time to talk about some more. In making this judgement the mentor-coach should be able to call to mind and may, though not necessarily, share again with the client information/evidence from the story that was told in Stage 1 (Context) that will either favour the choice made by the client or give the mentor-coach cause to doubt it.

We're talking here about specifics, not just hunches. The hunches are tested in the light of specific evidence.

How much will it matter?

If the evidence suggests that the wrong choice has been made, another judgement call is needed from the mentor-coach. This is, how much will it matter right now to leave what appears to be the more important matter that the client has put to one side?

It may be that the answer is not obvious. The importance of the matter left aside may be crystal clear, but tactically it could be wise to accept that the client is not ready in the first iteration of the cycle to handle something so big or crucial. Confidence and trust may still be relatively delicate and as yet a sense of empowerment is only beginning to form.

In this case, no matter how important the issue, better to leave it aside for a while rather than blow away the whole process by scaring away the client with big issues.

Someone else's responsibility

An acid test of the appropriateness for the client of the chosen issue is whether or not it is something over which they have influence or authority. If they choose something over which they have no authority or opportunity to make a difference, it is not an appropriate issue for this process. This is a baseline test.

A client who has entered the mentoring-coaching process feeling stress or distress at work may well look to someone else to change the situation. If their disposition about that stress changes while telling the story or in Stage 2, they may well decide that there are things (they may not know what they are) that they can do to change the situation. If a client remains convinced that they can do nothing about a particular situation, more work is needed in this stage, either to help further develop their disposition or to find another issue to work on. A client may later come back to this point and decide that they can do something about an issue over which they had felt helpless. This is infinitely preferable to trying to persuade them that they *have* to face up to something. It is worth stating here that persuasion – certainly any direct persuasion – is outside the list of helpful mentoring-coaching behaviours in this model.

Victim mode

If the client is adopting the role of victim he/she will be likely to look to others for a solution and want to say what others should do. It should be noted that even when a client sees a particular issue as something that has to be dealt with by someone else – perhaps the line manager – he/she may welcome some mentor-coaching as to how to raise this with that person in discussion. There are other kinds of reasons why the client may identify issues for someone else to solve. Some of these are considered in depth in the second part of this book. Stage 2 can take a while to process in this kind of case, but it is relatively uncommon.

Controlling our own destiny

People generally are pleased to receive help in thinking things through to a position where they can increase their personal influence over their own destiny.

> Education is about helping people, individually and collectively, to increase their control over their own lives. Community education makes that commitment explicit. (Pask, 1992)

Underlying the whole methodology of mentor-coaching is the belief that our humanity is enhanced by increasing our personal influence over our own destiny. It also happens to be a tenet of a truly democratic society and a fundamental characteristic of the purpose of education. This is part of the reason why, in this model, mentor-coaches do not tell clients what to do, do not guide them (except for guiding them through the stages of the process), do not advise them and do not make suggestions.

There is no sense in which it is argued that these things are bad things *per se*. It is simply that these things have whatever place they need in some other process – not this one. This will be explored a little more in a later chapter when the wisdom within this process of doing as much as possible through questions is considered in greater depth. Lest the reader become impatient with what seems like deliberate avoidance of a simple technique, an indication can be offered of the kind of situation where telling, advising, guiding and so on might be appropriate, namely any situation that might be an emergency where rescue from immediate or pressing dangers is required. Mentor-coaching would clearly not be appropriate if the building catches fire! Similarly, it would not be helpful if very damaging behaviours need to be halted. It could be very pertinent, however, in developing an awareness of how to avoid fires and what to do in the *hypothetical case* of one breaking out.

This stage is complete when the mentor-coach checks carefully that he/she has understood clearly (in the client's words) the issue in which the client – after very careful thought – wants to be mentor-coached.

Statement of the issue

Much of the rest of the process of mentor-coaching from this point on hinges crucially around absolute clarity as to the issue it is to focus on. Thus the National College for School Leadership's model for consultant leaders has a process in which a statement is written beginning with the words, 'I need to . . .'. We do not recommend such a formulation because it appears to allow for the focus to switch straight to action. Rather it can be extremely helpful if the client is given space and time to work out – with probing questions from the mentor-coach if needed – a concise (perhaps no more than 20 to 25 words) written statement of the issue. Such clarity will greatly enhance the remainder of the process and guarantee its focus.

Questions the mentor-coach might ask in this stage

As the process moves forward, suggestions for questions to the client become more difficult to make. This is because each person and their context are so unique. So the following suggestions are offered tentatively. They give an idea of what might happen and how the writer might frame certain responses to imagined situations.

What the reader will have to do is think of how s/he might respond to situations s/he has imagined while reading. When actually working as a men-tor-coach you will be attending fully to the person and this will prompt certain lines of questioning that will be generated by hypotheses formulated while attending/actively listening. For example, the fourth and fifth questions in the following list would, if used, be derived from some observed behaviour by the client and some reflections forming in the mind of the mentor-coach. All the questions should be thought of in that light.

- What are the things you have been most pleased with in your work in recent months?
- What has pleased you least in the last few months at work? (Note the language: the mentor-coach does not ask, 'What are you *dis*pleased with?' Think through why the question is formulated as it is.)
- Are there any things that have not gone so well?
- In the last few minutes you've talked about . . . and . . . and . . . that all seem to be live issues. Are there others that I've missed?
- When we talked about . . . (a person or a facet of work), I noticed some tension/uncertainty/anxiety. Correct me if I'm mistaken. Would it be helpful if we talked more about that? Is this the issue that you would most like to be coached in? Or is there something more urgent/

important? (Note that this is a string of questions that would have to be adapted in the light of the responses to each part.)

- Of all the things we have talked about, which is the one that it would be most helpful to you to talk (more) about in this (or the next) session?
- You've mentioned . . . (person or facet of work) that you hadn't mentioned before. It would be helpful to me if you could say some more about that.
- One of the things I've noticed is that all the issues you've talked about are issues for other people (e.g. the children, your team, your line manager) to address. Talk to me about any issues that may end up 'on your plate'.
- What are the things at work that, if you could, you would want to change? (The mentor-coach must listen out for the parts of the answer that might be things the client might in the end be responsible for.)
- What things could you/do you need to do differently at work?
- What is the next challenge for you in your work?
- What is the most challenging thing for you in your job?
- You've mentioned a number of things that seem urgent. Which of them are most important?
- You've been sounding a bit 'put upon'. How far do you want to/could you be more in control of your own destiny?
- What will be the consequences (for you or others for example, your team, your clients, the children, the patients) if nothing changes?
- Why is that? How do you know that? (Such questions need handling carefully if the note of challenge is to stay within reasonable bounds.)

The end to be achieved with an appropriate selection of questions is for mentor-coach *and* client to discover the issue that it would be most helpful to the client to receive some coaching on at this point in time.

Issues for the reader to reflect upon

- The 'correct' stance for a mentor-coach is to eschew fixing things or advising the client, but what is your natural inclination? How easy would it be to change that?
- What might you do if neither you nor the client can easily discern the issue?
- How far can you rely upon the declared statement of the client as to the issue that needs to be addressed? How far and in what ways might this need to be tested?

- What would you think it most helpful to do (and *not* to do) if the issue seems to be staring you in the face while the client cannot seem to see it at all?
- What does the notion of 'alignment' convey to you? How is it important in this stage and how might you and the client best be guided by the concept?
- How tolerant are you of the 'victim mentality'? What sort of things might you need to bear in mind if you challenge it?
- Is it issues or people that need sometimes to be challenged? What are the practical implications of your answer to this question?
- How would you judge whether a silence was becoming unproductive?
- What do you sound like when you become challenging? How easy is challenge for you? Is it too easy?
- How are your values going to come into play in this stage?
- What do you need to do to ensure that a climate of dependency does not creep into the process?
- How might you recognize that a 'decoy' issue was being offered you?
- How would you manage the situation in which a client tried continually to evade responsibility?

5 Stage 3: responsibility

A short but vital stage

This is the shortest chapter so far. It is frequently the shortest part of the process for reasons set out later. In at least one respect it is also the most important. If the client does not see that some change is necessary and that it is his/her responsibility to identify and, with help, work out what change is needed and how it might be brought about, the whole process is pointless.

Double loop learning

It can also be argued that there is only a minimal point in working out how to bring about a particular change to a particular situation – single loop learning. The object of this process is not only to solve particular issues but also to help the client to develop a paradigm shift that involves being able to approach a whole range of situations with confidence. There is a methodology that is widely applicable: 'If I can deal with this issue, then I can deal with other situations, both similar to and dissimilar from this one'. Some writers refer to this kind of learning as 'double loop learning': 'By double loop learning we mean learning that results in a change in values and theories-in-use, as well as in strategies and assumptions' (Argyris and Schon, 1996).

Who is responsible?

Many issues faced in the workplace seem to be someone else's fault. It is certainly the case that when you face a particularly difficult or complex issue, there are often others involved in some way. So, before proceeding into the coaching part of the model, it is vital that the client is clear about who is primarily responsible for the matter that has been identified at the end of Stage 2 (Issues).

No point, if it's not me!

We are not necessarily talking about sole responsibility for a whole set of actions. Nevertheless, if the matter identified in Stage 2 is something that the client can do nothing to influence or change, because they have no access either to the person(s) who hold the formal responsibility or to any of the critical factors in the situation or have no authority over it, no amount of mentoring-coaching of the client is going to make any difference. An inappropriate issue has been identified. The time has not, however, been wasted. Realizing that he/she cannot change that particular factor may be a great relief and a very important piece of understanding for the client. It may also help identify to whom he/she needs to talk if the matter is to be addressed and also how he/she might go about raising the matter with that person.

Wanting to do something

Nevertheless, any issue to be carried forward into the coaching part of the model must be something that as a practical matter the client could do something about. Equally important is that the person must *want* to do something about it. This desire may not be automatic as a result of Stages 1 and 2 (Context and Issues). The model provides for the mentor-coach to help the client first of all to see a *need* to do something about it. Recognition of a need for something to be done may well be the critical stimulus for the desire to take some action.

Don't rush in!

It is not necessary at this stage for the client to have any clear notion as to what action is possible. Indeed, such a notion could unhelpfully pre-empt the next stage of the process. Nevertheless mentor-coaches and clients do sometimes rush into deciding what to do before Stage 3 has been completed. When this happens, the whole process often comes unstuck because the client is not fully convinced that he/she is the one who should take responsibility for the change(s) that need(s) to be brought about. A further danger is that no picture has yet emerged as to what things will be/look/feel like if appropriate change is brought about. It is also sometimes the case that a single idea is latched on to without a wide consideration of all the available possibilities. In Stage 3 the mentor-coach is simply(!) ensuring the motivation and responsibility of the client.

Now I know I need to, I really *want* to

If an impetus has begun to develop as the key point of focus emerges, the client is often energized simply by that emergence: 'Now I know what it is that needs to change, I really want to find out how to bring about change'. The mentor-coach needs to be on the lookout for whether the client is up for the challenge of the change.

Other people may have a part to play

If this impetus has not done the trick, the matter of responsibility and owner-ship may need to be worked through carefully. If there are other people who could play a part in bringing about the necessary change, it is important that the client is helped to pin down the critical contribution that *they* can make – and preferably that *only* they can make. Clients may, for example, hold the view that 'Somebody needs to . . .'. Low-key but possibly challenging responses by the mentor-coach are appropriate here. For example, the 'hang-ing' question 'Somebody?' invites them to narrow down – eventually to themselves – precisely who it is who needs to take action.

What if nothing is changed?

The client might not accept the invitation. In this event the mentor-coach may want, for example, to raise for consideration what impact the issue could have if it remains unaddressed.

The mentor-coach may want to explore the range of possible protagonists in the relevant scenario. This is strictly *not* so that mentor-coach and client can find someone else to take responsibility but so that the client can see that if anything of significance is to change, then it is he/she who must in the final analysis be prepared to take action, even though he/she and their action are only part of the picture. Clients may even need the comfort of knowing that they are not alone in the whole situation.

I *suppose* it's me

Sometimes a client will accept rather uncertainly or even grudgingly that s/he is the one who needs to take responsibility. For example, in answer to a ques-tion like, 'So, who is the person who needs to take action?' the reply may be, 'I *suppose* it's me'. Depending on how it is said – the tone, facial expression, body language and so on – this might not sound like real ownership or commitment to change. This kind of answer probably shows that responsibility has not so far been seriously grasped. The mentor-coach may need to try again, perhaps by gently repeating the one word, 'suppose', as a question. This might bring some reluctance or uncertainty to the surface that can then be further explored. This stage has only really been secured when the client, by a combination of words, tone, facial expression and body language, signals that s/he is really up for bringing about some change by his/her own personal efforts.

Most clients see the point of this stage fairly readily, but it is as well to be prepared for the person who consistently tries to evade responsibility and may even prefer the comfort of a good 'whinge' to the excitement and reward of making a difference! In the extreme the possibility of such a disposition may need to be surfaced – very carefully! Such people are not frequently encountered in mentoring-coaching, and if they are encountered, it usually becomes clear in Stage 1.

Three prerequisites

So, to sum up some of the above points: however ready to be coached in a particular matter the client appears to be, the mentor-coach should ensure that the client articulates that:

- action to bring about change *is* necessary,
- he/she is not willing for the current situation to continue
- it is he/she who needs to initiate the action.

These are the three prerequisites for mentoring-coaching and time will be wasted by proceeding to the coaching half of the model if they are not secured.

How do you feel?

What the mentor-coach is trying to detect is precisely how the client feels at the thought that things really could be different. S/he might ask that question directly. If the answer is 'Excited', 'Really good', 'Really relieved' and so on, there is evidence that responsibility is being or is going to be accepted. 'Doubtful', 'Uncertain', 'Not very confident' for example, indicate there may be more work to do in this stage. The excitement and confidence may come as the next half of the model unfolds, but this should not be presumed. If the answer is uncertain, the mentor-coach needs to invite the client to explore the nature of that uncertainty, doubt or low confidence. It may be simply that the client is unable yet to identify exactly what change is necessary. That is acceptable as a basis for moving forward. But unwillingness disguised as uncertainty is not helpful as a platform for progress.

What change?

It was suggested earlier that it is not necessary at this stage for either mentor-coach or client to know precisely what the change is that needs to be brought about – merely that *some* change is necessary.

Both people may have some ideas. Equally both may at this point have no idea at all. Any strong idea as to precisely what the change will be may actually be very premature. In this particular process it is recommended that judgement be suspended on this matter until the next stage has been undertaken and that no decision is reached until the end of Stage 5. The reasons will become clear as the next two stages unfold.

A red light

In the diagram of the model used for training the stage that represents this particular piece of progress is normally represented in red. You can think of it as a red traffic light that turns green only when the client has signalled ownership, responsibility and a determination to bring about some change.

Some questions the mentor-coach may ask in this stage

- In the situation you chose to explore in more depth, what are the likely consequences for you if nothing changes?
- Who are the people who need to take action in this situation?
- What part do *you* need to play in bringing about change?
- Is this something that only you can change, or are you hoping that someone else will sort it?
- How keen are you that something should be done about this?
- In answer to the previous question you said, 'I suppose it's me'. What is the feeling that lies behind that word 'suppose'?
- When you consider the prospect of a real improvement in this situation, how do you feel?

Issues for the reader to reflect on

- How will you know that your client has really accepted responsibility for change?
- What are the sorts of things that could be or become barriers to his/ her acceptance of responsibility?
- To what extent should a mentor-coach 'push' the client towards the acceptance of responsibility?
- What are possible reasons for not trying to pin down particular courses of action at this stage?
- To what extent and why might it be a waste of time to proceed beyond this stage if the client does not grasp firmly his/her responsibility for change?
- What do you make of the possible 'internal dynamics' of the move from *needing* to be somewhere to *wanting* to be there (in terms of this model)?
- How important are feelings in this stage? Besides talking about them how else might the mentor-coach gain insight into the feelings of the client?
- What do you currently understand by the term 'double loop learning'? Why is it so much more important than single loop learning? (NB: double loop learning is not the same as either 'deep' or 'profound' learning. See Part Two of the book, Chapter 20, for more consideration of this issue.)

6 Stage 4: future

Now begins the second half of the whole process. If the first half is about pure mentoring – primarily thinking things through – the second half is about action, that is, about coaching, which is defined in this model as '*thinking through how to move from where I am to where I need/want to be*'. As in the first half of the model, there are three stages in this part. Note that thinking things through continues to be the activity that occurs in this half.

The body takes the lead!

Interestingly this feels like a much more active part of the process. It is often conducted with mentor-coach and client on their feet for a lot of the time, working at a flip chart stand. This is very positive in that it signals that we are now focusing on action that needs to be taken. Its almost as though the body is taking over the lead from the brain!

Stage 4 has two distinct parts: envisioning the ideal future and brainstorming possible steps towards it.

The ideal future

At the close of Stage 3 (Responsibility) the mentor-coach, having ascertained that the client really wants to bring about some change, will invite her to imagine that she has woken up one morning to find that the scene has changed to one where the issue being explored in Stage 2 (Issues) has been completely resolved and that everything in that particular aspect of the work is now as good as it could possibly be. She might want to close her eyes to imagine this.

Drawing (upon) the future

The client needs to be encouraged to assume that all barriers – time, cost, energy, the co-operation of others – to such a happening no longer exist, and that there is nothing to stop this ideal picture becoming a reality. Nor is he/she to bother at this point about exactly how it is to happen – he/she is simply to concentrate on what it would look/be like. *And then to draw it.*

This is a technique rich in potential. It is used widely in a large variety of contexts and there is a substantial rationale that has evolved for it, accompanied by a significant body of research. The main point of the rationale is that it helps free up the imagination and creativity of people who make such drawings. It is a particularly valuable tool for working with well-educated, articulate people who are very used to putting everything into words – either orally or in writing. It may also be especially useful to people who find it hard to form the precise words to express what they long for.

Words versus pictures

Although we can use both talking and writing as parts of the process of thinking and learning, they can be constraining too. Once we have spoken a set of words, we sometimes find it hard to take them back or alter them, and sometimes it is hard to think of the precise word we want to convey feeling, among other things. There are different constraints to do with drawing – as is pointed out later – and the reader will see that both drawing and talking are advocated as parts of the focus for thinking.

> There are levels and kinds of meaning that precede words. (Heron, 1996)

Besides freeing clients from some of the constraints of words, drawing also taps into other kinds of creativity. It is not entirely without risk however.

'I'm no good at drawing'

Two main risks are worth comment here. The first is the risk for the mentor-coach that the client will be, to one degree or another, reluctant to have a go at a drawing. This arises from the conviction that many people hold that they cannot draw. It is most important that mentor-coaches develop their own way of handling this. Essentially, there is no particular focus on the quality of the art-work! Stick people and other simple kinds of drawing are very welcome. Having said that, it is important that it be a drawing rather than a chart, diagram or mind-map, though this is not because we see no place in the thinking process for such tools. They could very well be of use as part of the two final stages of this model. *There should be no words, except perhaps to label something.*

The best, if not the only, way

Mentor-coaches often ask in training whether the drawing is the only way of tackling this stage. In truth, the answer is that it has been found to be the *best* way. Experience suggests that when mentor-coaches in training are asked to try it out, they sometimes resist, and even, at first, categorically refuse. Usually they can be persuaded, for the sake of their future putative clients, to give it a go. When this happens many of the fiercest resisters have the integrity to say that they found it a powerful, enlightening or rewarding experience.

It is worth recognizing, however, that if the resistance in the client is very strong, the mentor-coach may decide not to put at risk the trust and confidence that has been built up in the first three stages by trying absolutely to insist on it. But mentor-coaches should be in no doubt that if alternatives – such as diagrams, pictures painted in words orally – are used, the outcome will, to a significant degree, be less rich.

A further point in training arises over whether the picture needs to be on A1 paper. Can't it be smaller? The answer will have occurred straight away to the reader who perceives the need for expansiveness. Many people feel very constrained and confined by the circumstances within which they have requested mentor-coaching. Without provoking a feeling of 'paper agoraphobia'(!) the mentor-coach uses the A1 sheet to invite a feeling of constraints and narrowness being removed. Again, the body takes the lead.

Unintended elements

The second risk is that the client will draw things in the picture in a way they did not consciously intend. In fact, this can provide valuable material for sensitive exploration in the conversation that follows and is one of the more significant reasons for strongly encouraging the production of a drawing.

A private activity

It is a good idea to give the client some space and privacy to do the drawing. This is the one part of the process that the client usually does on his/her own.

Often a client will arrive at the end of Stage 3 (Responsibility) at roughly the time that a session was due to end. In this case the drawing can be done between sessions. If not, the mentor-coach might go off and make some tea or just simply have a stroll outside. Ideally, the drawing should be on a sheet of flip chart paper. So flip chart pens are appropriate here and it is very helpful if this stage can be carried out on a flip chart that is on a stand, to enable it to be an active process that can be worked on during the session and also looked at from a little distance, say, a few feet away.

A sort of vision

One of the reasons that people find themselves stuck in all sorts of unpalatable situations is that they have either lost their personal vision of their context or did not ever develop one in the first place. Using this technique invites the client to formulate a vision, albeit a particular kind of vision that may have bearing on a limited part of his/her (working) life.

A paradigm shift

It may, however, involve the generation of a paradigm shift for the client. For example, in an instance where the client was being bullied in the workplace, and had subsided into the role of victim, the drawing of the picture presented her as a very strong person confronting and prevailing over the bully in a very positive and constructive way. Subsequent stages helped her work out how she would bring this about and she broke free of the victim mode so convincingly that the mentor-coach was certain she would not easily relapse into that mode in any new circumstance. She adapted her vision of herself at work in a very important way.

Talking the picture through

Having thanked the client for taking the risk of producing a picture the mentor-coach then engages in conversation with him/her over what is in the picture with an invitation such as 'Talk me through what you have drawn'. The mentor-coach should not interrupt while the client does so. When the client finishes the mentor-coach may want to ask all sorts of questions generated from particular aspects of the drawing or the account the client has added. This conversation commonly takes place with mentor-coach and client on their feet, sometimes standing close to the drawing and sometimes standing back. Sometimes the client alters the drawing in some way to make something clearer or to put in something that s/he only thought of as they were talking. The decision to add or change something must belong to the client. The mentor-coach takes no ownership of the picture or what is in it and expresses no judgement about any aspect of it. S/he should not, therefore, say things like, 'Now I want you to . . .'.

'Where are you in the picture?'

One particularly relevant question might be, 'Where are you in this picture?' if that has not already been volunteered. Questions about the significance of where other people have been placed and how they are represented can also be relevant.

What's missing?

The picture is sometimes as revealing for what is missing from it as for what is in it. This is worth looking for carefully and exploring as necessary. Sometimes something positive has accidentally been left out. So, if that positive element has featured in Stage 1 (Context) or Stage 2 (Issues), the mentor-coach might say, 'I notice that . . . does not feature in the drawing.' (NB: *not* 'Why is . . . not in your picture?') The client must have the freedom and space to comment and, if s/he so decides, to alter the drawing.

Sometimes the client has deliberately left something – often a person – out of the drawing. This is frequently because s/he has decided that the ideal would be for a particular element (a person) not to be there in the future. This can yield fruitful thinking in the next stages. Sometimes a client leaves him/herself out of the drawing. In such a case it would be very important to explore the thinking – again without undue pressure from the mentor-coach.

No list

It is not worth trying to list all the possible types of question that might come to mind. It must be sufficient here to note that what is going on in this conversation is *dialogue* – a search together for *meaning*. It is the meaning of the picture at a practical level and in terms of feeling, ownership and creativity that is being explored, and careful questioning will bring this out.

An active process

Many clients testify that they feel energized by this process. They can feel themselves beginning to move in a positive direction. As indicated earlier, the dialogue often takes place with both persons standing and the picture fixed to a flip chart stand. This both prompts a rise in energy levels and symbolizes that energy.

The mentor-coach will need to get a clear sense of the extent to which the client is being energized at this point. Someone who is highly energized will not take a lot of prompting in the rest of this half of the process, and may even need encouraging to pause at various points before rushing forward. The client who fails to display much energy here may, conversely, need (and may overtly seek) high levels of support. If this support is readily available, the client will lapse into dependency, so this will have to be managed very carefully by the mentor-coach if the process is not to go awry. Such cases are best handled through careful and gentle questioning.

Some questions the mentor-coach might ask in the first part of Stage 4

- 'Talk me through the picture you have drawn'.
- 'I notice that . . . occupies centre stage'. (Note that this is a sort of 'hanging' question.)
- 'Who (or what) is this?' (pointing to a particular part of the drawing).
- 'What is happening here?' (again, pointing to an aspect of the drawing).
- 'Is there anything (or anyone) missing from the picture?'
- 'Where are you in this picture?'
- 'Highlight for me some of the main differences between what's in the picture and what is happening at present'.

Readers will be aware that there may be no need for these questions. They are possibilities for helping explore the picture if the client is finding it difficult to know what to talk about or *how* to talk about the picture.

Issues for the reader to reflect upon

- What might be the issue of resistance at the start of this stage? What thoughts have you got on how you would resolve the issue?
- Play back in your mind some of the possible thinking behind the use of drawing in this stage? Why is it important to try not to use words in the drawing?
- What reasons are there for standing up to discuss the drawing?
- If the client wants to alter or add to the drawing during the discussion, what that is positive would this signal? Is there any downside to this happening?
- How will you, as mentor-coach, know that this is a really rich picture?
- How will you know that the client has included all the appropriate facets of the future, unencumbered by any reservations?
- How will you know that the picture and the discussion have achieved their objective? How do you perceive that objective?
- If the drawing does not include *all* the things that were discussed in Stage 2, what might be the possible reasons?

- What if the drawing leaves out all together the client him/herself?
- To what extent are we expecting to see 'hands on, brains on!' at work here? (What do you take that saying to mean?)

It may be important to consider what happens if the picture is drawn between sessions. One possible benefit is that the client can have more than one attempt at the drawing. Clients may feel more comfortable knowing this. On the other hand this may give rise to a client being anxious to get the drawing 'right' – whatever that may mean. The mentor-coach should stress that the drawing should as far as possible be a relaxed and relaxing experience, no matter how absorbing.

A further point of interest is that in between sessions clients may be moving on in their thinking and may as a result draw a picture of a resolved future situation that is slightly different from the one they would have drawn, had they done it 'in session' as it were. This is generally a good thing, for it indicates that the client is continuing to *think actively* about their situation and how they would ideally like it to be. Remember, the whole process is about thinking things through, and if a client is getting into the habit of doing it on his/her own, he/she is on the way to autonomy.

Possible steps towards the future

Meaning

The discussion in the first half of this stage is aimed at discovering the meaning generated by the picture. The mentor-coach will engage in a struggle to grasp it. This is very important. It carries a danger, namely that s/he, as mentor-coach, will decide that it is her/his understanding of what the picture means that matters. It is not. The most important outcome is that the client grasps the meaning for *them*. So the mentor-coach may have to have two meanings in mind. It is the second meaning – what it means for the client – that the rest of the process will be primarily concerned with, though it may be appropriate for the first meaning to be drawn upon from time to time in order to challenge and question.

Stick it on the wall!

When the meaning of the drawing has been agreed – and remember that at this stage it must be the client's *meaning* – the picture should be fixed to a wall space nearby, where both persons can see it and refer to it as necessary. This is so that the flip chart is available for the next part of the process and so that the client can again take up a pen.

More energy

The point of this part of Stage 4 is for the client to generate as many possible steps as he/she can think of that could lead to making the drawing a reality in the future. All the ideas for action should begin with a verb – these are things it is possible for the client *to do*. This, along with both mentor-coach and client standing each side of the flip chart, will aid the generation of energy.

Unlocking creativity

Everyone can in fact think of lots of possibilities – far more than they initially believe themselves capable of. As life has become more complex (especially in the highly regulated climate of education in the last two decades), lots of people have become used to waiting for the prescription from on high – be that their line manager or higher still. So some skill is required to unlock that essential and powerful creativity that is inherent in being human.

Capacity building

It is in questioning that the essential skills lie at this point. There is a great temptation for many mentor-coaches at this stage to start offering suggestions and advice. The whole process and its underpinning philosophy collapse if this temptation is not strongly resisted. One might just as well have skipped everything that has occurred till now and cut to the chase in the first instance. Making suggestions and giving advice does little, if anything, to build capacity for the individual and their organization. Building individual and, thus, organizational capacity is what this model is about.

Questions build capacity. (Pask, 2005)

Advice and questions in disguise

Having grasped that questions are the order of the day, inexperienced mentor-coaches use what look like questions to cover advice and suggestions such as 'Have you thought of/considered . . .?', 'When that happened to me, I . . .', 'Can you see any merit in . . .?' These are not really questions, but suggestions in disguise. 'Who might you need to talk to about this?' *is* a question. So is 'Will you need to talk to anyone about this?' It can often be followed by a simple one-word, 'And?' or 'Who else?'

> As a mentor-coach you help the client to generate novel solutions and strategies. (Joy, 2002)

The point here is that the role of the mentor-coach is to *help the client* generate the ideas, not do it for her/him.

The picture as a resource

The picture is a useful resource for questions, for example, 'I notice that you have drawn . . .?' put interrogatively, inviting the client to think about a particular facet of the drawing to stimulate some thinking about possible actions. In the first half of this stage such a question is applied to help clarify meaning. Here the same kind of questions have the purpose of prompting ideas. Notice that some of these are hanging questions – a single word, perhaps repeating something that the client has said that may indicate an idea lurking somewhere at the back of their mind.

A possible technique

There may be a number of suggestions that the mentor-coach might like to make. They should be treated simply as triggers to attend to certain possible areas of thinking.

> To help develop this skill, think of a particular situation you have come across and some possible ways in which it might be addressed. First, write an action you might want to suggest. Then try to formulate a question you could ask – as open a question as possible – that would prompt a client in facing that situation to think of the sort of idea you had in mind.

Thus, the mentor-coach should frame a question that will help the client focus on that area. S/he may then formulate possible steps that lie in that area *but not necessarily the one the mentor-coach had in mind.* This is good, for a train of thought has started. If it does not lead to the precise idea the mentor-coach had in mind it does not matter. If *any* idea appears on the flip chart, the technique has worked. It is important that the mentor-coach does not try to play 'Guess the answer I'm thinking of'!

Brainstorming

It is vital that the rules of brainstorming are observed in this part of the process. Every idea, however practicable or wild, should be written up on the flip-chart. There should be no discussion of an idea's merits at this point and nothing should be rejected. The main aim is to liberate the client from what had previously acted as shackles to thinking and creativity. The ideal character of this part of the process is for the client to achieve 'flow' – that wonderful feeling of empowerment that stems from having been able to visualize a bright, unencumbered future in which the issue has been resolved.

Cathartic events

During this part of the process clients sometimes recall in a quite dramatic way the situation that they are in at present, with all its potential irritations and frustrations. When this happens they may come up with some ideas that encapsulate those frustrations like 'I could resign' or – at the sudden thought of someone they feel is badly letting them down – they might say, 'I could strangle him' or 'poison his tea'. They are likely to say it, rather than write it. It may be worth encouraging them to write it if they are thinking of it, even though such thoughts are clearly not intended to have a presence in the ideal future picture! The purpose here is to allow for emotional discharge that might otherwise get in the way later. Stage 5 will dispose of the product of such a discharge quite safely!

Twenty-plus answers

If this stage goes well, it is not uncommon for the client to come up with more than 20 ideas. If the process seems slow, the mentor-coach must be patient and be willing to hold significant silences while the client rakes through various corners of his/her mind. (This is not the stage where much talk is to be encouraged.)

The outcome should be a good range of possible courses of action.

Questions the mentor-coach might ask in this stage

- 'You talked about . . . a moment ago' (this does not sound like a question. It is more of a prompt).
- 'Are there any ideas that might be suggested by your picture?'
- 'I notice in your picture . . .' (another prompt).
- 'Who might you need to talk to who can help bring your picture to reality?'

- 'Who else?'
- 'Is there anyone you need to involve?'
- 'Anyone else?'
- 'Who might give you support to achieve your picture?'
- 'Is there any resource you might need?'
- 'Are there any really wild ideas you want to put on the flip chart?'
- 'What strengths do you have that might help you?'

Reversal

As your experience of mentoring-coaching grows, you will discover a range of techniques to stimulate the generation of ideas. One such idea is to invite the client to think of the very worst thing that could happen, including, 'What would make the situation a whole lot worse?' and try to turn that on its head – to see whether this 'reversal' stimulates useful thinking.

Provocation

Another technique is to invite the client to look out of the window and tell you what is the first thing he/she sets eye on. Then to ask the client to say another word he/she associates with what they see, and to keep this association going to see whether an 'Aha' moment occurs. For example, one school leader could only come up with sanctions as ideas for generating behaviour change. She was unable to see that she was locked into a negative and punitive way of thinking. She was invited to look into the next room (as there were no external windows) and set eyes on a plate full of chocolate biscuits. It took her only moments to think of the idea of rewards as a change in mindset.

These ideas – and others of a slightly more off-the-wall kind – are perhaps worth trying out as experience develops, rather than in the first stages of a career in this field of work.

Issues for the reader to reflect on

- Why must it be the client's meaning that we are seeking to generate in this second half of Stage 4? How difficult will it be for you to put to one side your own ideas during this search for meaning?
- What are the disciplines and challenges of brainstorming? Are there any parts of this process that you may have to manage actively?
- Questions in this stage need to be open but relatively focused.
- How strong for you is the temptation towards (or habit of) giving

advice? It becomes stronger in this stage, especially with clients who lack either general confidence or apparent creativity.

- How will you react to ideas that seem to take the client back to the present but that could have a cathartic impact?
- Why is it very important for the client to hold the pen and do the writing?
- What is the value of both parties standing up focused on the flip chart in this part of the process?
- How ready are you to hold reasonable silences early in the brainstorming part of this stage? How good are you usually at holding silences and hanging back?

The issue of supervision is addressed as part of Chapters 9 and 16.

7 Stage 5: deciding

Pen in hand

Like the previous stage, this part of the process continues with the client holding the pen, standing at the flip chart. At no point should the mentor-coach take hold of the pen – it is the symbol of control and ownership. The physical feeling of grasping the pen is also *the feeling* of being in control.

The rejection process

During the previous stage the client may have come up with a number of ideas that are not practicable and some that would not contribute at all to the building of the ideal future as envisaged in the first half of that stage. It is not for the mentor-coach to point this out. The writing and the thinking that has led to them have both formed a very valuable purpose. Similarly, if they are consciously and actively eliminated by the client, a constructive purpose has been served – they have been considered and rejected.

Not stating the obvious

Equally, there may be an idea on the list that is the obvious first place to start. *It is not for the mentor-coach to point this out either.*

The role of the mentor-coach here is to invite the client to consider the list very carefully and think first whether anything found its way onto the list that he/she knows they will not do or would have altogether the wrong effect. The most obvious examples of this might be things that were simply the expression of emotional discharge, for example 'Resign' or 'Wring so and so's neck!' Though these are residues of the 'old' situation, they should be allowed onto the list in Stage 4 (Future) so as to get rid of them, as it were, and avoid interrupting the flow. As the client goes systematically through the list, he/she will include them of their own volition for crossing out – and probably smile as he/she does so!

An old mindset resurfaced

Clients may also notice things they have listed that would actually palm off responsibility again onto someone else. These might be crossed off, too, and, if not, the mentor-coach may want to explore that issue by questioning. It is vital that plenty of opportunity be allowed for clients to come to their own decision, and before any questioning about things that might be better eliminated, all other business in this stage should be conducted – including plenty of silence and 'space' to allow clients to deal with that old mindset themselves!

The central purpose of coaching

There may also be things that a client honestly believes herself incapable of. She may be right, but these, too, should be explored to some degree before being crossed off, for it may simply be that she doesn't know *how* rather than actually not being capable, an important difference. Indeed, things that she believes herself incapable of should be the focus of special attention, including a variety of versions of the question 'Why?' It is the matter of *how* that is the central business of coaching so the mentor-coach needs to be particularly alert to sense that the item might be eliminated for this kind of reason and gently and persistently challenge that reasoning. So, if it is something that appears to have positive potential to bring about the desired future, the client's desire to cross it off should be explored very carefully. It may be that the nub of the whole situation will come more clearly into focus as a result.

Grouping similar ideas

The next thing a client may notice is that several ideas are either similar or lie in the same area of thinking. For example, there may be several individuals who need to be consulted or informed. These could be identified as a group of ideas, but once again the grouping should be done by the client with minimal prompting from the mentor-coach. It is perfectly in order for the mentor-coach to ask a question like, 'Are there any other things on the list that are similar to those you have so far grouped?' and 'Are there any other possible groupings?' Notice that the only interventions here – as in most other places in this process – are questions.

Still attending to the person

A particular reason for 'attending' very closely to the person here is that there may be items in a possible group of similar matters that have individual and particular significance for the client, for example, gaining serious attention from line managers. There may perhaps be some emotional difficulty attached to such an item. It will in all likelihood be necessary to let the client keep it separate from other items so he/she can – with help from the mentor-coach – work out how to produce a strong focus on it in order to get a positive outcome.

Prioritizing and sequencing

The essential part of this stage is for the client to try to prioritize the actions that need to be taken and arrange them in sequence. These priority actions should be part of the outcome from considering the *importance* and *urgency* (see below) of each action in the priority list. The mentor-coach may genuinely not know this for herself, though the exploration of the context and the picture may offer up lots of clues. So Stages 2 and 4 (Issues and Future) may be revisited a little at this point. Sometimes something emerges from this revisit that had not come to light until now. This merely proves the worth of those stages and of the process of revisiting them. In turn, a new possible idea for action may emerge. It can be added to the list. The list is never closed.

The client keeps control

During this process actions may get prioritized that don't seem appropriate to the mentor-coach. This is where tentative but rigorous challenge may be needed. The critical skill here once again is questioning. Tone, facial expression and body language are also critical at this point. The mentor-coach must not signal disapproval or in any way pressurize the client into abandoning an idea. The latter must remain and feel in control.

Readers will note that this and the previous stage normally take place around a flip chart with writing on an A1 sheet of paper in lists with crossings-out and symbols to group and prioritize. Some readers will be aware of the importance/urgency matrix (Figure 7.1). It is possible to conduct Stage 4A (Future Picture) on a flip chart but to have the importance/urgency matrix drawn up on another sheet and invite the client to do the brainstorm on to post-its. Stage 5 can then be carried out flexibly on the matrix.

This can have an added bonus of helping the client to think in terms of what is urgent and what is important. However, there may still be a number

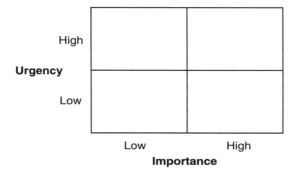

Figure 7.1   The importance/urgency matrix.

of things in the top right quadrant of the matrix that need prioritizing. In addition, this is a tool that is more appropriate in helping clients manage time more effectively. It is a possible option in this stage but mentor-coaches need to think carefully about the advantages and disadvantages of using it.

Exploring and taking risks

What is needed by way of questioning and challenging is the exploration of how the client would envisage going about the action in focus, what its purpose would be, the intended outcome, associated risks and possible unintended outcomes. In other words the client thinks and talks it through. If he/she calculates that the risks and possible unintended consequences would work against his/her vision, he/she will happily abandon it. If he/she does not, then the mentor-coach may have to persist in the exploration, depending on whether there is significant potential danger physical or otherwise, for the client or others towards whom there is a duty.

It is possible that the idea is simply of doubtful potential but the client is keen to risk it. He/she must be allowed to do so, as long as the mentor-coach has insisted on them thinking it through. The client may not achieve what he/she wants but may learn much that is of value.

The picture of the ideal future drawn by the client in the previous stage is a very valuable resource in this stage. Both in prioritizing and assessing the worth of particular ideas it can be very helpful for both mentor-coach and client to ponder the contents of the picture and the relationships of the different parts.

Accountability

In the final analysis the client may decide after systematic and rigorous critique with help from the mentor-coach, to go ahead with something the mentor-coach would not herself do in that situation. The client must retain the right to do this and must be helped to retain responsibility, and accountability, for their own decisions and actions. The mentor-coach remains accountable for the mentoring-coaching process but *not for the content and not for decisions*. The whole process is about helping the client to take responsibility – *and this always includes accountability* – for the decisions and for the actions that follow. This is why Stage 3 (Responsibility) is so important.

Authenticity and integrity

It is very unlikely that the client will insist on pursuing a course of action that is either illegal or potentially disastrous, especially if the mentor-coach has questioned rigorously including such questions as 'What is the law on matters such as this?'. If he/she does, the mentor-coach may have to declare that they cannot help the client with Stage 6 of the process. Authenticity and integrity are core values in mentoring-coaching and will come into play here. As a genuinely last resort the mentor-coach may need to say, 'That is something you should/must not do'. This is an extremely rare occurrence never encountered to date by either of the writers. However, it is a question often asked in training.

At the end of this stage the client will have a small number of actions to take in an order of priority that he/she owns. It is this short, prioritized list that is the purpose and, therefore, main outcome of this stage.

Questions a mentor-coach might ask in this stage

- On the list you have produced, is there anything that you have written down that you know would not be appropriate – that you know you are not going to do?
- Are there any things here that might be appropriate that at this time you don't know how to do?
- Are there any things that you know would have a negative impact?
- Are there any steps you have listed that appear to be similar to other things on your list? Would you like to group them?
- What appears from this list to be the most urgent thing to do? What is the most important thing on the list? How clear for you is the difference between the urgent and the important?

- Is there an obvious place to start?
- Can you highlight the three or four things on the list that might have the most beneficial impact on the situation? Is there a priority order among them?
- You are considering doing … What do you perceive to be the consequences or risks involved in that particular course of action? What is attracting you to that idea? How is X likely to respond to that particular action? (X is a person or group.)
- Is there any relevant regulation or law about that kind of solution that you should consider?

Issues for the reader to consider

- How easy is it/will it be for you to allow the client to retain control once a list has been produced, particularly if there is an obvious place to begin and the client doesn't light upon it without difficulty?
- Why is it so important for the client to hold the pen?
- What value is there in the client writing up ideas for action that are a bit 'off the wall' if s/he is only going to cross them out in this stage?
- Why should the mentor-coach not take any part in identifying the starting place in this stage – even if it is obvious?
- If the client begins to cross off the list ideas for action that s/he does not believe s/he is capable of, how might the mentor-coach explore this? What is the crucial responsibility of the mentor-coach in this situation?
- What value is there in grouping similar ideas?
- What part do feelings have in this stage of the process? For example, how does the client need to feel as a result of engaging in it?
- If the client opts to take action that you consider unwise, how might you handle that without going into expert/adviser mode?
- What are the advantages and disadvantages of using the urgency/importance matrix in this stage?
- Are there any circumstances you can think of under which it might be necessary to tell the client to do – or not to do – a certain thing?

8   Stage 6: action

One at a time

Having identified one or more steps that will begin to bring the ideal future into being, the mentor-client will now need to think through precisely *how* to carry out those actions.

The actions should be considered one at a time, unless a group of actions have been identified that need to be carried out either simultaneously or in close sequence. Future sessions with the mentor-coach may simply involve a review of how the first action was received, what impact it had, and, if successful, the client may then simply need to return to Stage 6 to think through how to take the next action and so on. It's important to remember, however, that the context may change in some way from session to session.

More double loop learning

Clients may even be able to plan subsequent actions on their own without any/much help from the mentor-coach, using the thought patterns and structures they learnt while planning the first action.

So it is important that the mentor-coach helps the client articulate the steps of this planning for action as clearly as possible. The issues to be addressed are things like what exactly is going to occur, who will be involved, where will it take place, when will it happen and so on. Matters like time of day, the exact nature of the environment and even the forms of words that will be used. An example might be helpful.

Dealing with a difficult team member

If the first action is to be a meeting with a difficult team member, for example, the client will want to consider how the meeting will be convened. Will it be by memo, through a third party (like one's secretary) or face to face? What will the client say the meeting is to be for or will be about? Will anyone else be involved? Where will it be held and what will be the rationale behind the venue chosen? Will it be informal – over a cup of tea, for example, or even a beer? The extent of the in/formality could be critical. It needs to be decided consciously and for a reason. The nature of the power relationship will be a feature in the thinking of both mentor-coach and client.

This example could yield a whole lot of further questions and the reader will have his/her own ideas.

Careful thinking, confident action

Essentially, this is the stage at which careful thinking needs to occur that will lead to the action being taken confidently and to a successful outcome. This is, in fact, the climax of the coaching part of the process and may well focus on the fine detail of the action (just as in tennis, for example, a coach may help a player to think about precisely how the fingers are wrapped around the handle of the racquet). This is often thought of as micro-coaching.

Micro-coaching

Involved in the micro-coaching may be an opportunity to explore the possibilities through a small element of role-play. In this – using for reference the example instanced earlier – the mentor-coach might offer to play the role of the difficult member of staff so that the client can try out various forms of words for convening or for starting the meeting. And although it would not be possible to role-play all possibilities and contingencies in relation to the other person's likely behaviours, thinking about some of the likely responses could help prepare the client psychologically for the encounter.

Several tries

During the process, however, the client may need to make several attempts to address the detail of what needs to be done, and how it might be done. In the same spirit the mentor-coach may need to provide a degree of challenge, using the kind of 'hanging question' we referred to earlier. For example, the mentor-coach might simply repeat a word used by the client, but in a questioning tone. The main point is that in the 'real' situation to be confronted there will only be one chance to get a difficult conversation started. If it starts badly, it will not be possible to wind the clock back and start the conversation all over again. In the mentoring-coaching situation, however, it is possible to do precisely that and thus familiarize the client with at least some possible scenarios.

The sound of my own voice

What will be of interest to the mentor-coach just starting out is that as the client tries out various possibilities, the sound of his/her own voice will often be enough to alert him/her to the possibility that something else – some other way of taking the action – might need to be tried. This will certainly happen if the client is practised in the skill of reflection and, if not, the mentor-coach will use the technique of the hanging question – the repetition of the exact words used so that the client can hear it in the mentor-coach's voice.

Procrastination

One of the things that sometimes happens in this stage is that the client engages in some form of procrastination – perhaps coming up with loads of reasons (some of which may seem entirely plausible) why the meeting or other action that has been identified earlier as both urgent and important cannot be set in motion for several days or even weeks. This might indicate that there is a doubt as to how confident the person is about whether they can in fact do what is necessary. It could indicate that commitment is waning and the sense of ownership and responsibility needs reinforcing.

Revisiting Stage 3 (responsibility)

This could make it necessary for an earlier stage in the cycle to be revisited. It would be pointless to continue and let the client depart from the session without this lack of confidence or waning ownership being addressed. The client would simply take no action and the 'latter state would be worse than the former'. By 'revisiting an earlier stage' we do not necessarily mean going through Stages 3, 4 and 5 all over again. It may be sufficient for the mentor-coach simply to ask again some of the questions proposed for Stage 3 to check again whether the client really does want to bring about change in a currently difficult situation.

Covering the escape route

Every honest adult knows that there are lots of reasons open to us to delay doing what we need to do or to put it off all together – from pressure of business (much of it perhaps trivial) to faltering courage. It can be really helpful, therefore, if the mentor-coach completes the cycle with an offer to make contact – by telephone, if possible, rather than email – immediately after the planned action is due to occur to enquire how it went. There is both moral pressure and moral support in such an offer. The client will not want his/her mentor-coach to observe a failure to implement the commitment made, or to be seen to let the mentor-coach down. In addition, the fact that the mentor-coach is going to be available to help reflect on how it went signals positive support.

Then what?

What happens next will depend on the degree of success experienced by the client during the implementation of the plan of action. If things did not go according to plan but still produced a positive outcome, the mentor-coach might help the client analyse how the success was actually generated. The point here is for the client to be helped to understand exactly what s/he did that produced the success and the dynamic that was involved. More double loop learning!

The plan came unstuck

Conversely, if the plan came unstuck and the hoped for outcome was not achieved, it is even more vital for the client to understand why. It is possible that the plan worked out with the mentor-coach was not in fact adhered to, or that some element in the whole equation (context) had been overlooked.

Back to the context?

This can all too easily happen and serves to emphasize the value of doing a really good job in Stage 1 (Context) of this whole process. Participants in training programmes often observe that Stage 1 seems very long. The payoff, positive or negative, is frequently delayed until much later in the process, for example at Stage 6. It is really important to pay strong and focused attention to this factor. As was pointed out earlier, it will not be possible to wind the clock back in real time, so letting a mess occur at the point of action because the mentor-coach has not done a thorough job at Stage 1 (Context) is something everybody needs to strive to avoid. Nevertheless, if this is what has happened, something must be done to retrieve the situation as far as is possible.

Not the client's fault

If such a situation as described in the previous paragraph should occur, the mentor-coach will be tempted to think (or even worse, say), 'Well, if you had told me about . . . I would not have agreed to your plan'. It needs to be clear that the responsibility for the *process of mentoring-coaching* lies with the mentor-coach. So, no stage should be regarded as complete until the mentor-coach has thoroughly checked that all potentially relevant factors have been considered. That is the nature of the mentor-coach's responsibility. We are however talking about responsibility – not blame. It will sometimes be the case that a plan failed for reasons that most people would not have been able to foresee.

Still thinking

It may be that all that can be salvaged from a failed plan is some new learning about the situation/context. Often it will be possible to try something else to address the situation – something from the list that had been generated in Stage 4 (Future) and prioritized at Stage 5 (Deciding). The thinking will need to be really rigorous here to ensure that any new plan of action is successful, otherwise the client will be in danger of a serious loss of confidence. One let down is likely to generate learning; two are likely to damage confidence.

Most plans work

Experience to date reveals that most plans made under the conditions we have described so far, using this model conscientiously, do work – often to a remarkably successful degree.

Back to the start

When this happens, the client often moves into a new and frequently more confident phase of work or life and is ready to engage with new challenges that the mentor-coach can help them think through. This necessitates a further complete iteration of the cycle, though much of the context will already be known.

Several iterations of Stage 6

Sometimes the success of the first planned action signals that it is now time to think about the second of the actions brain-stormed in Stage 4 and prioritized in Stage 5. Many difficulties that people need help in thinking through are complex (hence the need for help) and to resolve them several actions may be necessary. So one major iteration of the mentoring-coaching cycle may involve several iterations of Stage 6 – the action stage – to provide for mentoring-coaching in respect of several actions that are to be taken, with only cursory use of most of the earlier stages.

One complete cycle

Essentially, the process – or one iteration of it – is complete. Most contracting between mentor-coach and client involves an agreement that there will be several (commonly six or more) sessions of approximately one hour in the first instance, following which there may be more sessions agreed or some less structured continuing contact. At the very beginning it may need at least two sessions of one hour to complete the first cycle, with the opportunity to carry out the visualization activity between the first two sessions. Further sessions may be taken up with iterations of Stage 6, but if an entirely new issue is addressed (perhaps from among those discussed in Stage 2 – Issues), it may need at least a whole session, but not necessarily the two sessions that would be scheduled for a single cycle at the start of the mentoring-coaching relationship.

Finally, it is worth restating that the whole process is about thinking – thinking things through. So although the mentor-coach is there to *help* the thinking process and although there is thinking about *what needs to be done and how to do it*, both the thinking and the action are crucially the property of the client

Questions the mentor-coach might ask at this stage

- What will be the consequences if nothing is done about this issue?
- Whom do you need to involve in this matter?
- How might you go about involving him/her?

- When do you need to begin to take action?
- If you need to meet with X (where X = a difficult team member), when will be the best time to meet?
- How will you convene the meeting? Will you do it yourself? Will it be by email, telephone contact, memo, face to face?
- What will you say the meeting is about?
- What would be a good time of day for you? For him/her?
- What do you think his/her reaction will be to the request for a meeting? How do you think s/he feels about your relationship? Or this issue?
- How formal or informal will the meeting be?
- Where will be the best place to hold the meeting? Will a particular arrangement of the furniture be helpful?
- How exactly (i.e. the precise words, tone and manner) will you begin the meeting?
- Can you formulate a realistic plan for how you would like/expect the meeting to progress?
- What would count as a good outcome?
- Will anyone else be present at the meeting? Will you need to have a record of any agreements you make?
- Is there anything else you might need to do before the meeting? Does anyone else need to be informed that the meeting is to occur?
- Would it be helpful to role-play some of this?
- May I telephone you the next day to see how it has gone?

The reader will note that the specific example referred to earlier has been used to focus many of the questions. The assumption is made that the reader will be able to translate the spirit and principles of this example and the questions derived into other similar situations. The example that was chosen is relatively typical of the sort of issues that clients often want help in sorting out. In other words, it is often the management of relationships with others, especially in leadership roles, that people most often need help in thinking through.

Most people who work in a responsible position are capable of thinking through things that are subject to simple rational processes. The problem is that this largely applies only to matters that are inanimate. The moment the personal is introduced then emotions come into play, along with political and cultural issues. This makes everything that much more complex and challenging – hence the need for help in analysing and identifying the necessary action. Hence, also, Part Two of this book.

Some issues for the reader to consider

- Why is it important to adhere even at this stage to the principle of asking questions, rather than advising, telling or suggesting?
- What has the phrase 'double loop learning' come to mean to you?
- What value does the 'hanging question' have in your view?
- Why is it important to consider in this stage only one action at a time?
- Besides dealing with a difficult team member, what other examples can you think of that might help you in your thinking how to apply the principles relevant to this stage?
- Does the idea of getting the client to hear the sound of his/her own voice suggest anything deeper to you about human awareness or consciousness?
- How much might it matter that the plan of action evolved in this stage may come unstuck?
- What form of words would you personally use to 'cover the escape route'?
- Has this chapter thrown any light for you on the importance of any of the earlier stages of the cycle? If so, which stages and why?
- Given successful implementation of the plan of action, under what circumstances might it be unnecessary to return to the start of the whole cycle before using Stage 6 again straight away?
- Consider the context in which you might be working as a mentor-coach. What sort of arrangement with regard to the number and frequency of sessions might be appropriate for you and your client initially?

Mentoring-coaching or pace-setting?

In the book, *The New Leaders*, Goleman et al. (2002) distinguish coaching and pace-setting. The distinction is worth pondering, especially in the light of the now fairly common practice of advisers, consultants and line managers in schools inviting less competent colleagues to a demonstration lesson – with perhaps a difficult class or on a challenging aspect of the curriculum. On its own the demonstration of a successful lesson is a waste of time and can actually leave the observer in a worse condition than before. (Hence pace-setting is seen as correlating negatively with high standards.)

Supported by a coaching session – characterized by the sort of coaching behaviours described in this and the previous two chapters – a demonstration can be very helpful. The important part of the process is the shared, structured thinking that takes place around the demonstration. Indeed, a less competent/confident colleague might need to observe a successful demonstration, discuss with a mentor-coach what happened and why, then try similar things out with reciprocal observation, followed by further discussion around what worked and why, what went less well and why, and what the client might do to build on the incipient successes. Note that throughout the process the client does the thinking and makes the decisions with help on the thinking from the mentor-coach/demonstrator. The mentor-coach is not an instructor!

9 Evidence

How can a mentor-coach be sure about how and when to proceed?

One of the issues that often troubles inexperienced mentor-coaches is how one can know that one has successfully helped the client to identify the issue (Stage 2) that it is most important to address at this point in time. Similarly, how can the mentor-coach be sure that the client is really willing to take responsibility (Stage 3), has chosen the most appropriate starting point on which to take action (Stage 5 – Deciding), has a clear plan of action and will conscientiously implement it with real commitment (Stage 6 – Action)?

No way of knowing in advance

These are not questions only for the inexperienced mentor-coach. Someone who has worked successfully for years as a mentor-coach will enter each new mentor-coaching relationship with the same set of questions. There is no way of knowing rationally in advance that any particular individual will progress smoothly through these (or for that matter any) stages of the cycle. Each person is unique. Each person's situation is unique.

Each mentor-coaching interaction is unique

So even though a number of similarities in situation, personality, temperament, experience levels, intellectual ability, professional energy and so on may present themselves, each new person and his/her situation must be approached without presupposition and with complete openness and attention to the person.

A simple answer to a difficult question

How then will the mentor-coach answer the questions posed in the first paragraph of this chapter? The answer is by attending to the person and collecting evidence. Simple? Yes and no.

Inner voices can make a lot of noise

We have indicated earlier that there is a cognitive process occurring in the mind of the mentor-coach. The process is founded on accurate and well-developed listening skills – listening for precisely what is said – in words, tone, facial expression and body language, and clarifying with the client both the intention and the meaning of what is being communicated. The obstructions to this for the mentor-coach consist of the clutter that one may bring to the relationship, especially one's own experience, feelings, pressures, perceptions, anxieties, ideas, and even one's physical state; indeed, in some ways, one's own whole world view. These are things that most people cannot expect simply to abandon, but to be an effective listener and, therefore a capable mentor-coach it is necessary to be able to still the mind and put them to one side for the duration of the session.

Stilling the mind

The reason for that is that one will not be able to hear what the other person is saying if the inner 'voices' of the mentor-coach are making too much 'noise'.

Provided that the mentor-coach's mind is stilled the process enabling us to answer the questions set out earlier can come into play without undue interference. Stilling the mind is not always an easy, instant process. A mentor-coach is just as likely to be very busy and concerned with a range of his/her own day-to-day issues, big and small. This could be no more (nor less) than a difficult journey through traffic or on delayed transport to arrive at the appointment on time. It may be necessary to construct and defend a small space or period of time to do whatever helps to calm the spirit and still the mind: make some tea or coffee, listen to a piece of music, some deep breathing or simply sit still for five minutes with eyes closed. Each mentor-coach will need to identify the best way of managing this process.

What counts as evidence?

Facts count as evidence – provided they are genuine facts. These may be facts about the person of the client, his/her situation or context, the history of the client and the accounts the client gives of the behaviour of others. The reader will have become aware before completing reading the previous sentence that a client might relate the four kinds of facts listed earlier in a way that is far from objective, and that we can only really count as facts the *perceptions* the *client* has about those things.

Perceptions are facts

The question as to whether we are dealing in *facts* may not be as important as the fact (!) that the client perceives them to be facts. It may be important in some instances simply to accept the story being told by the client, at least for the time being. Because everyone has blind spots, it will become important as the mentoring-coaching interaction progresses to uncover the blind spots by probing the perceptions. The main point at issue here is that perceptions are facts of a kind.

Feelings are facts, so is body language

Equally, feelings are facts. Ascertaining with respectful sensitivity the nature of the feelings of the client is part of the process of evidence gathering. (It will become clear later that the evidence gathering process is something the client must engage in with help from the mentor-coach.) Facial expressions, tone, volume and body language of a varied range are also facts and, therefore, evidence.

How to gather the evidence

Beginning with effective listening – including clarifying, paraphrasing, checking for accuracy of fact, and probing to establish meaning as well as actuality – the mentor-coach will gather a great deal of evidence about the context of the client and the situation s/he is working in. It is important, though, to be clear about what the evidence is, hence the word 'actuality' in the previous sentence. Is the evidence in question a 'hard' fact, a perception or belief by the client, a feeling, a fear, an unqualified generalization, an assumption, a stereotype, or even a prejudice? It may not be clear at first what the exact nature of the evidence is, but that too should be noted mentally by the mentor-coach.

What to do with the evidence

Many mentor-coaches worry at first about whether they will be able to retain the evidence they are offered, let alone use it. The previous paragraph is illustrative of some of the difficulty. The truth is that using it is the best way to remember it. So, summarizing, clarifying, paraphrasing, reflecting back and so on are all aids to memory. They are also ways of testing for accuracy and part of the process of beginning to build hypotheses.

Forming hypotheses

Sometimes patterns will emerge from the information offered and the way it is communicated, and sometimes bells will ring in the mind of the mentor-coach that will in both cases suggest hypotheses about, for example, the crucial issue. (NB: hypotheses will form about the other three stages addressed in the opening paragraph in just the same way.) The hypotheses will probably form semi-consciously as a result of hearing evidence from the client. The processes for reflecting back evidence are part of the more conscious means through which hypotheses are developed. They help bring possibilities to the consciousness of both parties. What is crucial is that any hypothesis should be clearly articulated in the mind of the mentor-coach, and then tested.

Sharing hypotheses with the client

The means of testing a hypothesis fall into two main possibilities. The first is to share the hypothesis with the client. This has some dangers. The dangers lie in the perception of the client about what is happening and the nature of his/her relationship with the mentor-coach. In the early stages of a mentor-coaching relationship there can be a kind of unresolved dependency derived from the notion that 'This person is wiser/more knowledgeable/more experienced than I am'. A carelessly shared hypothesis from the mentor-coach may sound or feel like a clear diagnosis to the client. When testing a hypothesis the sound of certainty is completely inappropriate. The hypothesis may be wrong!

Be tentative

If the mentor-coach decides to articulate to the client a hypothesis s/he wants to test, it must be articulated only very tentatively and with a neutral tone supported by respectful hesitancy. For example, the mentor-coach might begin, 'I am wondering whether . . .', 'It sounds a little bit as though . . .', 'Correct me if I am wrong/I may be quite wrong here, but could it be that . . .?' If this precaution is not taken, an articulated hypothesis may be latched on to by a worried, confused or troubled client – whether it is accurate or not! It is not being asserted here that articulating a hypothesis to the client is generally unsound, but it would be if the client latched on to it without it being tested, or without alternative hypotheses being considered. For these reasons one might want to consider a different approach.

Try hard to disconfirm the hypothesis

The second possibility is, that having articulated the hypothesis to oneself, the mentor-coach will test it through gathering of further evidence, initially by simply listening further to what is being said and eventually, perhaps, through further questioning that might need to be probing and even challenging. A number of appropriate questions are offered above in each of the chapters that will confirm – or disconfirm – any hypothesis. It is important to stress that the mentor-coach needs to be open in a very disciplined way to the *disconfirming* of any hypothesis.

The rigour of scientific method includes trying really hard to *disconfirm* a hypothesis. This is a much safer approach than trying to confirm it. It is always possible to find some evidence to support a hypothesis, and difficult to be really objective in assessing whether one has enough evidence to confirm it. Very often, however, one simple clear question can be all that it takes to disconfirm it. Essentially, some balance is needed. If several attempts to disconfirm a hypothesis fail and there is a reasonable amount of supporting evidence, the mentor-coach can proceed, but will need to be alert to anything that may transpire later that would once again challenge it.

Caution

What was written about in the previous paragraph is what is going on inside the head of the mentor-coach. S/he is trying to disconfirm a hypothesis, not disprove or challenge out loud what the client is saying. In other words, this whole process is quite private – only the mentor-coach is taking part in the attempt to challenge or disconfirm anything. This will be going on internally, while externally there is an exchange that is part of the evidence gathering process.

The mentor-coach does not lead

By these means the client might be led to a clear view of what the issue is that most needs to be addressed. The central point of this whole argument is that it is not the mentor-coach who is doing the leading – it is *the evidence*. It is perfectly reasonable – it may even be necessary – for the mentor-coach to play back some of the evidence to the client as s/he works his/her way towards a firm view of what most needs to be addressed, his/her responsibility in the matter, the priority for action and the plan that is to be implemented.

The evidence leads the process

The key influence upon the client in this whole process is not the mentor-coach. It is the evidence. The mentor-coach's task is to help the client articulate, recognize and collect it, and then use it with integrity to think things through. Much of what is happening when summarizing, clarifying, paraphrasing and reflecting back are in progress – especially summarizing – is that the mentor-coach is laying out in front of the client the evidence that has gradually been emerging. This is so that – *led by the evidence* – the client can think things through, including the action s/he needs to take in order to bring about change and, in the second half of the model, bringing to reality the picture of the ideal future with regard to the issue in focus.

Some possible questions to help check the evidence

- 'Always?' 'Never?' 'Everyone?' (Useful when bold generalizations are offered, including statements like, 'I never seem to be able . . .' or 'It always seems to go wrong for me when . . .').
- 'What is it that makes you think that?'
- 'How did that come to light?'
- 'How much evidence is there of what you have just described? Precisely just how often does that happen?'
- 'Have I understood you correctly? What you are saying is that . . .'
- 'What evidence do you have for what you are saying?' (This needs to be used carefully and with a tentative/supportive tone. Direct challenge to veracity is to be avoided.)
- 'Who else shares the same perspective as you on this situation/issue/problem?'
- 'When you say you are not the person to deal with this, are you saying

you are not responsible/don't have the authority? Or are you talking about skill/confidence etc.?'
- 'What is your thinking as to how this came about? Do you think others in your team agree with you?'
- 'What other sources of support are available to you?'

Some of these may feature in specific stages of the process. They are examples and the list is by no means complete. Yet again, the questions must stem from full attention to the person.

Some issues for the reader to consider

- What risks are entailed in any decision to articulate a hypothesis out loud to your client?
- What does the uniqueness of every mentoring-coaching interaction signify for you?
- What does it imply about how you will need to approach each session?
- Are you clear about what it means to have a still mind?
- What are likely to be the most effective ways for you personally to still your mind immediately prior to a mentoring-coaching session?
- Have you a clear view as to what constitutes evidence?
- What is your current level of confidence in your ability to identify and gather evidence?
- Why is it important to be tentative? What are the phrases you personally might use at the beginning of a sentence to share a possible hypothesis in a tentative manner?
- Why is it safer to try to disconfirm than to try to confirm an hypothesis?
- How difficult might you find it to have all this happening inside your head without overtly involving the client? (There is a paradox here: the more difficulty you recognize to begin with, the quicker will that difficulty be overcome.)
- What impact does it have upon your thoughts and feelings to know that it is not you, as mentor-coach, that leads the process but that it is led by the evidence?

The first part of this book has been concerned with the exposition of the model of mentoring-coaching and each of its stages. It has also been concerned with the skills and subskills required to employ this model to good effect, and, in particular, with the matters of effective listening and questioning. It may be particularly helpful for some of the Chapters 3 to 9 to be read and re-read as experience of the process of mentoring-coaching is built up.

The method used has included suggesting types of questions and some examples of various types at each of the stages. The reader has also been invited to consider some questions for him or herself. The aim has been to engage the reader actively in the business of thinking through what it might mean to be a mentor-coach. This activity – thinking things through – is what mentoring-coaching is about. It would have been foolish and entirely contrary to the spirit of this model to have tried to describe or, worse still, prescribe what it might mean for each individual to be a mentor-coach. Mentor-coaches – hopefully with some help from the text of this book – must essentially work out for themselves what being a mentor-coach will mean for them. The pattern of the writing changes in Part 2.

Supervision

In Chapter 16 the matter of creating an organizational culture of mentoring-coaching is considered in detail. Before closing Part One it is important to stress not only the need for training in the use of this model – to which reference has already been made – but also the need for supervision.

The authors themselves have found that mentor-coaches occasionally have genuine difficulty in this work, sometimes because of the complexity of the situations being considered and sometimes because of a sort of vicarious stress. They are uncommon, but it is invaluable to have someone else who is practised in this work to whom one can refer (subject to the importance of maintaining confidentiality) in order to reflect on the situation/relationship that is developing with a client.

Where there is a culture of mentoring-coaching, such an arrangement will be an integral part of it. Even so, the pattern of supervision should not normally be in line of management – for the same reasons that a regular mentor-coach is not usually the line manager of the client. Where there is no culture of this kind, it may be necessary to arrange supervision from outside the organization. No mentor-coach should ignore this need.

PART 2
Digging Deeper

This is a book for practitioners. It is essentially about the *practice* of mentoring-coaching. Most benefit is likely to accrue for the reader who has persisted so far, if the book is set aside for a while before Part Two is explored.

Many of the behaviours required of the mentor-coach (and for that matter the client) are counter-cultural and will not come easily, even with intellectual commitment. They require practice. The ideal reader is one who has undertaken training in the process and is therefore able to use Part One as a reference and *aide-mémoire* before and between a number of iterations of the cycle to help begin to embed some of the critical skills and subskills involved.

Once the skills begin to seem familiar (note that they hardly ever become easy), the practitioner of mentoring-coaching will realize that beneath the general run of practice lie depths of insight into human experience and understanding that it could be very helpful to explore. So we suggest that the reader who is encountering this model and the associated ideas for the first time go away to practise the skills and the model before proceeding to Part Two where the deeper exploration occurs. It is an exploration of some of the forces and characteristics that may be at work in the person of both the mentor-coach and the client – in the mentor-coach within the mentoring-coaching relationship and in the client in the same context, as well as in his/her field of work, especially in their working relationships.

Part Two of the book aims to address a number of those forces – for example, why is it harder to work as mentor-coach in some circumstances than others? It does not contain a compendium of such questions. Rather, it looks at ideas and frameworks that have either evolved from the work undertaken by the Institute of Education or from work undertaken by people in similar fields. Some of the work drawn upon goes back over a hundred years, to some degree from a theoretical point of view. (However 'theory' – sometimes seen as an off-putting term – consists merely of generalizations from practice that have been systematically tested and re-presented as frameworks for thinking). It is also hoped that Part Two will encourage deeper thinking by readers about their role as mentor-coach or client, and help them to reflect about themselves and their own behaviours.

In particular, it explores some terms associated with mentoring-coaching that may help reinforce parts of the fundamental concept. This should help ensure that the theory supports the establishment of sound practice. 'Dialogue' is an example of such a term. 'Empathy' is another. Both are further examples of terms that travel far more easily than the concepts they represent.

Chapter 10 looks at the relationship between mentoring-coaching and the very popular, though sometimes superficially understood, notion of *Emotional Competence*. It also considers the issues of values and ethics within the mentoring-coaching process. If mentoring-coaching is not to become manipulative – a tool to deliver compliance and conformity – it is vital that the values and ethics that might both enable and constrain the process are put sharply into focus. In exploring this aspect of the work of mentor-coaches the book is indebted to a range of sources, though each text encountered and referred to expounds thinking that is congruent with a lifetime of practice and critical analysis.

In Chapter 11 the concept of dialogue is explored, leading to an argument that dialogue occurs in its true sense only where a shared search for meaning is in progress. Chapter 12 looks at the concept of empathy. Many people use the word today as though it is 'sympathy with knobs on'. This chapter argues that it is something qualitatively different from sympathy, and lies at the heart of the disposition of the effective mentor-coach.

In Chapter 13, important ways humans store and catalogue information from experience are analysed. It argues that this is a useful capability but one that can have dangers, unless consciously considered and understood. It needs to be grasped clearly by both mentor-coach and client. Building on the two that precede it, Chapter 14 examines both the positive and negative senses in which people can be bound (consciously and unconsciously) by previous experiences. The steps we take in our thinking that lead us to interpret new experiences in the light of previous occurrences and come up with conclusions, can either hold us fast to our values on the one hand, or imprison us in false perceptions on the other.

Chapter 15 progresses to the dangers faced by mentor-coaches and clients in the business of challenging, or not challenging, as the case may be. In particular, the way in which challenge can be too stern, leading possibly to the client's clamming up, or non-existent, which can result in collusion. Various views on how to challenge are considered. Experience suggests that a lone individual committed to the way of working espoused by this book is likely to become increasingly frustrated and, eventually, even to give up. Only if there is a conducive culture within the organization (be that team, section, department, school, division or other organization) is an individual likely to be able to sustain the change of behaviours required by adopting a mentoring-coaching approach. Chapter 16 considers some of the ways in which this might be done and includes a short case study of one remarkable organization that has achieved this.

> Creating and managing culture is the single most important work of leaders. (Schein, 1992)

Chapter 17 explores aspects of thinking around the roles of mentor-coach and client and how one can find, make and take them. Role is not the same as job, post or position, so the chapter tries to distinguish terms and consider the processes by which roles are found, made and taken, while Chapter 18 delves briefly into an aspect of psychology to consider the deeper forces at work that might help or hinder a person from finding, making and taking their role, particularly in the mentoring-coaching dynamic.

This book claims repeatedly not to be about a deficit model, and it is much more than a problem-solving tool. This is a vital claim, and one way of approaching human development (personal, professional and organizational) is through *Appreciative Inquiry*, the focus of Chapter 19, which illustrates a profound commitment to think in positive growth forms. For both mentor-coach and client, both within and beyond their relationship, such philosophy and methodology can pay significant dividends. The chapter explains how to apply Appreciative Inquiry as a powerful mentoring-coaching tool.

Chapters 20 and 21 explore briefly the ways in which the model is related to concepts of learning and leading. Mentoring-coaching has been described as the 'quintessence of pedagogy'. Some of the implications of this are discussed in Chapter 20.

Chapter 21 challenges notions of charismatic leadership and indeed other styles that tend to accompany it. A recent book by Sean Ruth (2005) contends that the main work of a leader is listening. This sits congruently alongside the philosophy and values underpinning mentoring-coaching. It can be argued that the best means by which a leader can create and manage culture is to work consistently and constructively with team members as mentor-coach. The team itself will then become empowered and enabled to undertake the substantive business of the organization.

Finally, in Chapter 22 a summary is offered of the arguments for the hyphen! Mentoring and coaching are often seen as similar – even identical – processes/concepts. Indeed, one eminent exponent of coaching suggested at a recent conference that the only difference between mentoring and coaching is the spelling! This book is based upon theory that challenges such superficial ideas.

However, the concepts are linked in a very special way, particularly in the model advocated, and this chapter explains how practitioners can consciously associate them as they work with their clients. The aspiration is effectively to promote the journey of a deeply respectful concept in human relationships, to the benefit not only of both parties to this process but also of those with whom they, in their turn, also relate and work.

The whole book is presented as a work for people from the educational context. It is 'educational' in a wide sense, and it draws some – but not all – of its genesis from education in the formal sense. Those who have been trained in the use of the model advocated frequently claim a profound impact from it upon all kinds of relationships, both professional and personal. It is truly generic in that sense, and could apply to any employment context. It can help readers to regain some of that ground of our humanity that has been occupied in recent times by those who seek to control the lives of others. The point behind the writing is that it unlocks a door to that elusive but highly attractive notion of 'transformation'.

10 How clever does a mentor-coach need to be?

To be effective in the role of mentor-coach certainly requires a person to 'have all her wits about her'. One could associate this with wisdom, but that would suggest an outdated concept of the mentor-coach – a guru of some sort. The 'wits' in question are in the main learned competencies, though there is no suggestion that they can be learned easily or speedily. The potential for them needs to be evident from the start of the work in this role. This chapter explores the nature of some of the requisite competencies and sets out three groups of them that might come into focus: rational, emotional and ethical. The development of all the necessary competencies is a lifelong process. It is one that continually enhances human consciousness for each person engaged in it, and reveals more of what it means to become a person.

Mental skills

Much of the talk of hypotheses, analysis and evidence gathering in the previous chapter raises once again the question what kind of person one needs to be in order to become an effective mentor-coach. Earlier chapters dealing with the skills of questioning, observation of body language, recognizing feelings and so on might also suggest that one needs to be alert and mentally well organized. There are a number of skills in terms of memory, and all those things to do with attending to the person: listening actively, summarizing, clarifying, paraphrasing and reflecting back. All these things imply that a special level of competencies is required. So it could be argued that only a clever person can do this.

The word 'clever'

Most people recoil a little in the face of the connotations of the word 'clever'. Readers may think of 'too clever by half', 'clever clogs' and possibly 'smartypants'. Even without the more extreme connotations, the word seems to suggest someone of a high level of rational intelligence. This is not what the word literally means. The word 'clever' is derived from the verb 'cleave' meaning 'to stick to' in the way that, for example, some versions of the Christian marriage ceremony refer to a man and a woman cleaving 'unto one another so long as they both shall live'. So, literally a clever person is someone to whom things readily stick. Traditionally, a clever person is someone to whom knowledge sticks so that s/he can re-present it when needed, for example in a written examination. With regard to mentoring-coaching one might want to think of a much wider range of things that need to stick – and to stick in a different way.

Rational competence: necessary (to a degree) but not sufficient

A person who is clever in the traditional sense (without the extreme connotations) – what one might refer to as rationally intelligent – will have a characteristic that is very valuable in the context of work as a mentor-coach. One might go further and say that having a significant level of rational competence is essential in the role of mentor-coach – necessary but not sufficient. And what is meant here by the word 'significant'? We are not talking of high levels of innate intelligence, but rather of mental or intellectual (another word with connotations) *skills* that one can learn.

Competencies can be learned

These skills are functions that most people can train their brains to perform, if they want to and if they persevere. They are, however, very important, even essential, functions in this role, but it is reiterated – they can be learned. It is also reiterated that although these rational skills are necessary, they are not sufficient. So what else is needed?

The point has been made earlier that each mentor-coach, each client and therefore each mentoring-coaching encounter is unique. As we consider other kinds of 'competencies' that are needed in order to work as a mentor-coach, it is important to note that each will be displayed in unique ways by each person, and the combination of these unique evidences of competencies adds to the distinctive character of the individual. *There is no formula and no 'one-size-fits-all'.*

Other groups of competencies

It is possible to refer to two other kinds of groups of competencies that are needed if one is to become an effective mentor-coach. They are represented in Figure 10.1 along with rational competencies.

Emotional competencies

A possible definition

In the last decade or so a great deal has been written and talked about emotional intelligence, though not always to positive purpose. It is essentially 'the capacity for recognising our own feelings and those of others, for motivating ourselves, for managing emotions well in ourselves and in our relationships' (Goleman, 1996: 39).

Intelligence or groups of competencies?

Daniel Goleman is perhaps the best-known, though by no means the only established writer on this subject and the interested reader would do well to

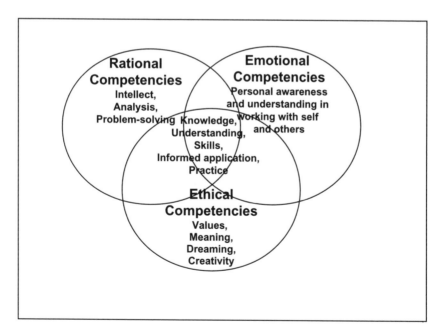

Figure 10.1 Competencies.

read his key texts on this subject. He divides emotional intelligence into 18 competencies that can all be learned to a degree over time (Goleman, 1996). He relies – as does this book – on David McClelland's (1973) definition of competency that has been slightly adapted as 'some characteristic of a person, evidenced in (patterns of) behaviours that differentiate levels of performance in a given role'. The patterns of behaviour distinguish the best from the rest – and in this context the best practitioners. Note the distinction between skills and competencies. A skill is the ability to do something. *A competency is the consistent habit of actually doing it.*

Goleman (1996) goes on to group the 18 competencies identified under four main headings: Self-awareness, Awareness of Others, Self-management and Relationship Management (Figure 10.2). Rather than repeat the whole of Goleman's exposition here, our purpose will be served best by highlighting some reasons why these four groups of competencies are so important to a mentor-coach.

Feelings are impacting on us all the time

It will have become clear by now that one cannot help a person to think through who s/he is, their morale purpose, context and issues without feelings of some sort entering the equation at some point. Indeed, because of the physiological nature of feelings, they enter the equation on first contact between any two persons in any situation – whether we recognize/like it

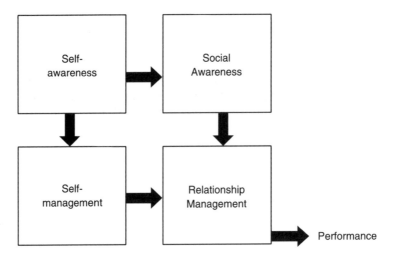

Figure 10.2   Aspects of emotional intelligence.

Source: Adapted from Goleman (1998).

or not. They also enter the equation between us and other entities in our environment – animate and inanimate.

These feelings impact upon us internally and upon all our relationships. For example, one of the critical emotional competencies Goleman (1998) identifies is self-confidence (within the domain of Self-awareness), which can be defined as a clear sense of one's own worth. Readers will know people who have an over-inflated view of their worth and, conversely, people who in all sorts of ways rate themselves less highly than could be justified. In both cases there will be an internal feeling at work, of which the person who under-rates themselves is likely to be more conscious. In both cases that feeling and the effectiveness of the competency will impact upon relationships with other people – an unhelpful impact. Having a clear and accurate sense of one's own worth will help a person to be at ease with themselves and with others. So the relationship between the mentor-coach and client will include a range of potentially complex emotions, of which self-confidence is but one example. In the same way the emotional competencies – at whatever the level to which they have developed – will impact upon the personal and working context of the client that is the subject matter of the encounter.

Choices about what to do with our feelings

We have a very important choice about emotions in the whole of our lives. We can let them have their sometimes random way with us, which is best done, albeit with increased risk, by simply paying no attention to them; or we can look out for or listen to them and try to recognize what is going on in this aspect of our being. Goleman (1998) argues that it is by listening to those emotions in ourselves that we can begin to understand and get a sense of the emotions that others we relate to may be experiencing. These two steps then enable us to take action to manage the emotions we have recognized in ourselves and to manage our interactions with others. This is not an entirely linear model: we can be working on all of them at the same time, but we shall make little progress on the other three if we do not *focus first on self-awareness*.

Everything hinges on the three competencies in the Self-awareness quadrant of the matrix set out in Figure 10.2: emotional self-awareness, accurate self-assessment and an accurate sense of self-worth.

Emotional competencies are essential to the mentor-coach

This short exposition will have made it clear to the reflective reader that these groups of competencies that make up what has come to be called emotional intelligence are important characteristics to bring to the role of mentor-coach. Some further points may help reassure the readers to whom this is relatively new.

Knowing about it is not the same as having it

Not everyone who has read Goleman or knows about emotional intelligence is, as a result, emotionally competent. One does not have to search far to find people who are experts in the theoretical knowledge of emotional intelligence but who blunder about in their relationships in a potentially very damaging way. This is exclusively about *how people behave*, as distinct from what people know.

Everyone has *some* 'emotional intelligence' but some have (or, more accurately, display) more than others. Equally, one does not even need to have heard the name Goleman or the label 'emotional intelligence' to have a strong record of emotionally competent behaviour. These competencies have been around for thousands of years. Everyone who wishes to develop them can do so – with a combination of self-discipline and external support and feedback.

Many of our emotional competencies are acquired at a very early age and stem to a significant degree from how we ourselves were treated early in our lives and the expectations placed upon us about our behaviour. They can be developed further in childhood and youth through a whole range of activities, especially those that help us use and strengthen our imagination. For example, reading some more developed forms of fiction. Novels are capable of helping us reflect on our own inner world and introduce us in depth to the inner worlds of others. This supports the development of self-awareness and empathy – two vital emotional competencies.

The critical point is that to a very considerable degree we learn, or fail to learn, emotional competencies as we make our way in life. We can learn more by consciously and deliberately practising the behaviours that are the evidence of the characteristic. At the heart of the development process for these competencies lies the practice or habit of honest reflection and self-critique. In particular this comes from thinking about our behaviour (both before and after) and analysing honestly the observable impact of that behaviour upon others.

A relationship of trust and confidence

One very obvious way in which emotional competencies are required in mentoring-coaching is that at the very beginning the need is stressed to establish a relationship of trust and confidence between mentor-coach and client. This relationship has to be nurtured and developed throughout the process. Relationship management is the prime outcome of the use of emotional competencies and it is known to impact positively upon performance in a wide range of contexts, especially in professions that centre around the personal, as education, for example, does.

The process of mentoring-coaching is particularly rewarding in this context. One can develop further one's own emotional competencies by practising all that is written in this short book in the role of mentor-coach. More rewarding still is the fact that one can help the client to do the same through engaging with him/her in these processes.

To sum up, emotional competencies are largely not innate, though the potential for them is a central feature of human consciousness. We can and, if we wish to be effective mentor-coaches, *must* take practical steps to develop them continuously. Some writers claim that it is harder to start to learn it, the older we get. This may be true of all learning, but hard or not, the ability to relate emotionally competently is hugely satisfying.

Emotional competencies and learning to drive

Finally, some participants on mentoring-coaching courses worry that learning emotional competencies is somehow false – that it asks them to deny their own personality. An analogy with learning to drive might be fruitful. To become a driver one needs to put oneself into a very specific situation and learn distinctive behaviours that one has not had to use previously. At first, it can feel alien and many people are nervous about it when they begin. As we develop a positive sense of the value of certain behaviours and the danger of others, we gradually build a pattern that makes us competent as drivers. Eventually, with practice, we reach the stage where we drive really well with a diminishing degree of conscious thought. So it is with emotional competencies, especially while becoming a mentor-coach. At this stage much of our behaviour remains conscious and deliberate. With practice over time we can come to feel that behaving in new ways that are more emotionally competent is quite natural – a normal part of our being, so that we hardly have to think about it. All skill development is like this. Sooner or later the skills stick.

So besides some skill in terms of rational, analytical competencies, we need a range of emotional competencies. Is anything else needed? Figure 10.1 included something called 'Ethical Competencies'.

Ethical competencies

Definitions

Ethical competencies are essentially about being aware of and true to the values that give unique meaning and purpose to our individual lives and about respecting, in turn, the right of others to live their lives and work with integrity. Zohar and Marshall (2000), for example, incorporate this group of competencies into what they define as 'spiritual intelligence' (which may, but does not necessarily, involve religion):

> Spiritual intelligence is the intelligence with which we address and solve problems of meaning and value; the intelligence with which we

can place our actions and our lives in a wider richer meaning – giving context; the intelligence with which we can assess that one course of action or one life path is more meaningful than another. (Zohar and Marshall, 2000: pp. 3–4)

As was emphasized earlier, it behoves the mentor-coach to accept and respect the client as a unique individual and to help him/her in the process of developing in ways that are aligned with his/her own values and feasible for *him/her*. In developing clients must remain their own person.

In their book, *Spiritual Intelligence: The Ultimate Intelligence?* Zohar and Marshall (2000), both physicists, were first to label these characteristics in this way. They argue that there is an identifiable and distinct part of the brain in which the activity relating to them occurs. They claim further that it is possible by scanning to identify in the brain when the rational, emotional and spiritual are optimally aligned. The interested reader may want to pursue these lines of inquiry by reading their book. It is because of this detectable activity in the brain that they refer to this set of characteristics as 'an intelligence'. It may be more accurate – and more consistent with the thinking set out in this chapter – to refer to a group of competencies rather than an intelligence.

Four clusters of ethical competencies

For the mentor-coach there are four important clusters of competencies that can overlap and interact with the other skill/competency groups considered so far. In Figure 10.1 on p. 99 they are labelled Values, Meaning, Dreaming (sometimes called Envisioning) and Creativity.

The competencies as an outcome of mentoring-coaching

Each of these groups is a characteristic evidenced in the (patterns of) behaviours of the effective mentor-coach. The development of these characteristics in the *client* is an important outcome of the process, particularly when the model advocated in this book is applied with skill over a number of iterations.

Mentoring-coaching values

At this point it is worth briefly revisiting a key value behind the model – one that also relates to envisioning and meaning. Many models of mentoring and coaching appear quite 'instrumental' – by which is meant that they are almost exclusively about solving a problem or developing a particular skill that happens to be needed in the workplace. The model expounded here *is* positively concerned with tangible outcomes. Something must happen – something must change – if this model is used to any effect. This is the immediate point of the second half of this model.

There are, however, deeper and more important longer-term purposes that the reader will already have grasped to some extent. The part of that purpose that concerns us here is the way in which the model helps to clarify values, to highlight ethics, to envision and to make meaning. The mentor-coach must be engaging in these processes and must also be able to help the client to do so at the same time. In addition, over a number of iterations of the cycle the client will become clear not only that this is happening but also become aware of the means by which it can continue to happen beyond the mentoring-coaching relationship. This requires that the mentor-coach can envision this happening for the client at some point in the future, can help her believe that this is possible, and enable her to make meaning around this vision in the context of her understanding of what it means to be human, and how mentoring-coaching enhances that meaning for both parties to the process.

It might be helpful to distinguish between some of the four labels mentioned earlier, for example, between values and ethics.

Values and principles
Values are to be considered alongside the notion of principles. A person's values are statements of those things considered to be of intrinsic worth, worthy of esteem in their own right. Principles are similar – statements of fundamental truth held by a person, his or her beliefs. Some examples might help. A person might believe that trust is the only effective basis for human co-operation and collaboration. Similarly, one might hold that every human being should be accorded respect as of right. This is not the place for philosophical disquisition but it will be evident that values and principles are likely to be derived from a personal philosophy.

Many people manage happily in life without articulating a coherent philosophical perspective, but most people do actually have one. While mentoring-coaching may not often involve exploring personal philosophies it can frequently prompt consideration of values and principles. Sometimes it will be possible to find an effective way forward only if relevant values are explored. So a mentor-coach will need to be able both to explore and be alert to their own values in order to help their client do similarly.

So, just as emotional competency begins with some awareness of one's own feelings, ethical competency begins with awareness of and reflection on one's own values.

The rules needed to generate the ethos derived from values

The notion of ethics follows on from the concept of values. One's values and principles define the nature or desired nature, the *ethos* of the relationship or organization in which one is working. Ethics are essentially the rules necessary to bring that ethos or climate about, and the science called 'ethics' is the set of processes by which those rules are evolved from principles and values. The rules define the behaviours that we need to engage in. (How, then does 'climate' differ from ethos? In this book the climate of a relationship or organization is taken to be a statement of *how it feels* to be in it, how team members get to *feel* about the ethos.)

It might also be helpful to try to distinguish between ethics and morals, The two are often used interchangeably. This is not helpful. Ethics, as indicated earlier, is about the ethos of an organization derived from stated values. Ethics are rules of behaviour that will bring the required ethos into being. The word 'moral' has two kinds of definition. The first – straight from the Latin word *mores* – is to do with the customs of a family, tribe, community and so on. It defines right and wrong in terms of what has become acceptable (required even) over time to sustain those customs and the culture derived from or by them. This is close to, but not the same as, what is meant when we talk of ethics. The second definition is to do with *meaning* as in the moral of a story or parable. When writers like Michael Fullan (2001, 2005) refer to *moral purpose* they could be using the word moral as relating to either senses of the word. Readers might want to reflect what this means for them individually. 'Moral purpose' is yet another term that travels freely without conveying a clear understanding of its associated concept.

An exercise

Using the two examples given above of possible values – respect and trust – the reader may want to try jotting down a few rules of behaviour in the mentoring-coaching context (or in any other context) that would help to generate an ethos characterized by these two values. It might then be worth writing down what the climate would be – what it would feel like.

Harmony between values, ethics and solutions

The job of the mentor-coach includes helping clients to think through what to do, and that will require him/her to be capable of that process. It is essential that there is some coherence and consistency in this activity that consciously links the *action that will be taken* to the values and ethics that they imply. Zohar and Marshall (2000) imply that there is a high degree of satisfaction and positive feeling generated by arriving at solutions that are in harmony with our values and ethics, when our rational, emotional and spiritual intelligences are aligned. They capture this in their statement:

> It is in its transformative power that SQ (Spiritual Quotient) differs mainly from EQ. As Daniel Goleman defines it, my emotional intelligence allows me to judge what situation I am in and then to behave appropriately within it. This is working within the boundaries of the situation, allowing the situation to guide me. But my spiritual intelligence allows me to ask if I want to be in this particular situation in the first place. Would I rather change the situation, creating a better one? This is working with the boundaries of my situation, allowing *me to guide the situation*. (2000: p. 5)

It is this creative potential to envision an essential alternative from the present, to move from framing the present to reframing a preferred, feasible future that makes ethical competencies an indispensable part of the dynamic of mentoring-coaching.

'It's the behaviour, stupid!'

Finally, on the subject of ethics it is important to distinguish between ethics (or rules of behaviour) and the behaviours themselves. Clarity in ethics does not of itself provide ways forward (just as knowing *about* emotional competencies does not of itself make one emotionally competent). It merely enables one to test proposed actions or behaviour against those rules and to 'rule' in or out each possibility. Ethics will govern the behaviour of the mentor-coach throughout all stages of the model and will come into its own in a very tangible way for the thinking of the client in Stages 5 and 6 (Deciding and Action). (See Chapters 7 and 8.) It is the behaviour itself that matters and makes a person ethically competent.

What does the word 'meaning' mean?

'Meaning' is a potentially difficult word because of the many applications of the word 'mean' in the English language. In this context it is helpful to think of it equating to purpose, intention or significance. Mentoring-coaching involves clarifying role and purpose – moral purpose and ethical stance. In other words, it is about why a particular purpose is to be found in the role the mentor-coach occupies and what being in it implies by way of personal significance and responsibilities. It involves thinking about the meaning of certain actions or behaviours – meanings not only for the client but also for those with whom he/she works and to whom he/she relates. In a more abstract way it may also be important for a client to think through the implications of his/her intentions and actions in relation to vision, values and ethics and to test his/her intentions against them in turn.

An underlying thread

Dreaming, envisioning and creativity are very prominent in Stage 4 (Future) of this model (see Chapter 6). That is probably self-evident. These qualities or competencies are not limited only to one stage, however. They run as an underlying thread through the whole process, and are a critical anchor for both parties as they strive – literally strive – to think through all the things that this process is about. To become a mentor-coach is to envision a role, a purpose, a process, an outcome and even a relationship and a classroom/ organization/school/community/society that can be changed for the better, however that may be defined, as a result of taking that role.

A possible lifeline

That vision will sometimes become a lifeline in some very critical scenarios in mentoring-coaching. Equally, it may become the lifeline for the client as s/he wrestles with his/her context and issues in practice and with the process of thinking it through. However, not any lifeline will do; it must be one that is acceptable to the *client* and does not compromise his/her integrity.

These four terms – values, meaning, dreaming and creativity – were chosen to represent groups of competencies. They are neither abstract nor theoretical. If they are not evidenced in behaviours or patterns of behaviour, the neutral observer is entitled to believe they do not actually exist for that person. They are about the behaviour of the mentor-coach and, over time, the changing behaviour of the client.

What does ethical competence entail?

Set out here are some features of ethical competence that are derived partly from aspects of what Zohar and Marshall (2000) call spiritual intelligence. It is by no means a complete list. It is intended to be illustrative and to prompt further thinking by the reader. It includes:

- the capacity to be flexible
- a deep sense of purpose
- a capacity to face and use suffering
- the quality of being inspired by vision and values
- a determination not to cause unnecessary harm
- seeing the connection between diverse things (being 'holistic')
- asking, 'Why? or 'What if?' questions and seeking 'fundamental' answers.

Competencies not 'cleverness'

The term 'clever' was used at the start of this chapter to attract attention. It is certainly not helpful for a mentor-coach to be clever in the pejorative sense of that word, nor in the sense of being a wiser person than the client, but it is helpful if the mentor-coach is the kind of person to whom things stick – namely the things that we mean by the skills and competencies that are the main subject of this chapter. The reader is intended to be left with two critical thoughts about all this. The first is that the skills and competencies can be learned over time by anyone so motivated. The second is that it is the behaviour – *sustained patterns of behaviour* – that really matter.

Some issues for the reader to reflect upon

- Where do you assess yourself to be in terms of the competencies outlined in this chapter?
- Are there aspects of the subject(s) dealt with in this chapter about which it would be helpful to read further?
- To what degree would you say you are a person to whom the kind of skills and competencies required by a mentor-coach would be likely 'to stick'? How do you know this?
- Would you count yourself as a reflective practitioner? Are you able to reflect *in* practice as well as *on* practice? (Reflecting *in* practice is reflecting at the same time as doing, as distinct from after the event.)
- How aware of your own emotions are you on a day-to-day basis? Is this something on which you reflect?
- If asked, would you be able to articulate a form of personal philosophy that might include some understanding or proposition concerning the nature of humanity as distinct from other living beings?
- To what extent could you trace back your espoused values to such a philosophy?
- Would it be helpful to take time to write down, say, a handful of core personal values?
- When you have written down some core values, you might want to try to generate some ethics (rules of behaviour) that are generated from the values, and some examples, from your own experience, of appropriate and inappropriate behaviours in the light of the rules? Did behaviours by other people or some of your own behaviours come to mind first?
- How important to you is the notion of 'meaning'? Do you see

the generation of meaning as an important part of the learning process?

- One 'sacred text' asserts that 'without vision, the people perish'? Is it that important? If so, what are the means by which you can nurture the competency of envisioning?

11 Dialogue

Mentoring-coaching consists substantially of talk based on attentive listening. It is not simply a conversation, however, nor is it a debate or discussion. If the thinking that this relationship exists to serve is to be thorough, it must be unfettered by considerations of argument, disquisition, position, status and so on that are sometimes associated with those other forms of talk. Neither is it chat. A dialogue is a joint search for meaning and might well involve 'taking counsel together' – the dictionary definition of 'consulting'. The origins of the word dialogue suggest a process through which meaning flows. The way in which the mentor-coach can stimulate this process as part of helping another person to think things through is explored here and the notion of dialogic questioning is developed.

A distinctive interaction

In this short chapter further consideration will be given to the nature of the mentor-coaching interaction. It is likely that most readers will by this point have become aware of the distinctive nature of this interaction and be able to frame it in language of their own. What follows, therefore, is offered with a certain degree of tentativeness, for it is preferable that each person thinks through matters like this for themselves. This chapter – like the rest of the book and like mentoring-coaching itself – is intended to help that process.

A friendly chat in the pub

Course participants occasionally ask if mentoring-coaching can take place in the pub, or a similar environment. It is certainly the case that interactions in the pub can have some of the features of mentoring-coaching, but what is evident when this question arises is that the interaction is considered to be something as ordinary as 'a friendly chat' about some issue or other. Mentoring-coaching is something a bit special, and is something more than an unstructured, informal friendly chat (though we would not want to derogate friendly chats; they can be very enjoyable and a moderate amount of the appropriate beverage can be a useful lubricant!)

So what is it that is special about this interaction? Clearly, there are many things that are special about a mentoring-coaching interaction, not least the fact that one person is actively listening to another – an experience all too uncommon in our busy lives. If it is much more than simply a friendly chat, is it a conversation, a discussion, a debate or a dialogue? The purpose of this chapter is to explore which of these terms can most accurately convey the nature and purpose of a mentoring-coaching encounter.

A conversation

The literal meanings of the word conversation are 'to have frequent company with' and 'interchange of thought(s)'. We have conversation with people we know or are familiar with, and we let them know our thoughts. Dictionary definitions often imply something intimate in the word. So we have conversations with our friends or people on whom we can count in the sense that they are 'on our side'. It's a very pleasing experience to have such conversations.

Sometimes conversations go wrong, for example, when the interaction generates or reveals significant differences, especially differences of opinion about something important. We generally think of conversation, however, as something relaxed, and unlikely to involve challenge for either side. It is sometimes (though less commonly) used in an unfriendly and even threatening way. An example of this might be when a team member has made a possibly foolish mistake and the team leader says, with appropriate intonation, facial expression and body language, 'I need to have a conversation with you!' (A teacher might say something like this to an errant pupil!) So would the word conversation convey what we have been describing in this book? There may be a better word.

Debate

Lots of conversations take the tone of a debate. Yet in a debate differences of view are explored in an adversarial or semiadversarial way – sometimes informally, but often quite formally with a degree of structure that can be a little complex and may even involve having a chairperson, who for this purpose must be impartial and ensure that the rules are adhered to. It is the structure, the formality and particularly the adversarial nature of the interaction in debate that gives the term its distinctive meaning. The words most commonly linked with it in dictionaries are terms like 'fight', 'strive', 'quarrel', 'wrangle', 'contest', 'dispute', 'argue'. It is used also to mean 'consider', 'engage in discussion (publicly)' and 'think about'.

These last three meanings might apply to a mentoring-coaching interaction but it is unlikely that this term conveys much of the essential character of the dynamic we seek in this context. The connotations are too adversarial. There are winners and losers – sometimes decided by majority vote. Further, although a debate requires formal structures for thinking it can also require the parties to a debate to turn away from what they genuinely think for the sake of winning the argument. In this respect a certain falseness can enter the process.

None of this is to derogate the notion of a debate. Debates have their place, but not in the mentoring-coaching context.

Discussion

This is a word that sounds friendly and relaxed too, but is in its essence quite the opposite. It's in the same family as the words 'percussion' and 'concussion' with their connotations of something being hit. Indeed the prime meaning of discussion is 'driving away', 'dispersal' or 'shaking off'. Modern usage has softened it, though it remains a word meaning examination (if necessary by trial or argument), investigation, or sifting. These meanings might give it a place in the context of mentor-coaching, particularly at Stages 5 and 6 (Deciding and Action). However, in its truest sense it is hardly a word that suggests an interaction characterized by rapport, trust and confidence.

The modern notion that it is an exchange of views that could be open to development in the light of what is said is what suggests that, if it could be conducted in a friendly and relaxed manner, it would help a person think things through. The question remains as to whether mentoring-coaching is a process that is mainly about exchanging views. One might think of discussion as 'knocking something (an idea or proposition) about'. Again, there is a place for this in daily life but a client will be hoping for an outcome that is more specific and more helpful than just having knocked a few thoughts about or exchanged views.

Dialogue?

This is also a word that has accumulated shades of meaning over time. Its origins are believed by some (erroneously, as it happens) to involve a Latin or Greek word meaning 'two' somethings or other. So a dialogue is seen as involving two people or two sides, and perhaps a context where two people exchange words.

In fact the prefix 'dia' means 'through'. The second part of the word is not simply about words (from the Greek word 'logos' meaning 'word') but about truth or meaning. Literally a dialogue is something through which meaning is generated or flows. People sometimes point out that a dialogue is also adversarial. They are thinking, then, perhaps of the notion of Socratic dialogue, where there is a winner and a loser – something more akin to a debate, only the process involves one party questioning the other about something to which the questioner already knows the answers. It's rather like a game of verbal chess governed by the rules of formal logic.

Where a dialogue in its literal sense occurs, there are no losers and if it serves its main purpose, both (or all) parties are winners. It often involves all participants in changing their views or, better still, making progress towards a shared understanding.

Shared meaning or understanding

In mentoring-coaching the purpose of the interaction is to think things through – 'Who I am, my role, moral purpose, the context I work/live in and the issues I face'. This is essentially about 'meaning', and the work of the mentor-coach is to help the client come to a clear understanding in relation to those five matters.

One might ask whether the mentor-coach and the client have to agree about the meaning of what is explored. One might also ask whether the understanding arrived at by both parties has to be the same. Strictly speaking, it does not matter whether the mentor-coach agrees with the client about the meaning of what is explored, nor whether their understanding is the same. What matters most is the meaning arrived at by the *client* via the process of developing understanding. It is in theory possible that the mentor-coach neither understands nor grasps the meaning for the client developed during their interaction, but this is unlikely to be the case. If mentor-coach and client arrive at different understandings/meanings it is important that the difference(s) is (are) explored, mainly in order for the mentor-coach to be clear that the client is secure in the meaning s/he has arrived at.

In practice the task of the mentor-coach is to hold up a mirror for the client – to reflect back, summarize, paraphrase and probe. These activities will undoubtedly generate understanding by the mentor-coach. In fact the mentor-coach will mark each step in the development of the client's understanding by reflecting it back to him/her. The assent by the client to the words of the mentor-coach confirm what has been said. Or the client may correct what has been said. The mentor-coach will only know that the client has gained understanding if s/he herself also understands. So, it is very unlikely that the mentor-coach will fail to understand. One might go as far as saying that without the mentor-coach's understanding the process cannot have impact.

Meaning

There is slightly more possibility that the *meaning* that is generated (as distinct from *understanding*) will not be shared. It is possible for one to understand exactly what another person understands, and even to share the same experience but without actually sharing the meaning. Understanding is substantially a rational function, while meaning involves the rational, emotional and ethical dimensions.

An example may help. Two teachers might be present when a student engages in behaviour that is inappropriate. On the essential facts of what occurred and how it came about they may be in full agreement. That is to say that the story is agreed and the understanding is shared. The meaning, however, is an entirely different matter. For one, it may mean something essentially about the student and his/her peers. For the other teacher it may be full of threat and will highlight his/her vulnerability at a significant level. The experience will not *feel* the same for each person. This notion of the 'felt experience' is important in mentoring-coaching. The concept of 'meaning' includes the notion of felt experience. The mentor-coach must try to understand the felt experience but may not entirely share it. To that extent meaning is not shared either. The situation of mentoring-coaching is not exactly parallel to a shared experience of some bad behaviour but this example illustrates the point that agreement on the facts and a shared understanding of the circumstances are not the same as a grasp of the felt experience. More is to be found about this in the next chapter.

An increasing number of writers are beginning to promote more serious thinking about the human need for meaning – both in personal and working contexts. For example, Gobillot (2006) argues that the need for self-actualization (involving the search for meaning) is ever-present in all human beings and demands a response from the connected leader working in what he calls the people economy. He further argues that Maslow (1968/1999) is wrong to imply that it occurs only *after* lower-order needs (for example, food and shelter) have been met. If Gobillot is right the function of mentor-coaching must have pride of place in the people economy.

Dialogic questioning

The whole point of gaining clarity about the nature of the interaction, namely that it is a dialogue, is that it will guide the mentor-coach in formulating appropriate questions. If the purpose is to win a debate, simply to examine an issue, to persuade, or to advise, then certain types of question are appropriate. But if the purpose is to make meaning together and to generate understanding (by mentor-coach and client), the appropriate questions will be distinctive and serve this very specific purpose. It is important that the reader thinks about this. Equally, there are questions that will be inappropriate, and these are to be avoided. The sort of questions one might ask here are included in the list below.

The client's meaning and understanding

To sum up: the process of mentoring-coaching is a dialogue. It works best when the mentor-coach, by using the skills written about in this book – particularly but not exclusively dialogic questioning – enables the client to develop understanding so that there is a flow of meaning for him/her as the process unfolds. This is what matters. It will be greatly aided by the extent to which the meaning and understanding of the mentor-coach also grows. In the final analysis, successful generation of meaning and understanding for the client herself are the criteria by which the success of the process is to be judged.

Some examples of questions that may be dialogic

- 'Tell me more about . . .', 'Say some more about . . .'
- 'What could the cause of that be?'
- 'Why do you think that happened?'
- 'How do you think he feels about that?', 'What makes you think that?'
- 'When you did . . . what was your thinking behind that?'
- 'How do you think that came about?'

- 'What do you think makes him act in that way?'
- 'Of all the things you've talked about, what is it that matters most to you?'
- 'What is it that makes that the most important/crucial point for you?'
- 'Explain that a little'.

Gaining explanation and reasoning is very important and the word 'Why' is often what we want to ask. It is fairly important to soften questions that could begin with the word 'why'. There are other ways of formulating such questions, as illustrated above. 'Why?' can be more challenging than we intend, so, if used, it is important that the tone in which it is asked is carefully managed.

Some issues for the reader to reflect upon

- To what extent does it matter which of the four terms considered above you attach to this mentoring-coaching?
- What are the characteristics of each of the four terms considered?
- To what extent does it matter how far the features of the process characterize the interaction? In other words, if each of those four terms do actually distinguish different processes, which one gets nearest to describing what ought to be happening in mentoring-coaching?
- Can you envisage a situation in which the mentor-coach and client do not arrive at a common or agreed (the terms are slightly different) upon understanding in relation to the things being thought through?
- Similarly, can you envisage a situation where differences of meaning emerge without the process being obstructed?
- Do mentor-coach and client have to agree about everything?
- Do they have to share the meaning?
- What in summary does the notion of dialogue now carry for you?
- What is your understanding of the term 'felt experience'? What is its place in mentoring-coaching?
- When you use the word 'Why' on its own, do you know how you sound? What other ways, besides those listed in the previous box, can you think of for making the request for explanation or evidence less threatening?

12 Empathy

Three processes involving emotions can become tangled up with each other in the mentoring-coaching relationship: identification, sympathy and empathy. They can work either slightly below the surface of consciousness or just above it. When operating within the level of consciousness each of these can be appropriate, though the mentor-coach will need to question just how appropriate or helpful identification or sympathy with the client are. This chapter attempts a definition of each of the three terms and suggests that empathy – a concept very different from sympathy – is the mental and emotional disposition for which the mentor-coach should strive. Empathy is much more dynamic than sympathy or identification. It is evolving constantly and is never fully arrived at. As a process, it governs much else that is happening within this relationship – as later chapters show.

The internal dynamic for the mentor-coach

There will be critical points in the interaction where the mentor-coach will be conscious of his/her own feelings. It is vitally important that these feelings are recognized accurately.

In Chapter 10 there was reference to the importance of emotional competence and to the fact that Goleman (1998) in his framework for EI stresses that in practice it must begin with self-awareness. He goes on to identify that competencies matters, such as awareness of one's own emotions and accurate self-assessment. In other words, it is important to know what is going on in terms of our own feelings. This is particularly important in mentoring-coaching.

Having any particular feeling may be neither right nor wrong. Recognizing what the feelings are is important in helping us assess whether it is the feelings that govern our actions, or whether we are managing our feelings in such a way that we can choose – when appropriate – to surmount them. So recognizing a feeling, including being able to label it accurately, can be especially helpful to us in all our experiences, including our relationships. Thus we begin by accepting feelings as facts but not necessarily unalterable. We can train ourselves to develop feelings other than those we at first find dominant or habitual.

Know what the feeling is

There is a particular reason in mentoring-coaching for needing to know and be able to label the feelings we experience at different points in this process. It should by now be taken as read that the ability to recognize moods and feelings in the client is a necessity. It is the feelings of the *mentor-coach* that are the focus of this chapter. Different states of mind or feeling will cause the mentor-coach to behave in certain ways, so knowing precisely what the feelings are and how they might determine our behaviour is essential too.

When attending fully to another person and trying to grasp the meaning of their story a mentor-coach will experience feelings that in some circumstances may be very powerful, even possibly overwhelming. An account of very troubling circumstances – for example, a situation where there has been prolonged significant bullying or a deep sense of failure or inadequacy – may prompt a strong feeling of sympathy. If either the situation itself, some facet of it or the client's language in talking about it prompts a recollection of something the mentor-coach has experienced herself (or may even be experiencing currently) there is a possibility that the mentor-coach becomes so absorbed in it that she experiences something called identification – 'She's talking about me and my situation last year!'

It would be foolish to pretend that we do not experience such feelings or that we – being the very experienced, controlled rational persons we think we are (!) – would not experience them in the role of mentor-coach. The very fact of attending fully to someone makes it extremely likely that we would experience one or both of those feelings. *There is nothing wrong with having such feelings*, indeed sensitivity and a degree of recognizable vulnerability are likely to be characteristics of a successful mentor-coach. The danger lies in not recognizing them and, therefore, being unable accurately to label and manage them.

Sympathy

This word means simply 'feeling with' someone – having the same kind of feeling the person you are listening to is having. Note that it is not *the same* feeling but a similar one, based probably on some previous experience the mentor-coach has had that is also similar. It is important to strive to recognize the feeling that the client has, and the reader may remember that recognition of the *felt* experience is an important aspiration by any mentor-coach. The mentor-coach, when experiencing sympathy, may 'feel sorry for' the client.

It should be recognized that such feelings can get in the way of the clear thinking needed in this relationship. Sympathy is slightly different from feeling sorry that the client has suffered an unpleasant experience (i.e. feeling sorry *about something* as distinct from *for someone*), though that can also be pointless since the happening has by this time already occurred and one may as well get on with what its meaning and implication might be. An unpleasant experience results in feelings that can range from simple things like temporary frustration, to significant levels of fear or anger and the mentor-coach will be more help if he/she can detach him/herself from any of those feelings and help surface what exactly it is that *the client* is or was feeling. The mentor-coach may nevertheless find those feelings welling up. So should sympathy be offered verbally?

There may be nothing wrong in expressing sympathy, depending on how it's done. Equally, there may be no point in doing so. Clearly, anything patronizing like 'Poor you!' is totally to be eschewed. A short statement like 'That's awful' may be less patronizing, but may still have dangers and not be helpful. Sometimes the client will talk about something unpleasant and will look to the mentor-coach to make a statement that confirms he/she is right to feel angry or hurt and so on. For the mentor-coach to do so may not be as helpful as one might at first imagine, though there are some circumstances, for example where distress is not far from the surface, in which it can be helpful for the mentor-coach to respond to that need. So, in, for example, a case where someone is signalling that they are upset, you might want to offer recognition of that fact. This may be driven by a feeling of sympathy.

There is good reason for a mentor-coach to strive to take a minimal verbal part in the whole interaction and this applies here. Ownership by the client is the driving principle. In order to help achieve this you might strive to express sympathy – if indeed it is appropriate to do so – by facial expression and a gentle nod. It is after all the feelings of the client that are important. So a good way of handling your own feeling of sympathy might be to say something like, 'I am sensing that this has been quite awful for you', or in a less acute case, 'So what were your feelings about that and how are you feeling now?' The facially expressed sympathy with a gentle nod is very powerful if offered while attending to the reply. One might then ask, however, would it be accurate to label what has been offered as *sympathy*? It may be something else – something we shall consider later.

Identification

There is a feeling called identification that is similar to sympathy, and possibly a subtle but more intense form of it. The process of identification (in the intransitive form of the word) can really catch a mentor-coach unawares. You might be listening to someone very intently and hear an account of something that sounds similar to an experience or set of feelings of your own. If what you are drawn by is the similarity of the *situation*, it is less difficult to manage than if the *feelings* are similar and the situation different. It is a fairly straightforward rational action to remind yourself that, although the circumstances sound similar, the situation is unique because of all the variables that pertain – not least a collection of unique persons interacting with each other. If it is *the feelings* that are similar, the recognition will be harder and so will managing them. The reason is simple – feelings are a lot more powerful than rational processes, and as Goleman (1996) points out, feelings are accessed faster than rational thought because of the physical structure of the human brain. An example may help.

An example

A mentor-coach is working with someone in a professional role, similar to one held by one of the authors himself several years previously, early in headship. The client exhibited sustained signals of distress about the treatment she was receiving from all around – a range of bullying tactics by her governors and Local Authority, actions that felt to her like outright treachery from her own team and extreme antagonism from her staff at all levels. The mentor-coach had never encountered similar circumstances but had at one point, five years previously, experienced something that had provoked profound and disabling anguish for him. Although he knew that the circumstances were very different from those of his own situation five years ago, he slowly became aware that all those feelings from a long way back were welling up in him and for a very short while became disabled by them.

Should it be articulated?

One can think of no purpose other than totally distracting the client that would be served by the mentor-coach (or, for the sake of the example, the author in the previous section) telling all this to her. What was very important, however, was his ability to recognize that the emotional process called identification was occurring. This recognition gave him an opportunity to manage the feelings involved. He was able to maintain concentration and focus on attending to the person of the client. Having the feeling was not wrong.

Indeed one could argue that anyone who is genuinely open to another person is likely to be vulnerable in this way to intense feeling. The challenge is to know such things about oneself, to be alert to one's own current state of being and to recognize one's own emotions as they begin to develop. Failing to recognize that identification was taking hold in this particular situation or to manage it positively would have severely hindered the mentoring-coaching process.

A summary of the dangers

Sympathy and identification can each cause the mentoring-coaching relationship to be hijacked. If the purpose of that relationship is to facilitate dialogue – the generation of understanding and meaning that is latent in the circumstances of the client – the focus has to be wholly on that person and only on the feelings of the mentor-coach to the degree needed to ensure that they are being positively managed. There are more specific dangers in sympathy, to which reference is made later, than in identification where the mentor-coach may simply lose the plot. That is bad enough, for the journey being made together will go down the wrong track. Worse still, the client may end up losing trust and even respect for his/her mentor-coach if the product of identification is articulated. In the case of sympathy, if expressed in an inappropriate way, the client will merely (!) be short-changed. Instead of being enabled to think things through, the client will receive pity and possibly collusion, which is of no practical use, however temporarily comforting it may be.

Empathy: an appropriate emotion

What is needed in this context in the feelings of the mentor-coach is something stronger and of more practical use than sympathy without all the distracting potential of identification. The term that best describes this is *empathy*.

The term empathy is often used to mean the same as sympathy only more so. It is, however, a distinctive concept. If sympathy means 'feeling *with*' a person, empathy means 'feeling *into*' a person's situation and feelings. A definition may be difficult and even unhelpful here, for what we are referring to is a state of mind that is evolving, often through mental and emotional striving. Empathy is a process in which we commit ourselves to trying to understand what it might be or even feel like to be the other person in their particular situation. It's not a state that we in a sense arrive at, but more a journey to which we are committed. We cannot, and must not try to, become that other person and we don't end up fully understanding what it is like to be that other person. The best we can do is get the sense of it.

Carl Rogers (1975) writes,

Empathy has several facets. It means entering the private perceptual world of the other and becoming thoroughly at home. It means being sensitive, moment by moment, to the changing felt meanings which flow in this other person, to the fear or rage or tenderness or whatever he or she is experiencing. It means temporarily living in the other's life, moving about in it delicately without making judgements; it means sensing meanings of which he or she is scarcely aware, but not trying to uncover totally unconscious feelings, since this would be too threatening. It includes communicating your sensings of the person's world as you look with fresh and unfrightened eyes at elements of which he or she is fearful. It means frequently checking with the person as to the accuracy of your sensings and being guided by the response you receive. You are a confident companion to the person in his or her inner world . . . It means you lay aside your self; this can only be done by persons who are secure enough in themselves that they know they will not get lost in what may turn out to be the strange or bizarre world of the other, and that they can comfortably return to their own world when they wish . . . Being empathetic is a complex, demanding and strong – yet also a subtle and gentle – way of being.

Because empathy is one of the competencies in Goleman's (1998) Emotional Intelligence framework, it might be helpful if we remind ourselves of the meaning of the word competency as it was used in Chapter 10. One feature of empathy is what Rogers calls non-possessive warmth. This, too, is a competency. A competency is some characteristic of a person, evidenced in (patterns of) behaviour(s), that distinguishes outstanding performance in a given job or role. The focus, once again, is on behaviour. In the case of non-possessive warmth it is the 'non-possessive' behaviour that is of most importance. The warmth displayed will be what is referred to by Rogers (1961) as unconditional positive regard, but the warmth will not be stretched to the point where the helper – in this context, the mentor-coach – takes over the issue or feelings.

Again, an example may help. A client may be describing something he/she has achieved since the previous meeting, like real progress in relating to and teaching a hitherto apparently intractable class. The mentor-coach may be motivated by a feeling of warmth to say something like, 'That's brilliant. Well done!' In this instance the mentor-coach has identified and owned the judgement – possessed it, in other words. A gentle smile supporting the question, 'How do you feel about what you've achieved?' allows the client to retain total ownership while at the same time conveying unequivocally *his/her* feeling of pride and pleasure. The mentor-coach will fully understand the feeling but will not have shaped it in any way and will not have deprived the client of the pleasure of being the first person to announce it.

An example of a frustrating event will need to be managed in the same way: not 'You must be feeling pretty irritated' but 'How did that make you feel?' If the feeling is fairly obvious, it's okay to label it, provided it is done tentatively: 'I imagine that must feel pretty frustrating', or better still, 'I have a sense that it must (may) have made you feel pretty frustrated'.

Be tentative

To be direct, that is, not tentative, suggests you have *arrived* as a mentor-coach at empathy. In fact we never *arrive* at empathy. Empathy is more a state of making a journey. Remaining tentative leaves the space for the mentor-coach to progress further on the journey and the client to possess the issue/feeling/situation, but still allows one to display warmth.

As indicated earlier, what is sought here is 'unconditional positive regard'. Such regard amounts to warmth, but for empathy (rather than sympathy) to prevail, the warmth must not be such as to take any kind of ownership away from the client.

Summary

Empathy is the state of feeling that a mentor-coach needs to strive for. One way in which we can do this is to listen carefully *to ourselves* as we work in this special interaction. By this we mean listening carefully to what we are saying, how we are saying it and what we are doing, for example with our facial expression, hands, legs, arms and indeed all our body language. In addition, it means listening to what is going on in our head and heart and all those visceral things, like the inadvertent tightening of stomach muscles or a lump in the throat. Listening to our feelings is important too. As we develop this aspect of our listening skills we will naturally improve our ability to empathize with the other person – to whom we are listening simultaneously. This requires conscious and deliberate practice.

Empathic listening

The essence of this chapter is about the nature of our listening. The way in which we listen and communicate can develop a clear sense of empathy of which both participants are strongly aware. At the basis of our practice is the search for empathy, and listening and communicating with non-possessive warmth. In addition to all the other things that have been said about listening in previous chapters, it is also important to stress here that listening for intention and pattern, as well as for emotion or feeling, are ways of developing empathy.

Most people find it difficult to convey either information or ideas in the moment in a succinct, precise manner. We often need two or three attempts to make clear even a simple set of practical instructions. When complex issues – perhaps involving relationships, complicated behaviour patterns and strong feelings – are at stake we often find it hard to make ourselves clear. Part of the reason for this is that we are not clear about such things inside our own minds. That's why a mentor-coach can be so helpful in such situations – because their purpose is to help the client *think things through*. So when the client is stumbling through trying to formulate the words that will help order his/her thinking, he/she may not get all the words right that will express with clarity what he/she is trying to describe. Empathic listening by the mentor-coach will make it possible for the intention of the client to be discerned.

When the mentor-coach has a good sense of what the client is trying to say, it is important not simply to announce it. Once again it is helpful to be tentative and to offer your understanding carefully, perhaps beginning with a phrase like, 'You seem to be saying that . . . Have I got that right?' Total accuracy is not necessary, as long as what the client intends to express has been moved forward, though it will undermine the process and possibly the relationship if the mentor-coach is spectacularly inaccurate. The ability to help the client articulate clearly the intention behind his/her words is an important part of, and manifestation of, empathy. It also links directly to the purpose of dialogue discussed in the previous chapter.

Language patterns

A mentor-coach can be really helpful when he/she is able to identify patterns in the story the client tells. There may be a number of patterns. For example, there may be patterns in the words used in the story that will reveal things about the state of mind of the client, or about how she feels. An interesting example is when a person refers frequently to an unspecified group of people as 'they'. ('They say'; 'they expect'; 'they demand'; 'they think' etc.) Besides needing to clarify who precisely 'they' are, the client may also need help in seeing that he/she is allowing other people to take responsibility for directing events and circumstances around them that he/she might want to shape for him/herself.

Some words are quite indicative of feelings that may need to be explored, even if only used once – words like 'inadequate' or 'failure', for example. If used on several occasions, these words demand attention and can be explored simply by the mentor-coach repeating the word the next time it is used. The playing back of the word can be invitation enough, but it may be important to draw attention to the fact that it is being used a lot and that something of significance may lie behind it.

Behaviour patterns

Similarly, one might hear patterns of behaviour in a story, of which the client may be vaguely aware or possibly even completely unaware. This could be behaviour that emerges from behind the language used. Thus someone who uses the word 'they' in the way illustrated in the previous paragraph may also regularly abdicate responsibility and may signal that when this happens they feel powerless. It is enormously helpful to have some light shone on such happenings. Similarly, in recounting how he/she responds to difficult issues it may emerge that the client's usual tactic is one of avoidance – leaving his/her personal history littered with unresolved issues that make him/her feel that he/she is useless at solving any serious kind of problem. Once again, it is important not to pronounce on these patterns of behaviour or even to announce them. Rather, it is essential to approach the matter tentatively, with something that might begin, 'I am wondering whether there is a pattern beginning to emerge that might be helpful to talk about?' If this engages the client, the mentor-coach will continue to be tentative: 'In the detail of your story it was beginning to seem as though you often . . .'.

Patterns of feeling

A client may be quite direct in talk about feelings, especially once a relationship of trust and confidence has been securely established. The client may, however, still be unaware that there is sometimes a pattern to those feelings. Continuing the illustration from above as an example, the client who constantly talks about a group of persons as 'they' may well exhibit feelings of being hard done by, or even of being victimized. Although he/she may not believe he/she is being victimized, his/her thinking may often be in victim mode.

Regular patterns of feelings of this kind can be quite disabling, but the client may initially be able to see no further than a general sense of powerlessness and lack of any ownership. A mentor-coach who can help such a person recognize the pattern in the events and the language used to describe them can help further by supporting the client in articulating this pattern of feelings more precisely. Such articulation is the first step towards considering options and taking action. A mentor-coach who is herself unused to feelings of helplessness may have to work hard at suspending judgement, listening carefully for the patterns of language, behaviour and feelings in order to identify exactly what is going on. In other words the mentor-coach is invited here to imagine what it must be like to be someone else – a different kind of person almost from the sort of person she perceives herself to be.

Imagination

The ability to imagine is part of the skill or state of mind called empathy. People who find it hard to empathize with another often do so because they have a low level of ability to use imagination. Having imagination is almost certainly one of the distinct characteristics of human consciousness. Like all such characteristics it can atrophy if left unused or ignored, or it can be enhanced and developed if actively nurtured. This does not of course mean allowing it to run wild. What is meant here is allowing one's inner world to make space for the stories and experiences of others. What the mentor-coach is being asked to do is to imagine what it *might* be like (notice the tentativeness) to be that other person in their situation.

In Chapter 10 – on the competencies of the mentor-coach – an indication was given of some ways in which imagination can be nurtured, for example, by thoughtfully reading written fiction. The suggestion was that to do so might help develop reflective habits including self-awareness. All aspects of the arts can stimulate imagination and the development of self-awareness and at the same time begin to generate aspects of empathy.

Staying tentative

When this sort of mentor-coach begins to see/hear patterns of language, behaviour and feelings emerging he/she can be carried away by the sense of having a revelation. This must be actively managed in order to stay tentative: 'I am beginning to wonder whether you often feel . . . (powerless, victimized, picked on)' [The choice of word is very important, but even when you think you have the right word, the opinion must be expressed tentatively – even as a tentative question.]

Listening for emotion

We might as easily have begun with this facet of listening as reserving it to the end. Essentially, the story the client tells will not be a simple recounting of events or facts in the usual sense. It is as much the story of their *being* in that particular part of their life – and to some extent their whole being. So their feelings or emotions will be a critical part of the story, even when they are not explicitly expressed. In fact, many people don't especially want to talk about their emotions, even though they are as much a part of the story as the events – if not more so. Thus, we might want to be listening for the *felt experience*. It is important to be clear as to what this phrase means, as characterized in previous chapters.

Many of the things that happen to us as human beings seem to be the same, or at least similar to other people's happenings. What makes our experiences unique are the feelings associated with them. Thus going to the dentist is a very common experience but the *felt* nature of such a visit varies massively even when the treatment is the same. For some it is something so routine it is very easy to cope with, while for others it holds great terror, even in this day of relatively painless treatment. Similarly, two supporters of opposing sports teams may witness the same match. The felt experience of a supporter of the winning team is a very different felt experience from the supporter of the losers, even though the actual occurrence(s) were identical. The events a client describes to his/her mentor-coach could even be identical to some events encountered by the mentor-coach (though one is reliably informed that history never exactly repeats itself!); yet the experience might feel very different. So the mentor-coach must be listening empathically – trying to discern the *felt experience* of the client.

Conclusion

It is not sensible to think of specific emotional competencies in isolation. If it were, one might want to argue that the critical competency in the business of mentoring-coaching is empathy. It is worth noting in the context of this chapter that sympathy and identification are emotional states of being rather than emotional competencies.

Empathy is what a mentor-coach needs to strive for. It cannot stand alone. It begins with emotional self-awareness. Only when we can listen to our own emotions and recognize them for what they are and their likely effect on our behaviour can we manage them positively and begin to gain insight into the feelings of others. The process of gaining that insight is what is meant by the word empathy.

When we begin to gain it and to share that process with another in this very special relationship we call mentoring-coaching, it gradually develops in the consciousness of the client who thus becomes more aware of his/her feelings too. In him/her it sort of works in reverse. The awareness of empathy helps him/her to recognize his/her feelings – as though the empathy growing in the mentor-coach sparks self-awareness in the client. It is a very powerful dynamic within human relationships. It is wholly empowering and enabling.

Issues the reader may want to reflect on

- Daniel Goleman (1998) lists three competencies within the domain of self-awareness in emotional intelligence: emotional self-awareness, accurate self-assessment and self-confidence (or self-worth). How do you see yourself in terms of these competencies? Do you have evidence to help you with this assessment?

- How do those competencies help the mentor-coach?
- Are you aware of some of the precise ways in which your feelings impact upon your behaviours?
- How easy is it for sympathy to be aroused in you? What benefits may it have? What are its dangers?
- What are your honest thoughts about those occasions on which someone has offered you their sympathy? How might an empathic approach have been different?
- Can you think of an occasion when you have experienced emotional identification? What impact did it have on your behaviours?
- Try to sum up in your own words what empathy means to you. Do the same with the notion of non-possessive warmth.
- Why is being tentative so important?
- How confident are you that you are able to listen for intention? Try to think of an actual occasion when you have done so successfully. If that proves difficult, try it out in a conversation that has some 'edge' to it.
- How hard is pattern recognition in general for you? Try this out too in an interaction where someone you are listening to is seeking to engage your attention to a complex issue.
- What do you do to nurture your imagination? Why is important to do so? How does it help in developing the competency called empathy?
- Try in your own words to explain the concept of 'felt experience'.
- Can you see how empathy in the mentor-coach works to stimulate self-awareness in the client?

13 Images in the mind

The human mind is a most powerful instrument – capable of extremely complex functions, including the storage, consciously and unconsciously, of vast amounts of information. Part of the way in which it does so is to classify things so that they and information relating to them can be retrieved relatively easily. It does not always classify them using words. It can do so with images as well as labels. This is an impressive and very valuable capability, especially when one considers that such activity is often occurring just below the level of consciousness. Like all capabilities, it has a potential downside. Unless from time to time we draw our images and classifications to the surface of consciousness and deliberately question and refine them, they can bind both our thinking and our behaviour, creating attitudes that are helpful neither to us nor to those to whom we have to relate. This chapter considers this process and some of the issues it can generate in the mentoring-coaching relationship.

How we use images in the mind

One of the challenges in the role of mentor-coach is the fact that most human beings tend to manage the information stored in the brain by categorizing much of it. As we experience a variety of events and circumstances we form images of people and situations, which we store as a sort of 'job lot'. To some degree this is part of our survival mechanism – the means by which in ancient times we could match current situations and encounters to ones we had come across before – or that our parents and more distant ancestors had come across – and decide in a fraction of a second whether the being that suddenly stands in my path is one that I eat, or one that eats me!

In less extreme forms this practice of carrying images helps us to make decisions in the moment about how to handle each situation we come across, especially if it is one that is similar to another that occurred recently. We decide how to handle the current situation by referring at speed to the image we developed as a result of previous similar instances. The mental process occurs so fast that we are often quite unaware of it.

Images and stereotyping

This process is similar to the means by which stereotyping occurs. A number of similar experiences of people from, say, a particular profession or social background, can cause us to develop an image in the mind that conditions our likely mental and, possibly, emotional response to the next person we meet from that profession or background.

When we remain blind to the fact that we are stereotyping people and build judgements about them – based not on the available evidence about that individual but on the stereotype we carry in our mind – the images in question can become prejudices on which we end up basing our behaviour. For much of our behaviour towards others can easily be the product not of our encounter with that particular individual, but of the images in our mind.

How conscious are they?

The images we are referring to are not subconscious. They lie within the field of our consciousness, but perhaps just outside our present awareness. They are things we can know and understand if we want to – with very little assistance from other people and certainly without specialist help.

In the case of people who harbour and act on prejudices, they are deeply embedded and spring also from limited capability in dealing with difference. Thus, images are formed in the mind as to what 'normal' looks and sounds like. Deviations from normal become challenging in that they conflict with our image of normality and are thus placed in another category of image – often an image that is negative in character – but without awareness that that is what is happening.

Impact upon relationships

Most people hold an enormous number of these images in the mind and it is likely that all of our relationships with other people are susceptible to impact from the way that these images operate. We all want to believe that we do not

stereotype others and certainly that we are not prejudiced either in our attitudes or behaviours. This is not a chapter about stereotyping and prejudice,
but it is important to recognize that no one is free from the temptation to
engage in such processes and no single group has a monopoly of them. They
are referred to here because all readers will know something about them
and recognize that we are all capable of engaging in them. Prejudice and
stereotyping are products of a form of image in the mind.

Denial is useless

Just as with prejudice and stereotyping, the impact of our images in the mind
cannot be addressed by denying their existence or by avoidance. Nor are they
dealt with simply by pronouncing on them and making judgements about
them.

We need to be careful at this point. Although our minds are full of images
which impact upon the way we act, many of them impact positively or neutrally. For example, a reader may find the term 'adolescent male' prompts a
particular image that creates a state of mental alertness to a number of possibilities – some negative and some positive. The image may prompt such a
reader to proceed sensitively when dealing with adolescent males she/he has
to work with that may help forge constructive rapport. The fact that the next
group of adolescent males the reader has to work with do not match the mental image she/he then has may or may not present a challenge. Similarly, if our
approach to life is a flexible one, our images in the mind may have a much
reduced general impact on our attitudes to people and situations.

How easily images form

All of the above is relevant to the situation one might find oneself in as a
mentor-coach. As the client begins his/her story (or even before that point)
matters will be presented that the mentor-coach will receive in his/her mind
that will stimulate mental reference to images already stored there. The temptation will present itself for the mentor-coach to associate the person in front
of them with the image. Or it may be that a character in the story of the client
evokes an image. Some examples might help. Imagine the following persons:

- a head teacher
- a newly qualified teacher
- an Ofsted inspector
- an excluded child
- a teenager with EBD special needs

- a dinner lady
- a school bully
- a 'failing' teacher.

Did an image come to mind? Did the image suggest judgements or was it simply a picture? For many people a picture is almost inevitable and usually judgements follow fairly readily. Yet the picture and associated judgements may be of someone we haven't even met and may possibly never meet in the future!

Tuning in to our images

There is nothing morally wrong in an image forming, nor in judgements presenting themselves to us. It is what we *do* with them that matters. If a person is easily given to forming images in the mind (for example, in response to some of the categories listed in the previous paragraph) it is important that s/he recognizes this tendency in general in her/himself. This is an important step towards routinely recognizing individual instances of this occurrence. Recognition is, in turn, a key first step in personal change (where that is appropriate) and in managing our thoughts and feelings.

Most people who have a reasonable degree of self-awareness (a critical emotional competency for a mentor-coach) will not find it difficult to challenge any preformed image or category once they meet the person in question and seek to relate to that person as an individual. Indeed, the phrase we have used to describe the behaviour of the mentor-coach is 'attending to the person' – as distinct from any image in the mind. Thus as the mentor-coach attends to the person of the client the image that might have dominated at first will be replaced by a picture of the individual.

So far in this chapter reference has been made to images of people, but this characteristic of our brain function is active when we hear of or encounter situations as well. The brain may not only assemble a full image from only the beginning of a story, it will also begin to sift a range of possible behaviours that might constitute our response – as if survival might depend upon it!

A link with intuition

In his book *Emotional Intelligence* Goleman (1996) quotes Ledoux (1998) referring to intuition as an operation by which the brain searches its recesses for information that may be stored from previous situations or circumstances similar to one currently being encountered. So when we meet someone for the first time we receive 'data' that prompt the brain to sift for further data about similar people we have met before. It then presents that data to us in some form or other – sometimes as warning signal, sometimes as something positive. In other words it recalls an image on which – if we wish – we can act, either to defend ourselves or to welcome the person and become open to them.

Opinions differ on what to do with intuition. Some people trust their intuitions with no reservation. Others trust them selectively. Yet others rely on intuition only with great caution. In the mentoring-coaching relationship it should be possible to recognize an intuition and hold it tentatively while checking for further evidence. This is in fact a requirement upon the mentor-coach in relation to the client. Sometimes the intuition is confirmed, while in other cases it is corrected. Very few people have intuitions that are always entirely accurate, but the brain does not offer these signals without some reason, so it is never wise simply to ignore intuition completely.

Summary so far

All mentor-coaches carry images in the mind that they need to be aware of, especially at the beginning of a mentoring-coaching interaction. Such images must be managed in the same way that judgements have to be managed. They must be put aside or suspended for the time being. Note that this is not the same as ignoring them. It is about being open as much to the possibility that they will be disconfirmed as confirmed. The reader who wishes to develop his/her thinking further on this aspect of mentoring-coaching will find more on this subject in Goleman's (1996, 1998) work and in Peter Senge's *Fifth Discipline* (1990/1998) and *Schools That Learn* (Senge et al., 2000) where s/he write of mental models. Images in the mind – as referred to in this chapter – are seen as somewhat distinct from mental models and from intuitions for a number of reasons but there is a degree to which these two notions have been synthesized here.

A mentor-coach who is unable to suspend images they may have of their client will not be able to offer an appropriate degree of help in thinking things through. Unchallenged images in the mind simply obstruct clarity of thought.

The client's images

The images in the mind of the client are a further challenge for the mentor-coach. The client may see people in his/her story in a particular way – even to the point of stereotyping them or holding prejudices towards them. Similarly, s/he may have an unhelpful image of the organization or kind of organization s/he is working in. S/he may believe they are intuitions and have almost taken them for granted as part of some self-evident truth. This stance may be a major stumbling block in her path. S/he may believe that s/he sees the other person or the organization as they really are. It was argued earlier and is stressed now that no one sees things or other persons as *they* are. We can only see things as *we* are.

Images are about us

The truth is that the images we hold in our minds are as much (if not more) about us than about the people whose image it is that we hold. So if mentoring-coaching is about 'thinking through who I am', the client needs to be helped to understand his/her images in the mind, that is, images of other people in his/her story and consider the possibility that other images of that person may be equally valid. In other words, it may be that by opening his/her mind to other possible images of individuals who are part of his/her story the client will engage in the beginnings of the process of empathizing with that person. This may be crucial in the medium term to finding a way forward in relation to issues that arise from the story, especially issues that revolve around working relationships.

This may involve the mentor-coach challenging the client's images in some way, including approaches that feature in the next chapter, but here it is necessary to stress that it is through the matter of surfacing or helping the client articulate the images that the process of considering other images begins.

Images of organizations

Most of this chapter so far has been about images in the mind of *people* we encounter. Additionally, Gregory Bateson (1972) and others (Hutton, 1997; Hutton et al., 1997; Reed, 1999) have written in depth on the subject of the 'organization-in-the-mind'. This is a category of the image in the mind that is important for a mentor-coach to understand. Put simply, most organizations have an 'official form': they have a purpose and a way in which they are supposed to work, according to official documents, vision statements, policies, structures and so forth. Most people who are part of the organization and those who interface with it from the outside will have their own perceptions of the purpose and way in which it should work – of which they will not necessarily always be fully aware. Moreover, they may not be aware how their own perception on a daily basis may differ from the 'official' version, let alone of the dissonance this difference can generate both for them, and for others with whom they work. Yet the dissonance stems from the behaviour generated in part from the particular perception that has here been called the 'organization-in-the-mind'.

This is not something that happens only as one works down the lines of management. Seniority in an organization is no guarantee of clarity about its purpose or the way in which it is meant to work. A mentor-coach could find that a client with a senior position in an organization is encountering a deal of dissonance as a result of a lack of clarity about these things – both on his/her own part and on the part of others whom they lead/manage, or to whom they have to relate.

Clarity and team membership

Any team, say, a subject, key stage or year group team, or even a class or other student group within the larger context is an organization of the kind discussed here. How each member of the team sees it – in any number of respects – may need to be understood by its leader, and preferably by other members too. The issue that becomes the subject of the mentoring-coaching interaction can both impact upon the 'organization-in-the-mind' of each member in the team led by the client and be impacted by it. This can only happen, however, if the client is helped first of all to perceive his/her own image of the team and that of other members, and to begin to recognize the differences.

Which image is right?

A client who is a team leader will find it easiest to assume that as the leader his/her image of the team is the right one. Equally, each team member may see his/her version as the best. What matters is not which image is right or best, but that the client can perceive his/her own image clearly and begin to understand that there are other possible images in the minds of the team. Those images are part of the reality with which they and, therefore, the mentor-coach, have to work. These diverse images do not have to be harmonized in any detail within a team, but considering them may help the client to deal with conflict being experienced in the work place. Some harmony is essential and there are inevitably some 'bottom lines' but the diversity – and a clear understanding of it – may help a client who is a team leader get the best out of each member of her team.

Relationships as organizations

Everything written in the preceding few paragraphs about organizations and teams could be held to be applicable to relationships – indeed it is essentially about relationships that one is thinking here. It is upon the way in which people relate that our images in the mind of any organization has the most tangible impact. On one-to-one relationships these images, both of people and organizations, can have a very profound impact. Discerning the image and its impact may be what the client needs most help with – often without knowing that that is a significant need. A relationship *is* an organization – in a microcosmic sense. Research has shown that the most common types of issue, positive and negative that arise in mentoring-coaching are concerned to one degree or another with relationship management.

Resolving dissonance

In any working relationship (as in personal relationships) having an understanding of each other's images and how they cause each to behave gives to both parties a significantly enhanced range of options about how to treat each other and how to work together. This applies to their image of each other, their image of the relationship and the image they have of other people who impact on that relationship.

It has been found in mentoring-coaching that a very large percentage of the issues that arise at Stage 2 of the model boil down in essence to some relationship or other, within which dissonance has been generated. The coaching part of the interaction in these cases address *how* to resolve the dissonance.

Unless the unspoken images the client carries in his/her head are addressed the dissonance cannot be meaningfully resolved.

Issues the reader may want to reflect on

- Think of some images of people or 'types of people' you personally carry in your mind. Do you ever consciously try to challenge yourself about them? How easy or difficult do you find that?
- Do you recognize any stereotyping or even prejudice to which you may be prone? How does the question, and your attempt at an answer, make you feel?
- Are you aware of others with whom you work who appear to carry distinctive images in their mind? What examples of an impact on their behaviour derived from those images could you say you had observed?
- How far could your own images in the mind help or hinder your work as a mentor-coach?
- How intuitive would you say you are? To what extent might this help or hinder your work as mentor-coach?
- How would you go about helping a client to develop a conscious

awareness of their own images in the mind (images both of people and of the organization(s) they are part of)? What are the key skills you would need? To what extent have you already developed those skills?

- Can you see why mentoring-coaching needs, among other things, to be about helping the client think through the questions, 'Who am I?', 'My role', 'The context I work in'?
- Do all team members need to have the same organization in the mind or simply a better understanding of the different images held within the team?
- How helpful might it be within any kind of one-to-one relationships for both parties to be at least sensitive to the fact that the other person may hold different images in the mind from their own?

14 Chains of meaning

Chains can be used to hold fast something of genuine importance – as when attached, for example, to a ship's anchor – or to imprison and enslave. The phrase 'chains of meaning' is intended to focus attention on both of these possibilities. The meaning we attach to our experiences can help us to be anchored to values we have evolved, and to develop further action in the light of those values even when experience is turbulent. Equally, it is possible to become inflexible directly as a result of patterns of meanings we have allowed to evolve without critical scrutiny. This chapter examines how both of these effects can be brought about. It also considers ways in which we can work ourselves loose from chains of meaning that imprison us and inhibit our growth as fully human persons, both as mentor-coach and client within the mentoring-coaching relationship.

Dialogue and meaning

In earlier chapters of this part of the book, a number of issues around the general nature of the mentoring-coaching interaction were considered. In particular, the reader was invited to focus on the concept of dialogue. Conversation, discussion and debate are thought to be less useful words because of matters like the informality, lack of structure or adversarial nature of each of these alternative concepts. The term dialogue was chosen – ignoring the popular notion of Socratic dialogue where winning an argument is a dominant characteristic – because of the sense that it conveys of 'meaning flowing through' the interaction. Mentoring-coaching is aimed at the generation together of *meaning*.

Neither the mentor-coach nor the client come to this interaction without some sense of the meaning (or meanings) that attach to the issues about which they will be thinking together. One of the distinctive characteristics of humans is their capacity to engage in meaning-making or sense-making. This characteristic is symbiotically connected with the human capacity for language. Whether meaning-making precedes language as suggested by Heron (1996) or vice versa could occupy a lengthy discourse but it need not detain us here. The point at issue is that we have the capacity to make meaning and the interaction we call mentoring-coaching is, perhaps above all else, about that process. Yet, one way or another, we are doing it all the time as we go about our daily business. It is a constant in our mental processes.

Coherence

For many people the meanings being made are random. Each event has its own significance, and little attempt is made to connect the meaning of one occurrence to another. No patterns are looked for and things and their meanings don't have to cohere, or hang together. Others find that a very unsatisfactory way to think and need to connect – in a whole range of ways. For the first group the meanings of each occurrence offer little help in making sense of the next. Nor do they help much in making decisions about how to respond to new events as they happen. In truth, most people who go about in this way eventually find it so unhelpful that they seek out connections and patterns to help chart a path through what might otherwise be a very confusing set of turbulent experiences.

It is important to distinguish between coherence and consistency. Consistency is valuable in a number of ways – in spite of the fact that Winston Churchill is thought to have regarded it as 'the obsession of fools'. The consistency that has value is one that helps ensure that we act in accord with our principles. This does not mean acting the same way in all similar circumstances. It means that we can adapt our behaviour in response to those features of circumstance that are distinctive. We can refine our behaviour as we distinguish one kind of occurrence from another, but always in the light of values and principles we hold. Coherence is about our ability first to distinguish meanings and at the same time to relate occurrences and meanings to values. It might also mean that some of our values are refined in the light of new experiences and our interpretation of them.

Primary and secondary values

The reader needs to be clear at this point that there are at least two kinds of values that are being referred to: primary and secondary. By primary we mean those values we perceive to underpin the very core of what matters to us. Examples could be distracting here, but the reader will want to think about what his/her primary values are. One value very important to the authors of this book is respect. Even our core values may be refined by experience. Respect for what and for whom? Everyone? Regardless of his/her behaviour? Regardless of whether the respect is reciprocated?

Core values are less likely to be refined in the light of experience than those we refer to as secondary. An example of a secondary value might for some be inclusion – something much talked about by those who make educational policy. It is secondary only in the sense that it is probably derived from a primary value, for example, respect for other human beings as of right.

How one arrives at primary values – how we come to know that something is right or true, even how we come to *know* something – is a most fascinating matter and has occupied many great minds. It is very much worth pondering but might detain us for too long here and overcomplicate the exposition in which this book is engaged. It is worth noting, however, that some position on this may be important to many readers.

Mike Bottery writes in his excellent book, *The Challenges of Educational Leadership* (2004), of a range of epistemologies that people adopt – sometimes without knowing it – to establish what they believe to be true and right. His chapter on this is well worth reading, and anyone who has read it will recognize what we set out here as stemming from what Bottery calls a 'provisionalist' epistemology. A provisionalist epistemology involves recognizing that there is such a thing as objective reality and objective truth but that it is in a number of ways hard for any individual to be certain that s/he has fully grasped it. The best we can do is rigorously to strive to find what is true and yet be open to the fact there are things that as yet we have not encountered or discovered that may cause us to reconsider some of that truth. It is an epistemology because we are making a sort of (tentative) judgement about precisely *how* we can know these things. Meanwhile, we do our level best to live in the light of what we have provisionally identified as truth or values.

Values and coherence as anchors

There is a chicken-and-egg character to the relationship between values and coherence. It is certainly the case that our values are formed as we reflect upon what happens to us and to others whom we observe. This reflection is part of the activity we engage in to derive coherence. So we reflect, make meaning and distil meaning (or meanings) into values. Our meanings feel coherent when we have arrived at a value. Equally, however, we use the values we have evolved by that process to make further meaning (subject to the possible further refining of those values). We test what has happened to us by reflecting on it in the light of our values. We have a sense of coherence if our values have helped us make sense of it, or make meaning from or about it.

We have called this chapter 'Chains of Meaning' for a number of reasons. The first of these is that the word 'chain' suggests a sort of security. Having meaning in our lives gives us a sense that things are not entirely random and, therefore, no matter how difficult or turbulent experience may be we are unlikely to be 'swept away'. We are anchored to our values and the coherence they help us generate. There are other reasons for choosing the word 'chains' in this chapter and we turn to these later.

Values in mentoring-coaching

Many adults cannot remember, when asked, how or when they acquired their value set. Many people never think much about values, though that does not necessarily mean they don't have values, nor that they don't try to live by some principles in an instinctive sort of way. Values often emerge during upbringing. We can gain them, often unwittingly, from parents or some family member or significant other who influenced us in childhood or youth. Only when we have the opportunity to articulate them, or when some acute occurrence challenges us, do we consciously reflect on what they might be.

It has already been indicated that the mentoring-coaching interaction involves a shared search for meaning, and linked to that is the possibility of coherence being generated. It is important that mentor-coaches recognize that values play several parts in this interaction. There are important ways in which a mentor-coach will be guided during the interaction by their own values and by the values of mentoring-coaching as a professional and philosophical discipline. This has been broached in Chapter 10. The focus here is on the issue of how a mentor-coach might handle a situation where the values of the client appear to conflict with the values of the mentor-coach. The use of the word 'appear' in the previous sentence is intended to convey that people often say and do things, in all kinds of context, that could be driven by a particular value, that may be in conflict with what they truly believe, but they simply haven't given it enough thought. In other words, they may be talking or acting inconsistently and they may simply have developed very little coherence around the kind of issues or experiences that have at the moment been focused upon. They may simply not know that their words or actions have a possible value base and therefore have no chance to reflect on it.

Mentoring-coaching helps to clarify values

The opportunity to take that step – to reflect upon, to ponder the meaning of, and begin to generate some coherence around an experience or issue – is part of the essential purpose of mentoring-coaching. It's a key part of what is meant by 'thinking things through'. Sometimes a client will not have had the opportunity to articulate his/her thinking on this kind of level. In such a case s/he may discover that one of the issues arising is that implicit values s/he holds are actually sparking tension for him/her in respect of their current situation. Equally, it may be that some clear articulation of certain values by him/her (*not* by the mentor-coach) will be a powerful prompt of possible ways forward with regard to the issues that are in focus. Realization that one holds certain values and, with help, can clearly articulate them is a very strong instance of doubleloop learning, because it offers a key to how other issues might successfully be addressed. A mentoring-coaching encounter in which the client is able to clarify and articulate his/her value set would count as a very significant interaction.

It is perfectly possible that a client may be struggling with an issue because of an internal value clash. To refer back to an example already quoted may be helpful. You might hold strongly to the principle of respect for other human beings as of right and yet find that your beliefs about the notion of inclusion (especially its limits) are somehow in conflict with the original principle from which they are derived. Sorting out how to deal with such a clash could be extremely important as a basis for resolving a whole range of practical issues, especially in the field of education.

Sometimes the clash is between a feeling, or set of feelings, about a practical issue and some underlying value – whether it is implicit or explicit. To stay with our example, other human beings to whom we believe we should accord respect as of right don't always make it easy for us to accord it. Indeed, many of the issues that arise in a professional context, that in turn become the subject of mentoring-coaching work, focus on the practical business of relationships and the feelings engendered within them that can be very negative. Acting according only to those emotions could prove very detrimental to the persons involved and to their organization. Sorting out how to balance the feelings against the values – once they have been articulated – is not easy for many people and the help of the mentor-coach can be extremely valuable in such a process (hence our return to this issue already outlined in Chapter 10).

Value clash between mentor-coach and client

A clash in values between mentor-coach and client is much rarer than people imagine. A mentor-coach may hear a client say many things that suggest a possible value clash. Indeed, a client may describe action s/he has taken that her mentor-coach would have eschewed on account of the value implicit in it. This usually indicates that the client is not thinking very much about values and their importance, or about how consistent s/he is being in terms of the relationship between values, on the one hand, and thoughts, words and actions on the other. In this case the process of thinking the values through will be sufficient to resolve some potential discomfort for the mentor-coach and to provide some light for the client on the issues in focus.

On occasion, however, there may be a genuine clash between a value held by the mentor-coach and one held by the client. This clash could occur at the level of a primary or a secondary value. We will consider such possibilities using the example already referred to twice earlier.

Although we hold the principle of according respect for other human beings as of right to be a core value, we recognize that this value could be expressed in different ways or might not be held as a universal principle by everyone we work with. Some dissonance will be generated where this is the case. When such differences arise in mentor-coaching, it is best if clarity is achieved. By clarity we mean that it is important that the client be helped to articulate clearly exactly what it is that s/he believes – exactly how s/he would express the value in question, so that s/he can understand one of the key factors driving his/her own thinking, feelings and behaviours. It is as this clarity evolves that the mentor-coach may become aware of the clash (if one exists) or the potential for a clash. At this stage it may be important that the *client* is not deliberately made aware of the clash, though if s/he becomes aware of it, the mentor-coach must manage it according to the same principles that would guide him/her if, for example, the client requested straight advice. As indicated earlier, we often find in such circumstances that this process results in a reconsideration by the client of the values in question. But what if it doesn't?

How big a clash?

For the mentor-coach the question that can arise is 'Can I continue to work with this person?' It would be irresponsible for a mentor-coach to rush into a decision to withdraw from the relationship. It would be important to probe the values held by the client in a systematic and rigorous yet tentative way before doing so. A fundamental or big clash could well make continued mentoring-coaching virtually impossible. For example, continuing the theme of respect, a client who articulated clear values that limited their respect for others on account of gender, race and other issues of equality might end up wanting to take action that the mentor-coach felt to be entirely unethical. But if the values articulated supported such decisions, it is likely that the mentor-coach's position would have become untenable long before decisions about actions were arrived at. Nevertheless, it would be wrong to pass up the opportunity to subject those beliefs to calm and rigorous scrutiny. It would be a mistake for the mentor-coach to bail out too soon in such a circumstance.

This would, in our view, be the case even if the situation arose where the client took a stance towards the mentor-coach that were, for example, sexist or racist, though the writers are aware that it is perhaps too easy for them – as white males – to generalize here. The point perhaps still stands that if there were an opportunity to influence such a person's thinking, it would be a pity to miss it. If such thinking was entrenched, however, it would deny the very basis on which mentoring-coaching should occur.

Because the mentoring-coaching relationship is a voluntary one, it is important to stress again that the kind of occurrence we have written about in this section is quite rare. The kind of people who agree to enter such a relationship are usually people who are ready to think and who want something to change – even if they know nothing about what needs to change or how change is to be brought about. In other words, they bring a degree of openness to the interaction. Or it is often the case that the openness is generated by the development of the relationship of trust and confidence engendered by the process. In contrast, by definition almost, people who are entrenched in negative thinking towards other human beings are unlikely to want mentoring-coaching, unless somehow their entrenched thinking has made their lives pretty unbearable.

Enchained by meaning

On a somewhat less obvious and less troubling level than the sort of thing we referred to at the beginning of this chapter, a sense is emerging in which meaning and coherence can put people in chains from which they may need help to break free. This is quite distinct from the sort of security we suggested earlier that meaning and coherence can provide. Helping the client to break free of such chains may be a very important part of the purpose of the interaction.

> We see things, not as they are, but as we are. (Talmud)

This saying from the Talmud was referred to earlier to highlight the need for the mentor-coach to develop empathy, and to contextualize the concept of images of the mind. The saying has particular value for the client, who may need help in recognizing that his/her view of reality – important though it is – is only *his/her view*. Fascinatingly the client's view is also a part of the reality that faces the mentor-coach. Reference was also made earlier in this chapter to the notion of a provisionalist epistemology, by which is meant that all that we know can only be known provisionally. Absolute certainty is not available, according to this view of knowledge. Yet many people talk, think and act as though certainty is readily within their grasp. The fact that this belief in the certainty and accuracy of their own perceptions generates emotional and practical turbulence for them fails to dislodge them from their certainty. This is because they are unaware of, and are in chains to, the patterns and processes of meaning making that have brought them this far.

Filters

Everything that we hear and see has to pass through filters that we have developed through experience of the world from our earliest days. Indeed, some of the filters are generated genetically through the processes that have enabled our species to survive. For every individual there are distinctive and unique combinations of filters. They condition how we see the world around us and, in turn, influence the meaning we make from it. The process is circular. Every meaning we make has the potential to generate another filter or at least to modify our existing filters. An example may help.

An example

We all know or have heard of people in relationships that we – so we say – would fight our way out of, if we happened to be in something similar. In abusive relationships, for example, some women – and occasionally some men – put up with treatment that most of us would not tolerate. They put up with it because they expect or hope for change in the other person, or they think or feel that deep down there is something lovable about the person that no one else can see. Sometimes, as many working in education will have experienced, it's a parent who sees things like this in relation to their child – the child can do little wrong because he or she is really quite special, their child! In this kind of example a predisposition about a person acts to filter out things that other people might be able to see very readily.

The result is that what might seem to be facts are interpreted either positively or negatively to create meanings that, in turn, will act as further filters. So an abused person may, for example, not really focus on the abuse they suffer and instead be impressed by what they see as the strength displayed in the other person's behaviour. Or s/he may see behaviours that s/he takes to be a cause of hope that the person is changing, when others see that same behaviour as confirming the current, manipulative nature of the relationship. Similarly a parent of a spoilt child may notice apparently entertaining behaviour by the child and fail to recognize actions through which s/he is being manipulated by the child. These are fairly extreme examples. In mentoring-coaching, as in much everyday experience, our filters work in more subtle ways.

Links in the chain

The chains of meaning that can imprison us have two main parts consisting of a small number of links each. The first part is largely inside our heads and is made up of:

- the objective reality we encounter
- our filters
- elements of reality we choose to notice – our perceptions
- interpretation(s) of those elements.

The second part begins inside our heads but sets in motion a sequence ending with actions we take:

- we apply our interpretations to the situation
- generalizations we make from several instances of applying interpretations
- we generate values (implicit and explicit) and principles – our world view
- behaviour based on those values, especially the implicit values.

Objective reality?

Although we all see things as *we* are, rather than as *they* are, there is a reality that is to some degree objective. Thus, several people may witness a single event and come up with their own quite distinctive account of it. But with the help of modern technology (a video-recording) they could end up largely agreeing on the details of the occurrence they witnessed. However, we do not normally have that technology available to us at the time of most of the experiences we have in life, however common street cameras are becoming. All we have is our own perception as derived from reality via the filters in operation, largely just below the surface of consciousness. This is not to deny that there is an objective reality for much of the time (i.e. activity occurring outside of our own minds), much of which would be happening even if we were not there.

In the previous paragraph reference was made to filters operating just below the surface of consciousness. They are often quite subtle, so that although we know – often in retrospect – that we allow them to skew our perceptions, we are frequently unable to do anything about them at the time. By 'subtle' we do not mean complex. Something like a tendency to see the empty half of a half-full glass would count as a relevant example. Equally, unfounded optimism may operate as a subtle filter that skews perceptions of reality – occasionally with disastrous consequences. In mentoring-coaching an opportunity arises to probe those perceptions and to help the client to become more aware of the effect that the filters have upon him/her – to become more aware of the filters themselves and decide consciously on how they are best managed.

This may not be a simple matter. What we are talking about is the need to raise the filters and their impact on our behaviours (through the chains of meaning) to a level just *above* the surface of consciousness. Of course, this is not achieved by telling the client what the mentor-coach is observing (partly because the mentor-coach also has perceptions that are influenced by filters). It can only be achieved through the mentor-coach helping the client formulate questions that will probe the perceptions and allow him/her to develop new perspectives.

What's happened (is happening)?

The Learning Cycle developed by Kolb (1984) is particularly helpful here (see Figure 14.1 for our modified version of this model), in that we are talking about helping the client to consider in some depth the question as to what is happening (or has happened) in the situation that is the main subject of the encounter.

When using this cycle (most easily by starting top right and proceeding clockwise through the quadrants), many learners pass over too quickly the first stage. They assume that the details that come easily to mind when they ask the question 'What happened?' make up the whole picture of objective reality, when what is needed is consideration of the occurrences under scrutiny from a number of possible angles so as to avoid critical factors being filtered out. So, for example, when a client is describing an encounter with another individual whom s/he is finding it difficult to handle, the mentor-coach might ask a question like, 'If you were the other person [the pupil, parent, your head of department or head teacher] would your description of those events differ from the one you have just given? If so, how?' If this quadrant in the cycle is passed over too readily, the answer to the question 'Why did it happen?' will

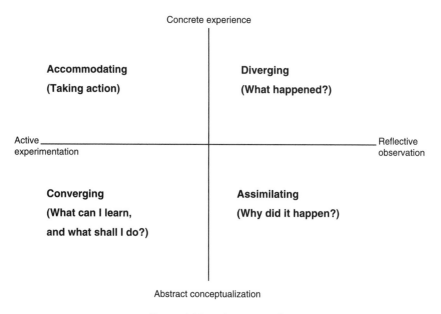

Figure 14.1 A learning cycle.
Source: adapted from Kolb (1984).

inevitably be flawed. The client will arrive at meanings that will not necessarily bear a great deal of relation to the objective reality of the encounter.

The relationship between David Kolb's Learning Cycle and the model of mentoring-coaching we are advocating is very strong. The mentor-coaching model is a managed model of experiential learning, that is, it is about one person helping another – by thinking things through – to learn from current experience and to plan and take action based on that learning.

In a whole range of situations it is easy to derive learning that is flawed as a result of perceptions based on a version of objective reality that has been filtered, without our full awareness, to a degree that leaves one unable to function effectively. In doing so, we interpret events in a way that other involved participants might not easily recognize. In other words, we create meanings that are poorly founded but that nevertheless impel us in the direction of action that might make a problematic situation worse, because we have become so detached from objective reality. If a mentor-coach can help a client to consider a range of perspectives on what has happened, it will be easy for the client to consider a number of alternative interpretations too. Making a poorly based meaning from a poorly based perception helps us become more securely imprisoned in situations, especially relationships, that are already troubling.

Applications

In this part of the chain we often find ourselves confirming the images in the mind that we already hold about situations of this kind or about people – individually and/or collectively. The meaning we have made in the first part of this chain is used to confirm further – as if confirmation were needed – that, for example, this is a case of a glass being half empty. Or, to introduce a further example, this is yet another instance proving that this member of the team is not to be trusted/is negatively disposed towards the organization/ wants to undermine my position/won't pull his weight and so on.

The next link in the chain can follow almost seamlessly from the process of the application of interpretations. It can, however, be the link that almost seals the imprisonment of its subject. The kind of generalization that might emerge from examples given in the last sentence of the previous paragraph will illustrate the point:

- The decision that a team member is not to be trusted may lead one to be wary of trusting other people generally – to a belief, for example, that 'If I really want something done, I'd best do it myself'. Delegation and shared leadership are thus negated.
- A readiness to conclude that another person is negatively disposed towards the organization may lead to a defensive general view of how the organization's needs should be approached. This, in turn, can stifle innovation and enterprise.
- Instances of believing that someone is out to undermine one's position may become a general feeling or belief that 'They are out to get me'! Trust is thus profoundly undermined.
- A conclusion that a person will not pull their weight may become a general view that people are lazy. Expectations plummet, and performance is thus severely eroded.

Every reader will know of organizations where this kind of thinking has had a damaging impact.

In general, a tendency to see the empty half of a half-full glass has a similar impact and is produced by a similar chain of thinking or of meaning-making.

Generating values/principles

It is not difficult to see how from such generalizations values might be generated – or indeed how values might be undermined. Values relating to empowerment, trust, respect, inclusion, care for others, openness, honesty and so on may all be strengthened or weakened by generalizations of the kind considered in the previous section. The examples used here would, of course, weaken the values instanced, while the process of challenging those generalizations might lead to their strength being increased. Principles will emerge that might reflect either a positive or negative world view – principles such as 'In the last resort other people will always let you down', 'If you don't put yourself first, no one else will', 'The essence of being is the will to power' (Nietzsche), 'Competition beats co-operation' and so on. A less misanthropic world view could equally be generated from a different set of starting points: 'People respond well to being trusted', 'Care for others reaps a generous response', 'Empowering others is generative – the increase in power is shared by the initiator' and 'Co-operation ensures everyone gives of their best'.

Behaviour

At the end of the chain is behaviour – things we say and do (as well as things we feel and think). The whole process, but especially the generalizations and the values we develop (remember they are often below the surface of our consciousness) or allow to evolve, determines what we do and say, and even how we do and say it.

The way in which chains of meaning can have an impact upon us is seen in its most raw form in our relationships with individuals in the workplace and elsewhere.

For example:

> I notice that Bryan keeps looking down at his notes while I am leading a team meeting to introduce a new development we have decided to work on. He is not engaging with what I am saying, and probably doesn't really want to be involved in the project. Come to think of it, Bryan doesn't really like change and new ideas very much – unless he's the one who thought of them in the first place. He doesn't like other people being given credit, especially people superior to him in the management chain like me. He's really not a team player. The organization mustn't depend on people like him. I need to make sure any part he plays in this new project is not too important. That's what you have to do with colleagues who are not good team players: sideline them.

The reader may want to try dissecting this account into the links in the chain identified in the section with that heading.

Padlocking the chain

It is important to recognize that it is the last but one stage, the process of generating values, that makes up the most imprisoning part of the chain of meaning – a sort of manacle with padlock.

What tends to happen is that the values – particularly the unspoken values (what Schein, 1999 refers to as our 'values in use') – become part of the filter system through which we see and hear future occurrences of a similar kind. Sometimes it is a new filter and sometimes it is simply the case that an existing filter has been strongly confirmed or reinforced. In any event, the generalizations and values/principles we have evolved through our chains of meaning condition how objective we are able to be when faced with further occurrences of either a similar kind or in a similar context. They influence how accurately and openly we are able to observe what has been referred to as objective reality.

Emotional competence as an antidote

In Chapter 10 we wrote of the importance of Emotional Intelligence in the mentor-coach. The sort of situations described in this part of the current chapter will be less likely to occur for people with reasonably developed emotional competencies. The reason is simple: it has a whole lot to do with levels of consciousness or, as Daniel Goleman (1996) puts it, awareness, particularly self-awareness. A person who is self-aware will find it easier to recognize the danger from the chains of meaning we have been describing in the second half of this chapter, and, having recognized it, will be in a better position to do something about it.

Other writing on this subject

Readers who have not come across these notions before may initially find this train of thought somewhat abstruse. Many readers will find that it rings true. It has been written about in terms that express a depth of experience from working in services and organizations that focus very much upon people, as all informed leadership and management must do. These experiences have, however, been tested against the writing and research of a number of well-established academic authors. For example, Kolb (1984), Bottery (2004), Goleman (1996, 1998) and Schein (1999) have been quoted in the text of this chapter.

In a similar vein, Argyris and Schon (1996) and Senge (1990/1998) and Senge et al. (2000) write in depth about similar issues. In particular, Argyris and

Schon build a notion similar to the chains of meaning described here based on the double bind theory expounded by the social anthropologist Gregory Bateson (1972) and linguist S. I. Hayakawa (1949). This book's exposition is a genuine attempt to formulate the experience in a distinctive way using language and imagery that ring true for the authors and for readers in the education sector in particular. The serious student of social psychology will want to pursue the writings of the eminent authors and researchers referred to in this section.

Issues the reader may want to reflect on

- How important does the ability to make meaning feel to you in both your work and more general life experience?
- Think about people you know well/work closely with. To what extent do they seem to need to make meaning from experience(s)? Does that appear to you to help or hinder them in their work and relationships?
- Do you know anyone who appears not to try to make meaning from a succession of experiences? What impact does it seem to have on the way they work?
- When you consider your own values, are you able to identify values you would count as primary and others you would count as secondary?
- On a day-to-day basis how conscious are you of trying to work explicitly to a set of values? Is there to some extent a different set of values that would be identified by an observer as your 'values-in-use'?
- Can you think of a point at which you evolved or altered any of your values? What was the experience that prompted that change?
- What are your own thoughts about whether there is an objective reality? If there is such a thing, how disciplined on a daily basis are you about trying to observe it?
- Are you conscious of some filters, including subtle ones, that can inhibit your hold on reality? How do they operate?
- How familiar are you with Kolb's learning cycle? Is it a framework that you could use more rigorously to develop your own learning? Can you see how ease of application of such a framework might help you as a mentor-coach in supporting the learning of clients?
- How far do you recognize the more pejorative sense of 'chains of meaning' as sometimes applying to you and your thinking?
- How many instances of the 'Bryan experience' (see earlier example) can you recall observing in working relationships – whether your own or those of others?
- Would you say you are more or less likely to notice the empty half of a half-full glass?

15 Challenge versus collusion

Some of the common descriptions of mentor-coaching make the process seem cosy and comforting. This can lead to collusive patterns of behaviour. On the other hand, few people manage to pitch challenge in a way that is not emotive. Many see it as potentially aggressive and so display impatience with the person being challenged. The focus of this chapter is upon challenge in proportion to empathy, where tone, volume, pace and body language are mainly neutral and otherwise invitational but, nevertheless, unmistakeably a challenge. The challenge is to the thinking, rather than to the person.

The first encounter that many people have with mentoring-coaching prompts them to think that it is a somewhat soft-edged process, especially if the mentoring-coaching is not directive in its nature. Directive mentoring-coaching (whatever that may be) is seen as hard-edged by contrast. When people say this they are thinking of advice, guidance or even instruction being given. Indeed, we have pointed out earlier in the book that there is a considerable degree of confusion as to what mentoring-coaching actually is. By the time the reader has progressed this far in the book, it should be clear that the model expounded here is based on clear concepts about the two terms mentoring and coaching and that the model is both robust and rigorous.

Mentoring-coaching is not telling, advising, directing and guiding. It is helping a person *think through* how to make progress from where they are now to where they need/want to be. Note the italics and the order of the words 'need' and 'want'. It is about the *person being mentor-coached deciding* upon the practical steps that might be taken and choosing those that need to be taken first in the light of what they will find possible and practicable. It is action focused and is aimed at bringing about change – improvement.

Mentoring-coaching vs pace setting

Some people confuse mentoring-coaching with what McClelland (1973) called 'pace setting'. So, for example, we have worked in education and other public services with many advisers, inspectors and consultants who have relied heavily upon the practice of demonstrating and modelling good practice – a good lesson perhaps, or a well-managed meeting. In some professions a common practice is to team up new recruits with more experienced colleagues so that they can sort of imbibe what good practice is.

Without analysis and exploration of what they have seen, however, the new recruit is left to 'pick the bones out of' what is or purports to be effective modelling in the unspoken expectation that they will not only thus know what good practice is but also be able to copy it for themselves. This is not mentoring-coaching. It is pace setting: declaring or demonstrating a standard but not actually providing help in achieving it. Research by Goleman et al. (2002) show that pace setting largely does not work, that is to say, it does not lead to change and improvement. It can frequently lead simply to confusion and 'deskilling'. The research suggests that pace setting is effective only where it is displayed to an already effective and highly motivated person or group, for example, in introducing a new development to such people.

Only where the demonstration of good practice is supported by analysis, exploration and practice by the client does improvement follow. Sometimes the second part of the cycle – practice by the client accompanied by analysis and exploration – has to be repeated in more than one iteration, before significant improvement occurs.

By 'analysis and exploration' we simply mean 'talk'. The purpose of the talk is to identify precisely what it was that was demonstrated, what the skills were that were applied and why that particular use of those skills amounts to good practice. This is only the first part of the process of mentoring-coaching and the talk to which we refer here is not talk by the mentor-coach but mainly by the client, which includes dialogue with self.

The next part involves the client trying things out and being observed (not necessarily all the time; it depends on circumstance including the nature of the work) and being helped by the mentor-coach to reflect on the efficacy of the practice. Once again, this is done not by being given judgements pronounced by the mentor-coach but through being helped to formulate tough questions to themselves about what they did – about what happened, why it happened, what needs to be learnt from the happenings and what will (need to) be done differently next time. It is the answers that the client comes up with that matter, not any judgements, guidance, advice in the mind of the mentor-coach, though questions can be used by the mentor-coach as pointers to areas on which s/he will help the client to focus.

Notice that at the heart of this part of the process is the client taking action. What now follows about mentoring applies equally to the coaching part of the concept.

What makes mentoring-coaching *appear* soft-edged?

If this is a hard-edged, robust and rigorous, action-focused model, it may seem hard to understand why it sounds what some people call 'touchy feely'. There may be four factors that could help to explain this:

- It is a person-centred model.
- The model rests on the ability of the mentor-coach to generate a relationship of confidence and trust.
- The ease with which empathy and sympathy are commonly confused with each other.
- The client has to do the thinking and come up with answers that may not in the first instance always appear to be the best answers.

What many employers and organizational leaders want from mentoring-coaching is improved performance, better and more productive practice, higher standards. They want it to be outcome oriented. They are absolutely justified in doing so. But in seeking this as the predominant characteristic of something they might call coaching, they are missing an essential link. What this line of thinking misses out is the fact that the improved performance and more productive outcome that mentoring-coaching might generate is not that of a machine or of some impersonal system. It is the improved performance and productive practice of *a person or group of persons*. So, it is essential that at the centre of any mentoring-coaching is the person – the person who has to do the thinking. Since it is about thinking – essentially a distinctively human activity – it cannot be other than a person-centred business.

The purpose of the relationship of confidence and trust

The second possible factor influencing a view of mentoring-coaching as soft-edged and derived from the person centredness of the model is the fact that its success hinges around the quality of the relationship between mentor-coach and client. In Chapters 3 and 4, reference was made to part of the aim of the introductory stage and the first full stage of the model, namely the development of a relationship of confidence and trust – a rapport between the two persons involved. To some people a focus on relationships is essentially soft-edged. If the relationship and its quality were to become the main or sole aim of the process that would indisputably be the case. However, this is only *a part of* what Stage 1 seeks to achieve – and there are five further stages.

The focus on the relationship and upon the person of the client has a purpose. It is not an end in itself. If it were to become an end in itself, the process would not just be soft-edged, it would in all probability be quite useless as a tool for generating improved practice and more productive outcomes.

Nevertheless, there is still a risk that the nature of the process will degenerate into something cosy as a direct consequence of the mentor-coach losing the overall focus, namely, *improved performance and more productive practice by the client.* The risk of this happening is higher if the mentor-coach, in pursuit of a relationship of confidence and trust, fails to challenge the client's thinking, when necessary, and begins to collude with him/her. This can happen more easily than some people are prepared for. (Note that reference here is to the mentor-coach challenging the client's thinking, rather than challenging the client. This is an important distinction.)

Chapter 12 referred the reader to three terms that might represent states of mind/feeling by the mentor-coach. What the mentor-coach is striving for in this relationship is empathy, something quite distinct from sympathy – with which it is often confused in modern parlance. It was pointed out that many people use the word empathy to mean very deep sympathy. Very deep sympathy is appropriate in some circumstances within human social relationships, but that is not what is meant by empathy. At any point in the mentoring-coaching encounter, but especially in the first stage of this model when the client is telling his or her story, the mentor-coach may well experience a feeling of sympathy. Many people have stories to tell their mentor-coach that involve distressing events or situations laden with feelings. Indeed, the need for help in thinking things through often has feelings, some stress or distress, attached to it.

Sympathy can sound like collusion

To *feel* sympathy is not wrong but expressing it may add little value. It may, in fact, have serious dangers and may actually reduce the value of the encounter. It could do this by sidetracking both mentor-coach and client from the main purpose of the relationship, which, it is worth repeating, is to generate improved practice. The main danger is a kind of distraction, namely that articulating sympathy may come across as a sort of collusion – that it may even *be* collusive.

An example may help. A client may be telling a story in which s/he is finding it very difficult to work with a pupil or colleague, whether a subordinate, peer or line manager. S/he may include an account of some typically weak practice and poor co-operation by that person, and refer to having displayed *severely dismissive* feelings towards him/her, perhaps even losing their temper. The mentor-coach may well feel that such poor co-operation by the pupil or colleague in the story was particularly reprehensible, but what help would it be for the mentor-coach to say something like, 'I don't blame you. She jolly well deserved it'? That may well be how the mentor-coach feels, but saying so distracts from the fact that the display of feeling described by the client may actually have made the situation (the working relationship with that person) even worse.

Conversely, a client who might be performing poorly might be telling the mentor-coach how awful it was to have his or her line manager lose their temper in that way would not be helped by the mentor-coach saying, 'How awful for you'. What is needed in this case is some help in understanding what brought the line manager to react in that way, so that the poor performance that prompted it can be addressed.

The truth is that most decent human beings will not enjoy hearing about someone else's distress, even if that person's own behaviour was the cause of the event generating the distress. So as humans we incline towards sympathy. So far, so good, but expressing it as part of deepening the relationship, is collusive and makes the mentor-coach a hostage to fortune. When the less than effective practice of the client comes to be addressed a little later in the model, s/he is entitled to say, 'But I thought you agreed with me. You were very sympathetic when I told you about it. It seemed as though you understood, but now . . .'. The effect is that the line of thinking that might lead to improved practice has been closed off. The relationship that was supposed to have been established and supported by the sympathy has in fact been undermined – trust has actually been broken.

Answers?

Another possible reason for perceiving the process as soft-edged is the fact that the client has to come up with answers. This is particularly the case in the second (coaching) half of the model. Sometimes on training courses a participant may say that if the client had got answers to offer, s/he wouldn't need a mentor-coach in the first place. However, having the potential within oneself to find an answer is a very different matter from coming up with one – or more.

So, when the client struggles to come up with ideas in the second part of Stage 4 but eventually comes up with something, it is important for the mentor-coach to find a way of being encouraging – to signal that the struggle is worth continuing. Here's another place where danger lurks for the mentor-coach. It would be so easy to respond with words like, 'Good', 'Well done', That's right', even though the first idea is not good or right or a qualitative achievement. In fact, the first thought could even be potentially catastrophic! But even if it is a good idea, for the mentor-coach to say so might cause the client to think or feel that he or she does not need to come up with anything further. In all these cases value will not have been added and the process could even have been undermined, perhaps fatally.

Collusion is an ever-present danger in mentoring-coaching. The process has to be razor-sharp to make sure the danger is avoided. If it is soft-edged, it will fail in its purpose, even if the client ends up feeling greatly comforted.

It is the ability of the mentor-coach to make appropriate challenges that will determine whether the danger is avoided.

Challenging the thinking rather than the person

It was made clear earlier that the mentor-coach challenges what the client is saying, thinking, feeling and doing. The mentor-coach does not, however, challenge the client. The distinction is important. At the heart of all positive practice lies a strong sense of self-worth and the mentor-coach must have this in mind when looking to introduce challenge into the interaction. It may be the case that the client will need to change and grow personally in order to perform more effectively in his/her role. This is unlikely to happen as a result of having his/her essential being challenged head on.

Most people change by very small steps. They acquire competencies by recognizing new skills and behaviours that are needed, by learning them and embedding them in their practice over time, with the help of feedback from trusted colleagues or a trusted mentor-coach. So it is through constructive challenge of the client's behaviours (using a wide definition of behaviours – what s/he says, thinks, feels and does) that the mentor-coach may begin to stimulate the process of change. This must be done at no cost to self-worth for the client. Indeed, if the challenge is appropriate in focus, timing and manner, it will be likely to enhance the client's sense of self-worth (sometimes also called self-esteem or self-confidence).

> Sympathy is a platform for collusion. Empathy is a platform for challenge.
> (Pask, 2006)

Challenge and empathy

First, however, there is the process of empathizing. In Chapter 12, empathy was described as the struggle to understand what it might feel like to be the other person in their particular situation. It is not easy, though with practice and self-discipline most human beings are capable of empathy. Engaging in the struggle that is called empathy is what earns the right to challenge. Further, without empathy the mentor-coach has no platform from which to judge precisely *when* and *how* to challenge.

When to challenge

The first part of the answer to the question of when to challenge is that the challenge will miss its target unless there are the beginnings of a relationship of confidence and trust. It need only be the beginning of such a relationship if the level of the challenge is relatively low. For example, in telling his/her story the client may well make a broad generalization – something like, 'Whenever I try to . . . he always . . .'. The mentor-coach might reply by repeating the word 'always' in a neutral interrogative tone. In fact, playing words or phrases back to the client in the first two stages of the model can be a gentle but clear way of establishing the principle of challenge from the beginning. In those first stages of the model checking for clarity and accuracy often implies challenge. The establishment of the fact that the mentor-coach is likely, however gently or neutrally, to ask questions and to challenge is a means of distinguishing this particular relationship from those s/he will experience in a social context.

So to wait until a sound relationship is established before offering challenge might not achieve what is required. What is being said here is that there is a sort of chicken-and-egg relationship between challenge and the development of rapport. It's spiral: build some rapport, enable the challenge; challenge gently, build some more rapport and so on.

It might not seem helpful to raise the question of when *not* to challenge but there are some important points of caution to consider. There is no point presenting challenge to someone who cannot rise to it for whatever reason. The reasons may be that the client:

- is temporarily wrong-footed by the train of thinking s/he is engaging in
- may genuinely find the circumstances s/he is facing too tall an order and may need to consider alternative routes around what needs to be confronted
- may be in a general state of a low sense of self-worth
- simply does not believe at this stage that there is a way forward
- does not have as yet the skills needed to rise to the challenge.

Sometimes a mentor-coach feels that s/he *ought* to challenge the client – because if s/he were in the client's position, s/he would behave very differently and must, therefore, get the client to do so. It is important to recognize that this might say as much about the personality of the mentor-coach as it does about either the client or the situation in focus at that point. This interaction is not intended as a forum for a display of virility or challenge by a mentor-coach. The only sure way to approach a judgement about when to challenge is to apply the rule that the level of challenge should always be proportionate to the level of empathy developed by the mentor-coach.

By '*level*' of challenge' the reader is intended to understand something about the 'how' of challenge as well as the 'when'. There is more on this later in the chapter.

What to challenge

On a more general point, the answer to the question of when to challenge is multifaceted and requires a careful judgement. Essentially, however, the mentor-coach will want to offer challenge to anything s/he hears the client say, senses s/he is feeling or thinking, or discovers that s/he is doing that could get in the way of him or her moving forward. By 'moving forward' we mean in the process of thinking things through and eventually in actions that s/he needs to take. The mentor-coach will want to challenge anything by way of obstructions to thinking, and, later, obstructions to more effective practice or positive outcomes.

Initially this will be very much about achieving clarity in the story, then in gaining clarity as to what it is that needs to be addressed – and so on through the model. At first the clarification may be about facts or events. A false picture of exactly what is happening will need to be challenged. If the mentor-coach does not engage in this challenge, the client will be deprived of the opportunity to engage reasonably closely with objective reality (see the previous chapter).

The challenge may be as subtle as an invitation to consider the situation under discussion from the point of view of others who are involved in it, especially where the situation involves conflict between the client and another person. For example, 'If he was sitting in your chair now, how would *he* describe the situation?' or 'How, I wonder, might the others in the team see/feel about this issue?'

Gradually the clarification may extend to include feelings and perceptions – those of the client as well as those of other parties to the events under consideration. An interesting occasion for challenge is provided when a client expresses reluctance to talk about his/her feelings. This is not a common characteristic but, when encountered for the first time, often causes difficulty for both parties.

Reluctance to talk about feelings

Some people consider themselves very rational and may see feelings as some kind of distraction. They may even try to argue that feelings are irrelevant, especially their own feelings. The causes of this view can be extremely varied, but it often signals discomfort with the thought of exposing their emotions to another person. To challenge this kind of disposition head on could be counter-productive. It would certainly provoke resistance and may undermine the emerging relationship of trust and confidence. Nevertheless, it is important that the mentor-coach does not collude with that position, for the simple reason that it may be due to unaddressed feelings that the issue under discussion has become intractable or unresolved.

A possible way forward might be to focus on the feelings of others in the situation. Having clarified the facts about the other person's behaviour, one might ask why the client thinks this person is behaving in that particular way. This might prompt a remark about the other person's feelings, and if not, the mentor-coach is entitled to ask about those feelings in a direct question. This could then lead on to a consideration of the role of feelings and perceptions as a part of objective reality. This may seem roundabout but it is challenge of a significant kind.

Thus, if a client is willing to engage in discussion of the feelings of others, s/he is likely to be more open to the fact that feelings are playing some part in the situation that has become the focus of Stage 2 of the interaction. It is then a short step to a direct reference to the fact that feelings influence the client as well as his/her colleagues. This, in turn, might enable the question as to whether his/her own feelings are a possible blind spot for the client. Some people are simply not prepared to allow for the fact that *anyone's* feelings should come into the work place. In this case it may be necessary to explore through questioning the *behaviours* in focus and discuss where those – sometimes irrational or arational behaviours come from.

In answer to a question posed earlier – 'How to challenge?' – it is possible to offer a valuable general answer. Nearly all challenge that is fruitful is presented in the form of a question.

The question can be aimed at seeking clarification and accuracy, be prompting or exploratory. These are lower-level challenge kind of questions. As empathy and rapport grow, the questions can be more robust and include *probing* questions – aimed at testing out a hypothesis by either mentor-coach or client. Further probing questions can challenge assumptions or interpretations the client is relying on and encourage them to consider alternative meanings to events they are recounting, and even to reconsider the chain of meaning and sense they have made from events, as explained in the previous two chapters.

The challenge in asking 'Why?'

The question 'Why?' can come across as a particularly strong challenge. Any question that asks 'Why?', in either a direct or indirect manner, is a challenge. It challenges the client to think beyond the readily available surface of a situation. When asked boldly, the question 'Why?' (e.g. 'Why did you do/say/feel/think that?' or 'Why did that happen?') can be too challenging and it has been argued earlier that alternative formulations are often wise. Examples would include:

- 'Can you explain a little more about that?'
- 'What might have led to that happening?'
- 'What leads you to believe that?'
- 'What caused you to take that course of action?

Without such alternative formulation, questions of this kind can sound like overt criticism.

How to challenge

It should by now be clear that we are still addressing the question of how to challenge. In essence the answer is, as is pointed out earlier, fairly simple: through questions. Questions help, like empathic responses, to make the challenge tentative.

We have said that mentoring-coaching is not telling, judging, advising, guiding, directing and so on. If it is about challenging a person to think things through, the most important tool is the well-judged and carefully expressed question. The word 'challenging' was used at the beginning of the previous sentence for the same reason that this whole chapter has been included in this book, namely that people often approach the role of client expecting someone else to do their thinking for them. So, the whole process of being invited and given support to think things through is a challenge. The fact that they have not been able to think things through on their own before this encounter makes the challenge a little more steep, though one which, when met, provides profound satisfaction.

Earlier chapters of this book and sections in this chapter have considered types of questions that could be asked at different stages, and you, the reader, have been invited in each of the chapters of this book to think of questions a mentor-coach might ask, and/or to consider questions that have been addressed to you personally. It is not, therefore, necessary to provide further examples of the types of questions that might challenge the client at different stages. The reader who remains in doubt about this might want to revisit the chapters in the first half of the book on each of the six stages.

Minimalism and a neutral tone

What might be helpful, however, is to emphasize that the mentor-coach's own emotions should play no part in the delivery of challenging questions. Nor should their particular temperament; people who are naturally inclined to challenge should be wary of their habits of challenge when they come into the role of mentor-coach and should consciously control their style and tone when probing in the ways already described. The more neutral the tone the better.

In addition, there are instances where the question can be delivered in a single word. The reference here is not to the challenge that consists in simply repeating a key word spoken by the client. Rather, one needs to have in mind a situation where the client has thought through almost all of the issue but stops short of the concluding part of the thinking that could open up the way ahead, or shine entirely new light on the situation. In that event the mentor-coach might simply, with a gentle smile, say, 'So?' This can even be done without any words – using just an open gesture of invitation accompanied by a smile.

Challenge in the zone of proximal development

This last technique – the single word or the gesture of invitation – may remind readers of the whole philosophy, perhaps best expressed by Vygotsky (1978), of moving the thinker or learner out of their comfort zone. Lots of people try to get others to leave their comfort zone and cannot understand the other person's reluctance. The reason for that reluctance is often that they are being asked to go too fast and/or too far. (There are situations when we need to go quickly well away from our comfort zone, for example, when there is an impending disaster that can only be avoided by quick and fairly radical action. These are not occasions when mentoring-coaching might prove very useful.) Vygotsky' s notion of the zone of proximal development is wise and useful in the mentoring-coaching context. Several small, graduated challenges are likely to generate a lot more progress than one huge challenge. The mentor-coach would do well to apply this principle. Needless to say, empathy is required in making any judgement about just how big a challenge any particular client can take on board in a single step.

The use of silence

Lastly, the place of silence in this context is worth considering. Silence can be collusive as well as challenging. Clients often make statements (express judgements) about people (including the client him/herself) that are too general, and often disparaging, to be allowed to pass without challenge, for example:

- 'I'm no good at that sort of thing'
- 'I'm too unimportant to have any influence on that issue'
- 'I wouldn't expect anyone to take any notice of me'
- 'She's quite hopeless at what I need her to do'
- 'He's totally negative when things begin to go wrong'.

While such remarks might be made in the middle of a flow of expression and are, therefore, not easy to challenge immediately, they cannot be allowed to pass unchallenged. The reason for challenging is that the client may be touching on or even actually displaying the very factor that needs to alter if change for the better is to be generated in that situation. Even if this is not the case, the generalized low esteem that is expressed in such remarks weakens the morale of the person who makes them. Challenging them implies that esteem can be raised.

Equally, a client might make one of the above remarks immediately before lapsing into silence. The mentor-coach might want to allow that silence to continue. It is likely that the client will be expecting the mentor-coach to challenge them, in which case it is best if the client is given the space to do the challenging. Or s/he may expect the mentor-coach to agree with him/her, in which case the silence can be a plain denial. The mentor-coach will need to be attending very closely to the client to be able to sense the most fruitful way to deal with this situation. Many mentor-coaches have found that sometimes a silence supported by a quizzical expression conveys enough of a challenge.

Summary

Throughout the model there are opportunities both for collusion and challenge. To avoid colluding and to make effective use of the skill of challenge in order to help move the client's thinking forward requires the mentor-coach to be constantly alert. To get the challenge right – the when, what, and how of challenging – demands persistent empathy, respect, sensitivity and non-possessive warmth towards the client.

Issues the reader may want to reflect on

- What possible contradictions are there in the term 'directive mentoring-coaching'?
- Does the concept of mentoring-coaching seem soft-edged or hard-edged to you? What is the rationale behind your thinking on this point?

- Can you explain in your own words why pace setting might be less than helpful, and how different it is from the concept of mentoring-coaching?
- What is the purpose of the relationship between mentor-coach and client?
- How sympathetic are you in general? How can you best manage some of the dangers inherent in sympathy?
- In what terms do you recognize a difference between challenging a person and challenging their thinking, feeling, behaviour and so on? How important is this distinction?
- Do you see a relationship between challenge and empathy in the dynamic of mentoring-coaching?
- What are the sorts of things that you feel might need to be challenged in the way of a client's thought, feelings, words, actions? How easy is it for you to envisage a form of words that might be appropriate in each of the cases you can think of?
- Do you know people who are reluctant to talk about feelings? Can you can think of anything that might explain that reluctance? If you were working as a mentor-coach with such a person, how might you deal with it?
- How challenging a person do you consider yourself to be? What are the possible implications about how you might need to manage your natural tendency to challenge – or not to challenge – in the role of mentor-coach?
- Can you see how minimalism and neutral tone might enable/apply to the principle of non-possessive warmth?
- Have you any thoughts of how best to challenge people to move out of their comfort zone, especially in the mentoring-coaching context?
- What are the advantages and disadvantages in the context of this chapter?

16 Creating a mentoring-coaching culture

We are all influenced far more by culture than we are able to recognize on a day-to-day basis. To try to change behaviour radically without attention to the culture in which those changed behaviours are to be displayed is to court serious frustration. Even the leader of an organization is unlikely on his or her own to be able to do this in a way that leads to embedded behaviours or new habits. Since in many organizations mentoring-coaching will appear counter-cultural, this chapter focuses on how organizations and their leaders might set about changing the culture to embed the necessary new habits of behaviour.

The interest most people have in mentoring-coaching is related to the work context. What they want, as was indicated early in the previous chapter, is improved performance, higher standards, better practice and outcomes that are enhanced, qualitatively and quantitatively. It has often been found, however, that for one or two people within an organization to be committed to such a model for managing work relationships fails to have anything like the impact on practice and outcomes that one might hope for. Indeed, those one or two people can find attempting to use the model and the associated skills both frustrating and eventually demoralizing.

A major part of the reason for this disappointing lack of impact is that mentoring-coaching is counter-cultural in many professions. In lots of organizations it generates a serious clash of cultures. The reader might not be surprised to find such factors in work places whose business is to maintain control – like the military or law enforcement (though there are some interesting cultural variations within such services). What is in a way surprising, is that even businesses that need a spirit of enterprise and innovation to survive the rigours of commercial competition in times of rapid change, often find mentoring-coaching challenging in a cultural sense. Perhaps more surprising still is that in public services like education and social work, where one might imagine that learning how to think clearly is a stock in trade, mentoring-coaching can still come unstuck because of a clash of culture, particularly in a climate where outside (media and government) pressure to comply and perform is intense.

External and internal commitment

Argyris (quoted by Fullan, 2001) writes of two differing kinds of commitment demonstrated by team members within organizations: external and internal commitment. External commitment is a willingness, even a determination, to do an effective job because of factors that lie outside the person expected to perform. These external factors can range from extreme pressure to comply with the management's expectations – up to and including bullying – to charisma in a leader demonstrating warmth and enthusiasm that inspires loyalty in team members, who may in this context be thought of more as followers. Neither Argyris, Fullan nor the present writers argue that all forms of external commitment are unacceptable. Many writers in fact argue that the charismatic leader and his/her impact are very positive. They are certainly preferable to the leader (and climate) that demands compliance through pressure, threat or bullying. The question at issue is whether commitment generated, for example, through charismatic leadership is sustainable, particularly after the departure of the charismatic leader.

One argument worth considering is that commitment is only sustainable at high levels if it is *internal*. High levels of *external* commitment may well be the cause of 'burn-out'. This is because the efforts of the followers are aimed at providing satisfaction for the external source – the person or body from whom the pressure to perform emanates. Commitment at high levels is only likely to be sustained if the person giving it finds that doing so generates serious satisfaction from within. Adults who constantly depend on the pleasure and approval of another person, even a charismatic leader, to generate satisfaction in response to their work are likely to find their own satisfaction shallow over time.

Part of the reason for the shallowness of satisfaction is that this dependence upon another person's approval stems from a basic (rather than developed) ego state. (This perspective will be developed in Chapter 18). Children can be persuaded to behave in certain ways in order to gain the approval of their parents, but even children who have complied with parental expectations prior to adolescence begin, as they go through their teens, to question their parents and want to know *for themselves* the reasons for certain expectations before they will comply. Indeed, this kind of agreeable behaviour cannot any longer be called compliance, but rather positive co-operation. Thus, young people who have been helped genuinely to think through how to run their lives usually achieve deeper levels of satisfaction that are sustainable over time. The same is true of staff in work organizations: internal commitment is another way of labelling intrinsic motivation – doing something because deep inside it feels right, worthwhile and fulfilling, rather than through someone else's pressure or approval.

An organization driven to a significant degree by internal commitment reflects some important identifiable features that are cultural.

What is culture?

Writers on the subject of culture do not all agree on a particular definition of the word. Nonetheless, there is some agreement, perhaps summed up in the simple phrase, 'the way we do things round here'. In his writing on this subject Schein (1999) points to different manifestations of culture: artefacts, myths, practices and procedures. He writes in addition of the way that culture reflects the *values in use* that have emerged over time – values that can be quite different from *the espoused or official values* of the organization. Egan (1992) expands on this theme and refers to a model of organizational practice that he calls the 'shadow side', in which the values in use hold sway but are not explicitly articulated. He argues that unspoken values are expressed through the things people in the organization say and do. By 'people' he means other individuals and groups in addition to the formal leaders and managers. He also argues that for the shadow side to be effectively dealt with it has to be adumbrated and articulated. It can then be managed and possibly changed over time.

There are cultures, including shadow side cultures, in which it is very difficult for mentoring-coaching to thrive and bring the benefits described so far in this book. For example, where the leader constantly seeks to exercise tight control through procedures of command and compliance; where there is an atmosphere of fear, allied to blame practices and risk taking is actively discouraged. In these kinds of culture, that often go together, mentoring-coaching will find it difficult to take root. As argued earlier, this can also apply where the leader operates on a charismatic basis that inspires loyalty and even enthusiasm through external commitment.

A mentoring-coaching culture

It might be helpful to clarify what is meant (and what is not meant) by a mentoring-coaching culture. The culture in mind would have both formal and informal manifestations that are equally important. In fact, one might want to argue that it is the informal manifestations that would indicate the presence of

something that could justifiably be called a culture. The more formal characteristics, the strategies and structures that might need to be put in place to
bring about that culture, are in some ways easier to describe and that is where
we focus first.

A number of organizations have at least an embryonic mentoring-coaching
culture as a result of focusing directly on the model expounded in the first half
of this book. They include several schools and some other public service organizations. What is written about here is a generic culture that is feasible in any
organization of almost any kind and size. There are clearly particular implications about strategy for large complex organizations, and, conversely, one
would expect a small organization to find the establishment of any new facet
of culture an easier matter, depending, of course, on the history and pattern of
relationships existing within it and the nature of its leadership.

Some quite large organizations that have worked with the model
expounded in this book (for example, a Local Authority with a budget in excess of
£250 million) have made significant strides in developing a mentoring-coaching
culture. What follows is a pattern that has worked extremely successfully in
some schools (with a turnover of perhaps £4 or £5 million). The reader may
want to have in mind his or her own school or work place while reading what
follows and be testing what is written against their own context and experience.

A change of culture must be desired by someone

In referring to the more formal characteristics of such a culture one has in mind
it is important that someone explicitly desires it. That 'someone' needs to have
significant influence in terms of leadership in the organization and it has a
greater chance of becoming embedded if the 'someone' is the leader of the
whole organization. The term 'organization' might encompass a department,
section, key stage or team within a larger entity as well as an entire school,
company or other institution. It is also envisaged that this leader recognizes
that there is a need for specific steps to be taken to bring this culture into
being. In turn, it assumes that there is some kind of vision as to what the
culture would be like and what would be happening as a result of such a
culture. This person would need to be ready to explain and promote the idea
and purpose of whatever was to happen. These things would work best if there
had been serious attempts to promote and co-construct a *shared* vision and
shared values.

It is worth pointing out that the lead on this does not necessarily have to
come from the head or the person at the top of the leadership and management hierarchy, though the person occupying that position must both
understand and explicitly support it if it is not to be randomly negated
on a frequent basis. Having said this, the generation of culture occurs most

effectively where the leader of the organization sets out consciously to bring it into being.

In the current public service culture in the United Kingdom there may be a need for the leadership both of the whole organization and of this initiative, to be courageous in developing such a culture. This is because such services, especially education, are heavily regulated at government level and subject to a complex network of accountabilities, where even calculated risk taking is often implicitly discouraged on a systematic basis.

> The most important work of a leader is to create and manage culture. (Schein, 1999)

The place of formal training

Formal training of individuals is a notoriously weak way of generating change within a given organisation (Osterman and Kottkamp, 1994). It appears to matter little whether the client for training is the leader or any other person in the organization. Something else needs to accompany it. Given courageous leadership, however, the visible process of establishing a mentoring-coaching culture has often *begun* with the leader experiencing a course to introduce the concept and associated skills, along with an understanding of a model to enable the formal process of mentoring-coaching to take place.

The work the writers have done in recent years for the London Centre for Leadership in Learning at the Institute of Education, London University has included the training of school and other organization leaders in those matters. This has involved courses of two, three and four days (some of them accredited) plus supervised practice in applying what is learnt to help deepen reflection and consequently the skills and behaviours. Many leaders who have taken part in such courses then want to set up a structure within their organization but often find they cannot do so without sending some other staff on the course or, as has happened in a considerable number of instances, they have enlisted the Centre's help in putting on a development event for the whole of the staff.

Any leader reading this will recognize that to have a two- or three-day course for a whole staff team is a very significant investment, especially as the course is best delivered to groups of no more than 24 persons at a time. Such investment is only made if the leadership (team) is committed to some sort of in-depth development of mentoring-coaching, and it gives a very powerful signal to staff and others of something profoundly cultural. The most obvious way to develop that commitment further is to establish a structure of mentoring-coaching relationships across the organization.

A structure of mentoring-coaching relationships

Such a structure rests on a belief that having a mentor-coach and some time in which to be mentor-coached is a kind of entitlement, or at least a recognition that everyone needs a mentor-coach. It is certainly the case, as argued earlier in this book, that we all need help at times to think things through and that access to a trained mentor-coach is a positive and potentially powerful way to meet that need.

Some organizations work to a cascade process, whereby the leadership team trains itself first and then offers its mentor-coaching services to the next rank of staff, who in turn undertake training and offer it to members of their teams, and so on down the lines of management. Thus, when everyone has had some training and some experience of being mentor-coached, it would be possible to argue that the structure is in place for a mentoring-coaching culture to grow. One would certainly claim that such structure and training would be a valuable resource for the development of this culture. The writers are aware, however, that similar approaches were taken to the development of tools like appraisal and performance management, often with little productive impact and without any kind of culture being developed.

> If you're going into appraisal, you're going out of business. (Deming, 1982)

The truth that the quote in the text box is expressing is that setting up formal structures – especially those that are hierarchically operated, and where people have something like appraisal, performance management or mentoring-coaching 'done to them' – can be culturally irrelevant.

There are other questions too:

- Can mentor-coaching work if the mentor-coach is the line manager of the client? How tangled up does it then become with issues of accountability?
- Do clients need to be trained – not simply to receive mentoring-coaching but so that there is a conscious context for mentoring-coaching that has some depth to it?
- Can mentoring-coaching work better outside line management structures?
- Would peer mentoring-coaching be equally valuable?
- Should anybody receive mentoring-coaching if they don't also give it?
- Ought everyone to be able to choose their own mentor-coach?

These questions illustrate some of the complexities that need to be faced if a formal structure of mentoring-coaching is to be established with a view to growing a mentoring-coaching culture. The questions need to be thought about carefully in the light not only of the rest of this chapter but in the light of the whole philosophy underpinning this book and the model it expounds.

Structures and systems don't necessarily breed culture

Nothing written so far in this chapter should be taken as making a case against setting up a formal, system-wide structure. The message on offer is that it would be wise to proceed with caution (which, in turn, may suggest a gradual approach) to mentoring-coaching systems. They don't necessarily breed cultures. In any community of learners, however, it can be strongly argued that *all the learners* would benefit from some structured learning about the model and related competencies if the objective is to bring about a mentoring-coaching culture.

The phrase 'community of learners' is intended to refer not just to organizations whose explicit purpose is learning – like schools, colleges, universities and so on – but also to businesses, social groups, and other public services that see learning together as a vital component of their well-being. So, for example, a school would hardly be able to claim a mentoring-coaching culture if it did not manifest itself in the whole life of the school – in the classroom as well as in the more informal activities of the institution. It might not be necessary to induct all the students into the model expounded in this book, but it would be important that some of the underpinning ideas were conveyed to them along with the fundamental skills through which those ideas could be most effectively implemented. Similarly, a social work team, a sales, design or production group would develop a culture of 'thinking things through' not necessarily by all going on a course, but by encouraging the relevant behaviours to permeate the working context and its network of relationships.

So a thorough and conscientious commitment to the training aspects of mentoring-coaching, at some level or other, of everyone in the community could be extremely valuable, but *it is the widespread use of the competencies of mentoring-coaching across the whole population of the institution that would determine the culture*. The following box reiterates the importance of understanding the notion of competency.

A competency is some characteristic of a person, evidenced in (patterns of) behaviours, that distinguish outstanding performance in a given role, job or responsibility. (Adapted from McClelland, 1973)

A competency implies habitual behaviours that have been developed

> *especially for a specific purpose, namely outstanding performance. It can only be called a 'competency' when it requires only a small amount of, or no conscious effort. It has become a habit.*

It is the development of new behaviours across the organization that forms the link between institution-wide training and the establishment of a culture of mentoring-coaching. All of the organizations the writers have worked with to develop a mentoring-coaching culture would be the first to say that their culture is not yet fully established – that they do not envisage a day when it will be, for it is a continuing process. They will still have to continue to think carefully about specific mentoring-coaching behaviours somewhere in the routine work they engage in for the foreseeable future.

Nevertheless, when any community displays at a variety of levels (whether of skills or of organizational responsibilities) the relevant competencies in its day-to-day formal and informal interactions, it can claim that to a measurable degree a culture of mentoring-coaching is alive and growing.

What are the relevant competencies?

Essentially, they are those competencies that encourage and stimulate the members of the community *to think things through.* This is not a matter of knowing and understanding a model. People learn to think things through by doing it. The two fundamental stimuli to thinking things through are questioning and listening. In a community characterized by serious listening and asking questions there is likely to be a great deal of thinking things through – certainly a lot more than in a community characterized by:

- giving instruction
- telling
- giving advice and guidance
- directing
- requiring obedience/compliance and
- knowing the 'right' answer and being able to regurgitate it.

The questioning has to be skilful and pertinent, with due attention to accuracy and evidence supporting the replies. The listening has to be thoroughly attentive listening based on real respect for the person being listened to. Under these two conditions, however, there will be a great deal of thinking things through – the essential behaviour that would count as evidence of a mentoring-coaching culture.

The reader will note that these competencies could in theory, and possibly in practice, be in operation in large parts of the life of any community without anyone ever having heard of the words mentoring or coaching, let alone having gone on courses about them. The point does not need to be laboured but, conversely, there are organizations where lots of people have done the course, everyone has a nominated mentor-coach and periodic interviews with their mentor-coach, but where for the rest of the time people have to do what they're told! The term has obviously travelled well while the concept has stayed absolutely still!

There is a good deal about the skills of listening and questioning in the first half of this book that the reader might want to refer back to. In addition, Chapter 10 examines in considerable detail the three groups of competencies that support the mentor-coach in this work. It is worth noting here that there is more to learning than listening and asking questions. Also there are occasions when responding persistently to a colleague with questions can be downright patronising.

> *Client*: 'What time is it?'
> *Consultant*: 'What time would you like it to be? (Adapted from Block, 1981)

Information – and explanation giving are very important practices in all walks of life for a multitude of purposes. Listening and questioning, particularly in helping establish meaning, come into their own if what we need is help in thinking things through.

In an effective mentoring-coaching culture team members will sense when information, training, instruction or explanation is required and when, conversely, it is more appropriate to respond with questions.

Questions empower people

> Judge a man not by the answers he gives, but by the questions he asks. (Confucius)

Leaders of organizations often complain that they are daily bombarded with problems to be solved, questions to be answered. This feels like a huge burden – the reason for the feeling is that *it is* a huge burden, but it is largely self-inflicted. It is caused directly by the leader assuming, consciously or unconsciously, that the team members cannot solve the problems they bring without his/her intervention – often taking over the whole problem. A mentoring-coaching culture assumes that most problems can be solved and most questions asked can be answered by the person from whom they originate. Help to draw out those answers and solutions comes in the form of listening and questioning. Thus are team members empowered to do what they are paid to do and *take responsibility for it, and thus are leaders liberated to lead.*

To sum up: a mentoring-coaching culture will be found where helping each other think things through is a significant behaviour of a majority of people in a given organization, and where the favoured way of delivering this help is through skilled questioning and attentive listening. It can be greatly aided, but by no means guaranteed, by structures that provide both training and regular times for people to learn and apply a clear model and specific skills. In the last resort, where such a culture exists there is thoughtful leadership, thoughtful systems and structures, and thoughtful behaviour by most members of the community in a majority of situations. The underlying impact will be enhanced human consciousness.

Following the questions for readers to ponder there is a short case study (see Appendix 16.1) to illustrate how one organization is proceeding with the continuing development of a mentoring-coaching culture. It is a peculiarly apt and singular study. The head of the school is a key consultant and facilitator on the mentoring-coaching team at the London Centre for Leadership in Learning, but what makes it singular is the very distinctive nature of the school and its clientele – families whose children face what are often acute special needs across a wide range of personal challenges.

One might wonder whether thinking things through is simply an additional challenge – even a challenge too far – for children, families and staff confronting acute special needs. Paradoxically, the level of the challenge, often complex, demands that very thing – carefully thought out approaches to life and its exigencies. It is rarely found in this particular field. Simply caring for the children can too often become the order of the day. The fact that it is to be found at Swiss Cottage *and* that it works well make it remarkable. The reader should be careful not to assume that because it can work at a special school, it can work anywhere. It is only effective there because of the rigorous thinking and systematic development of behaviours that are consistent with the values and principles that underpin it, and because of the sharp clarity of the way the school is led. It is that thinking and systematic behaviour in accord with values and principles that can work anywhere and are characteristic of a mentoring-coaching culture.

Some questions for the reader to reflect on

- What is your own way of defining the notion of 'culture'?
- Could you describe for your own satisfaction the nature of the culture of the school or organization you have most experience of? (Remember that even a family could be called an organization and will have its own culture.)

- Have you experienced moving from one organization and culture to another with a different culture? How did that change of culture impact upon you?
- Do you have experience of a change of culture being brought about within a single organization? How was the change generated/ managed? Who or what was most instrumental in bringing about the change?
- What do you understand by the term 'shadow side' of an organization? Could you describe the shadow side of the team, school or organization you are most familiar with?
- What do you understand by the distinction between an institution's 'espoused values' and its 'values in use'? Can you think of contrasting examples in your organization?
- Can you think of an instance in an organization when an initiative has occurred that has changed the structure or systems within it but has had little impact on the culture?
- What do you now understand by the concept of a 'competency'?
- How difficult would you expect it to be to embed changes in patterns of behaviour by a significant group of people? Under what sort of circumstances might you expect the new culture to be undermined by people defaulting to old habits?
- If you were persuaded that a culture of mentoring-coaching would be really valuable in the organization in which you work, what, after careful consideration, would be the steps you would most favour to try to develop it?
- What evidence (think of specific examples) would tell you that there was real progress in developing such a culture?

Appendix 16.1: A brief case study

Our mentoring-coaching culture at Swiss Cottage specialist SEN School

Introduction

Swiss Cottage is a highly successful specialist SEN school, with a national and international reputation, catering for the needs of 143 pupils aged from 2 to 16 years, including learners on the autistic spectrum. Pupils have a complex range of predominantly learning, physical and communication needs.

Swiss Cottage School was formed as an amalgamation of two special schools in 1995. Since the amalgamation:

- We have had two very successful Ofsted inspections (July 1998 and December 2002).
- We were named in the Ofsted *Most Successful Schools* list after both our Ofsted inspections. Because of this, we were named in Ofsted's 'Hall of Fame'.
- We first gained Investors in People (IiP) recognition in February 99 and re-recognition thereafter, most recently in July 2006. We gained a further IiP 'Leadership and Management' award and achieved the highest levels possible in our IiP Profile Report. We have been awarded 'Champion Investors in People Organization' status (2005).
- We became a Beacon School from January 2000 to July 2005.
- We were awarded Specialist SEN School Status (Cognition and Learning) for 2006–2010 with a grant from the DfES to improve learner achievement within Swiss Cottage School and to spread best practice in partner schools and community organizations.
- We have won a number of Awards (e.g. Sports mark, Arts mark, Achievement Awards for 2002 and 2003, ICT mark).

Our journey thus far

Relationship skills

We have an unswerving belief that focusing on developing and maintaining positive relationships is at the heart of our school's success. In April 1995 we agreed a set of guidelines to help us to manage relationships effectively – our Staff Relationship Guidelines. We printed personal copies for everyone; copies to go on the wall of every work space; copies for people considering applying to work in the school; provided training and support in how to manage effective relationships; and in monitoring of our practice. We review these guidelines regularly, and change them in response to reviews. They are now different from the originals, and focus on initiating and maintaining emotionally intelligent relationships.

Swiss Cottage school staff relationship guidelines

In general, we will:

- Treat ourselves and each other with dignity and respect.
- Give and receive praise from each other frequently – using descriptive language and just saying, 'Thank you'.
- Understand that we are responsible for our own behaviour – others don't make us '*do*' anything.

- Greet each other with a word and a smile – just practise this.
- See the funny side of things – laughing makes us feel better.
- Look for the 'good' reasons behind decisions/actions, and act accordingly.
- Look for solutions – not focus on problems – a 'can do' approach.
- Remember: most communication occurs through our body language – facial expressions, tone of voice, stance and so on.

If you feel you need help, approach:

- a peer
- a team leader
- a member of the senior team who has the skills to mentor-coach you in addressing this problem so you achieve a positive outcome.

Conflicts MUST be addressed – feelings don't go away.
To resolve any conflict, I will:

- sort out exactly what I am upset about
- speak to the other person, in order to resolve the situation (know your outcome)
- imagine why the other person said/did what s/he did (empathy)
- tell the other person what is upsetting you (and why)
- listen to his/her answer, trying to understand it from his/her point of view (empathy)
- agree a way forward
- forgive and let go.

We have worked tirelessly on these principles and practices since the school opened. We do not claim to have achieved a 100% emotionally intelligent workplace. Our guidelines are only as effective as the least effective member of staff. What we do, in response to any difficulties, is address them. This approach means that staff who do not want to work in this way leave the school, and others become more skilled in this area.

Learners

We have a Positive Behaviour Policy which, again, we work tirelessly on. In 1995 we agreed key principles, which we still adhere to.

Whole-school positive behaviour policy
At Swiss Cottage we believe that:

- pupils want to behave well
- pupils can learn to improve their behaviour
- mistakes are part of the learning process
- all adults can learn strategies to support pupils to improve their behaviour.

We adults can support our pupils by:

- the quality of our relationships with each other and them
- the quality of our teaching
- the scaffolding of support we put in place.

The scaffolding consists of:

- rights and responsibilities
- rules
- routines
- the language of choice
- rewards and consequences
- reparation
- descriptive praise.

Our values

Our values were last reviewed and agreed in 2005 by the whole staff. We undertook work similar to that on the Staff Relationship Guidelines. They are prominently displayed, included in the application packs and Induction programme for new staff and so on. Our behaviour is regularly evaluated and improved against these. We align our values, our SRG, our mission, our School Development Plan and our performance development system.

Our values

1   Respect:
- forgive and let go
- celebrate individual contributions
- listen: to understand, not to prove your point
- presume honourable motives
- understand the other's point of view
- be polite
- fully attend to the person
- ask, not tell
- engage in dialogue
- recognize and value individual difference.

2   Integrity:
- be honest – no secrets
- awareness of self and impact on others
- look for the positives
- tell the truth, sensitively
- do what you agree to do
- speak with the person, not about the person
- empathize, not sympathize – don't collude.

3   Positive attitude:
- prepared to go the extra mile
- 'can do' approach
- commitment to personal and professional growth, and willingness to learn from others
- happy to share skills and experiences
- have high expectations
- take pride in the school and your contribution to it
- solution focused
- no-blame culture.

Effectiveness of our positive culture

- Staff like their work (Investors in People; exit interviews; staff survey).
- Recruitment and retention rates are high.
- Staff attendance has improved year on year – currently 93 per cent.
- Staff report that one thing the school does well is manage its relationships (exit interviews).
- The atmosphere is positive – almost palpable. Visitors comment on it, as soon as they enter the school.

Our mentoring-coaching culture

We have now further developed our positive culture, by using mentoring-coaching skills and understandings to further improve the effectiveness of our relationships and the development of our learners and staff.

We have now made a fundamental shift from telling to asking by: making significant additional time available for some key processes; making the requirement for 'emotionally intelligent' behaviour explicit; providing 4-day mentoring-coaching training for 12 staff so far; providing a 1-day introduction to mentoring-coaching for the whole staff; using daily opportunities to practise mentoring-coaching skills; reviewing our practice regularly. We are at the beginning of our mentoring-coaching journey.

How we currently use mentoring-coaching at Swiss Cottage School

With our learners

Listening and helping learners find their own solutions, are fundamental to our Behaviour Policy. When learners have interpersonal difficulties, our job as adults is to facilitate the dialogue between the learners, helping them to identify the problem and to take responsibility for their part in it and plan what steps they can take to resolve the issue.

We encourage our learners to: name how they are feeling; choose a socially acceptable response; recognize the feelings of others and manage the interface. This is crucially important for our learners at SCS, as they can easily become dependent on the many adults in their lives. This also links to our Mission, Vision and Values.

With our staff

Following initial training we are using mentoring-coaching skills on the following key processes.

Performance development We call our system 'development' not 'management' as we use it to help staff improve their performance on key aspects of their job, linked to our SDP.

We allow up to 2 hours for the initial and final 1:1 session for teachers, with up to 1 hour for the mid-year review session.

The Performance Developer will listen and ask questions, helping the teacher to think through his/her Action Plan and to reflect on his/her progress. We use mentoring-coaching initially to help the teacher think through his/her role, values, responsibilities, and mentoring-coaching when we move into action planning.

We follow the same system for all staff, allowing up to 1 hour for meetings.

> A wonderful way of helping people to celebrate their successes. It's definitely changed my thinking.

Line management Again, this is similar to our performance development meetings. We encourage staff to reflect on their performance and plan action to improve their performance, in relation to their Job Descriptions/Person Specification.

> A really effective tool for holding people to account.

Lesson observations, followed by a learning dialogue   We were concerned that feedback following our lesson observations was less effective than we hoped for. The problem with feedback is that the person being observed can erect barriers to the feedback, not believe it, and, most importantly, do nothing about it. We do it differently now:

- Each member of staff has a copy of the Ofsted exemplars of grades 1–4.
- All staff know that we expect grades 1 or 2 from all staff.
- Observers (from the Senior Leadership Team) make running records of what they see happening based on Ofsted criteria.
- We allow up to 2 hours for the learning dialogue, which takes place as soon after the lesson as possible.
- In the learning dialogue, the teacher self-evaluates against the Ofsted criteria, helped by the observer who asks questions and refers to the observation notes s/he has made. The role of the observer is to help the teacher to make a realistic judgement of his/her performance against the Ofsted criteria, and to identify areas s/he needs/wishes to improve.
- We quality assure the observers, using our Local Authority School Improvement Partnership, and our senior staff.

> As a client, I have found Performance Development and observation dialogues so much more constructive. Instead of feeling defensive at being 'managed', I have been listened to and have been able to identify areas of development for myself. I have felt that I am more in control of my career development and am much more motivated to make changes that I have ownership of and that I recognize will meet the needs of my learners and my class team as well as the whole school.

Whole-school meetings   We hold these once a half term and now call them 'Shared Thinking Sessions' to signal the changed nature of these sessions. Instead of *presenting* to staff, we now involve all staff in thinking through a whole-school issue, for example, last year we reviewed and improved our Staff Relationship Guidelines; our Staff Attendance Policy and our Balanced Life Policy.

With 82 staff, we work in small, facilitated groups, in order to capture everyone's contribution. We also use this time to practise our mentoring-coaching skills. The result is that everyone is actively engaged, they share their thinking and they have ownership of the co-created outcome.

> Every member of staff attends these meetings and every single one of us has input into how we think we should work together to best effect. This way we all know that we contributed to creating key guidelines and we know what we expect of each other.

Staff attendance meetings   We have co-created a Staff Attendance Policy. We provide every member of staff with his/her attendance data termly. This provides an opportunity for us: to recognize staff with regular attendance, for staff to challenge the data, if necessary, so that we ensure that we have accurate data; to confront staff with the reality of their absence and to give them the opportunity to improve their attendance. We believe that this is respectful.

In the case of staff whose absence is unsatisfactory, that is, defined as being below the agreed school target, we have a scaled response:

- Level 1 – give them the data with a note so that they have the opportunity to improve their attendance.
- Level 2 – meet with them to help them think through how they will improve it.
- Level 3 – meet with them, as above, plus referral to the Occupational Health Unit, plus close monitoring, to help them improve it or face the consequence of not improving.

In the meetings we use mentoring-coaching skills: I ask; I establish rapport; I summarize; I help them think through their absence and identify a solution which will work for them and for the school.

> I leave feeling more confident. Afterwards, I think about it and do it.

Resolving issues
There are many opportunities every week to use mentoring-coaching skills to help people resolve issues quickly and effectively. Some are small and are easily resolved; others are more complex, and take longer. The approach is the same: listen, ask, summarize, and help the person find his/her own solution, in line with the school's mission, vision, values and priorities.

With parents
Parents come to us, or are asked to come into school, to address issues, usually to do with their children or their parenting. Both are potentially difficult situations. We use mentoring-coaching skills in these situations, in order to help parents think things through and find their own solutions. We treat them with

utmost respect; we challenge; we attend to them fully, and, as a consequence, they grow.

We have a complaints procedure, as required, but it has never been used. There is no need, if we really value our parents and encourage them to work with us.

At Swiss Cottage, we are on a journey, developing our mentoring-coaching culture on a daily basis. There are people at different points along the skills continuum but we are all working to improve our practice. We don't always get it right but we are asking people to keep a learning journal and commit to their own development. We see our staff as our greatest resource, and we are committed to helping them to grow.

We see mentoring-coaching as a means of accelerating real personal growth because it engages people's thinking and it energizes them. And we are committed to providing the best for our people – adults and children.

Next steps

- We will all continue to practise our mentoring-coaching skills, and review how well we are doing (what went well and even better ifs and action).
- All staff who will be working on our SEN Specialism will have the 4-day mentoring-coaching training, because they will be working with staff from other schools/organizations, and we believe that they need mentoring-coaching skills if they are effectively to help others to develop their practice.
- Under our new staffing structure, we will be working in Key Stage teams, and staff will be 'mentoring-coaching' buddies from within that team, to help them develop their practice further.

Quality assurance

The Headteacher will 'quality assure' the key mentor-coaches in the school, by sitting in on their sessions, followed by a mentoring-coaching session with the mentor-coach.

We will continue to offer formal practice sessions for the whole staff through, for example, our Whole-school Shared Thinking Sessions and we want to move to a position where staff are practising and self-reviewing as a matter of course, using their learning journals to capture their reflections.

17 Finding, making and taking the role

Role is often confused with notions such as job, post, position, function, person specification and a set of tasks or responsibilities. It is distinct from these other concepts in that, whereas they are all *given* or even dictated by someone seen as in charge, role cannot be given. It has to be *taken* – taken, that is, by the person him/herself. It is an expression in action of the person. There are three roles in focus in this chapter: those of mentor-coach, the client and client as (most commonly) employee. The nature of these roles is examined and contrasted with the concepts with which it is sometimes confused. The process is then considered by which a person acts with integrity to find, make and take his or her role.

It may be helpful at this point to think about the processes and time that it takes for a person to become established in the role of mentor-coach. At the same time it is worth reflecting on the fact that across a whole spectrum of trades and professions, and in education in particular, many people who might benefit from mentoring-coaching come to the interaction with little or no conception of role or what *their* particular role is – both as client and in the work place.

What is role?

Part of the issue at stake here is generated by confusion as to what role is. In the world of work terms like person specification, job description and role definition can get mixed up and even be used as though they mean the same thing. In addition, leaders and line managers, as well as the people they lead, often focus simply on the function or place in the organization that an employee is supposed to fulfil and take that as a given. So even in work disciplines, such as education, that prefer to be called professions, it is common to find that leaders and team members put most of their thinking simply into the tasks that are expected of them. These tasks are derived and driven by the organization, and the average employee often has little control over what these tasks are, once they have accepted a contract of employment – a contract that normally focuses on the job description.

Job description and person specification

A job description should set out the functions a post or an employee has, the lines of accountability, what precisely it is that a person is responsible for, including specific tasks to be carried out, the limits to their responsibilities and a carefully defined degree of flexibility that may be built into their contract.

The contracting process will usually include a person specification. This is a systematic attempt to list the professional qualifications, abilities and experience necessary in the post to be filled and some of the key personal qualities the appointed person will need in order to be successful in it. A sense of humour commonly appears in the list along with, in many posts, a variety of interpersonal skills and qualities like diligence, conscientiousness and so forth. There is also a list of qualities and maybe qualifications that may not be essential in the post but are nevertheless desirable.

Our purpose here is not to familiarize readers with employment law and good personnel management practice but to try to achieve clarity in distinguishing the terms person specification and job description from the concepts of role and role definition.

The person

Readers will – if only through earlier references in this book – be by now familiar with some of the work developed by David McClelland (1973) in the second half of last century around leadership effectiveness. In this work McClelland aimed to distinguish between the things that are given, like the job description and any formally agreed standards (agreed perhaps by national professional bodies or set down by government agencies) on one hand, and the personal characteristics or competencies brought to the post by the person who fills it on the other. (Note the definition of competency offered in the previous chapter.) McClelland's colleagues in Hay McBer (see Goleman et al., 2002) write also of the way in which *the behaviours* of leaders constitute a third element that, in turn, impacts on organizational climate – the critical factor that influences the quality and quantity of effort contributed by employees or team members to the performance of the organization. Somewhere in this model there is the effect of a person's *role*, though it is not made explicit.

A possible definition

So what exactly is role? It is easier to give examples of how different people having identical job descriptions take different roles than it is to define role, and some examples of these different roles in the same job will be given later. (Readers may also want to become more familiar with McClelland's work and can do so through exploring materials and ideas developed by the HayGroup (Goleman et al., 2002).) For the sake of clarity, however, a definition of role may be helpful. *Role is the part a person plays in life or society or in an organization.* It could be very fruitful to think of different roles that teachers in their class may have. It is peculiarly responsive to position and title, but *the prime factor in determining role is the person.*

It can help to think of role as in drama. An actor assumes a role and plays a part. It is a part in a story that has themes and underlying meaning. Most parts played by actors in plays have a script that they are expected by the author and director to adhere to. Even so different actors playing the same role in the same play – even using the same script – are likely to enact it differently. They will be influenced in this by conscious things like their own under-standing of what the writer may have intended and by themes and interpre-tations that they, with help perhaps from a director, have worked out. So one might see a work of Shakespeare on several occasions in several theatres and on each occasion observe the lead role being played differently. However, the prime difference in the way that the same part in the same play is played by different actors stems significantly from the uniqueness of the person acting the part.

In family life similar diversity of role may be observed in the instances of parents. The position of father in a family will have a core that is common to most fathers, but the reader will soon be able to pick out from families s/he knows the different ways in which that role is played. A lot of the features of the role of father will be adopted without serious thought, but fathers have choices about what they do in respect of their growing family – about their behaviours towards their children and their attitudes to them, even though some of the choices may become habitual over time. In some families, for example, the father may be the disciplinarian, especially towards sons, while in others the mother has to take that role. Some children who have grown up think and talk of their parents as their friends, while others talk of parents as somewhat distant in their relationships with them, perhaps conveying authority rather than friendship. All these things are features of role.

Professional roles

If we turn to professional contexts, we can quickly find examples of a wide range of roles within a single job. For example, at every level of the teaching profession there are specified posts and job descriptions and a huge range of ways in which each post is fulfilled. The reader will only need to consider the school, college, university or Local Authority she knows best to see how the role taken, for example, by subject leaders, headteachers, lecturers, professors and directors of children's services differs markedly from one context to another. To give a particular illustration, the role or part played by headteachers in adjacent schools may differ sharply. Some headteachers are seen by staff and pupils as a sort of wise friend; others as busy organizers and administrators; others present as distant and aloof – figures of remote authority.

One might think of other professions in a similar way. A police constable, for instance, is no longer usually an avuncular figure of whom one can happily ask the time. Nevertheless that is still the kind of figure that some police officers, especially those who pound the beat, try to project. Others see the need to be authoritarian and establish a reputation as someone not to be crossed. In each case there is the same job, the same rank and title, the same uniform and so on but a different role. One might in the same way explore the role of family doctor, tax inspector, shopkeeper, barman, banker, nurse, railway driver and so on. Every profession has common job descriptions at various levels and most have common person specifications too, but it is the individual who determines the role in each of those positions.

That is to say that they either allow the role to emerge at the dictates of others, at the behest of circumstance, or they shape it themselves. Shaping it can be largely unthinking and even semi-conscious – 'That's just me; it's the way I am' – or it can be a matter of quite deliberate conscious choice followed by systematic attempts to behave in a way consistent with the role that has been identified.

The dynamic nature of role

The other really important point about role is that it is dynamic. A job may stay the same over time – subject to such forces as evolving technologies – but role is likely to be continually evolving, requiring the person to adapt in order to respond to new people, new situations and even new ways of viewing the environment. Essentially, role does not remain static. It evolves and grows as we do both in the light of experience and reflection and in response to changing circumstances in the environment. This is perhaps the key dynamic

– personal growth. We develop greater clarity about, and commitment to our role, as we reflect and develop as persons.

The work of the Grubb Institute for behavioural studies has been influential in shaping the thinking outlined here and merits further study. One important facet of the issue of role is the concept of the 'person-in-role'. The way in which we adopt or shape our role – and we all take more than one role, as will by now be evident to the reader – is influenced hugely by who we are, the kind of person we are. The reader should not take this to mean the kind of person we were born as, though our genetic inheritance will have considerable influence over this. The concept of the person, too, is a dynamic one.

We are evolving all the time. Just as our physical composition is constantly changing with cells dying and being replaced and renewed, so also are our personalities. We can replace features of our person on a like-for-like basis, behaving according to old and rather static habitual patterns, or on a 'new-for-old' basis. That is to say, that as we meet new circumstances, we can respond in the way we have always done or we can consider the new situation and develop responses that we have consciously chosen as a result of reflection. We can evolve new habits of behaviour.

In their seminal work on the biological basis of human consciousness, Maturana and Varela (1987) write of the way in which organisms respond and adapt to what they call a perturbation in the environment. They link this to the Darwinian theory of evolution and describe how this capability to respond through adaptation influences the survival of a species. Survival, they argue, depends upon the ability of the organism to renew itself in the face of perturbation(s). The technical word they use for this ability to renew oneself is *autopoiesis*. For humans there is a possibility of conscious choice about this. For example, not only do we respond to being burnt by taking some sort of avoidance action in future similar circumstances, we can choose from a range of possible actions and, if we wish, we can think about the pros and cons of each of them.

Similarly, in the social, as distinct from the obviously physical, context, we can respond to external factors as they change either by what it has become common to call 'kneejerk' reaction (old-established and often unhelpful reaction) or by consciously deciding our preferred response, and our reasons for preferring it.

We can choose a role

So when we find ourselves with a new set of responsibilities or duties, a new job or new position (for example, subject leader, year co-ordinator, deputy head, adviser etc.) we have a choice as to whether or not we instantly rush out to perform the tasks we have been told are entailed in the new position. We may instead, or in parallel, decide on the role we wish to take and sort out what behaviours would with most integrity be appropriate to ourselves as persons and the position we find ourselves in within the organization or system.

The word integrity is introduced for a variety of reason. Previous chapters have addressed, for example, the question of the values we hold, but here the reader is invited to ponder how big a leap anyone can be expected to make from one role to another, or from not really having a role to finding one, without putting on some kind of act. To try to make a big change at one go may cause a person to stretch him/herself beyond what integrity can stomach. One has encountered many people who had attempted such a development professionally and found themselves facing intolerable tensions between themselves as persons and the role they thought they had to take. What is being inferred here is that finding a role with any sort of integrity takes time.

In addition, the role a person needs to find is one that accords with their personal desire rather than one a person feels others expect them to take.

So we come to the title of this chapter.

Role for a client within their work system

For many people you might work with as mentor-coach, role may be an issue that has received little or no attention. Yet lack of clarity about their role may be generating issues and problems that are difficult to resolve, to the point even of acute frustration, dissatisfaction and conflict. Such impact undermines motivation and effectiveness, and corrodes sense of purpose. One of the really valuable things a mentor-coach can do is to help another person – in thinking things through – to begin to focus on their role.

It must be stressed that this is no simple task. One does not have a one-off discussion with a mentor-coach and suddenly experience an 'Aha' moment that produces clarity about role. It may take a great deal of time and thought, even genuine struggle, to find one's role. Indeed, in their excellent chapter in *Coaching in Depth* edited by John Newton and Susan Long (2004), Bruce Reed and John Bazalgette describe the painstaking process of what they call Organisational Role Analysis through which their clients first find their role and then begin to take action that will help them make it.

Role is unique to each person

Two really important points have begun to emerge that must be noted here. The first is that the role is not lying there dormant waiting for someone to find it, wake it up and then adopt it! Because role relates uniquely to the person and is dynamic it has to be *made*, and it can only be made by that particular person.

What is made is unique to him/her and to that particular environment. That is to say that the finding of role involves formulating a conscious but tentative hypothesis. The hypothesis is the attempt by the person to match up with integrity their sense of who they are to their perception of what is needed in the position they have found themselves within a particular organization. The hypothesis is then tested by action, and either confirmed or reformulated as a result of what is discovered by trying things out.

The second point of note is that neither finding nor making a role can be considered as one-off actions. There is a dynamic interaction between these two parts of the one process. As one tests out the role one has begun to find, more of the potential role will emerge. The hypothesis will then be refined. It will then need to be carefully tested further. There is no single point at which one might say, 'Ah! I have found my role' or 'Ah! I have made my role'. It is more a question of a growing consciousness and growing confidence. Similarly, there is no point at which one can say, 'Ah! Now I have taken my role'. The gradually increasing confidence will come from a sense that there is a pattern of behaviours (perhaps even an habitual behaviour pattern) that accords and is in harmony with the role that is being conceptualized. However, the continuous present tense is vital – because role is dynamic, not static. Even when the role appears to have been taken, it will still be refined further in the light of experience.

An example

An example may help. In large schools it has been common for there to be senior middle management positions to co-ordinate the work of particular year groups. Holders of such posts have frequently felt the huge frustration of being the receptacle for all the problems that other staff encounter when trying to teach the children of that year group. Students themselves often see that person as the one who will field their problems, including their lack of motivation and bad behaviour. Parents, too, may see the year co-ordinator as someone to whom they can refer problems their youngsters generate, including, in some cases, problems that have little to do with school. Add all this together and the job (and implicit role) could be entirely unmanageable. Yet situations like this occur commonly, though more by default than design.

Year co-ordinators with whom the writers have worked often say things like, 'This is not what I became a teacher for', or 'I feel as though I am expected to be a social worker but without relevant training'. A mentor-coach can then ask what it was that led to the person becoming a teacher or rather (since it needs to be related to the present not the past) how they see their role as teachers and how this might relate to a different view of the role of year co-ordinator from the one they currently inhabit. Coming up with a new view will not, however, make much difference back in the work place. Suppose the client comes up with something like, 'Well, I think my role ought to be more related to learn-ing'. S/he will return to the place where s/he is seen by others as trouble-shooter and will be expected to go on shooting trouble. If s/he fails to meet this expectation, colleagues and students may lose faith in him/her.

S/he will need to try out one or two things to test whether the job will tolerate some gradual change in behaviours over time. S/he will then need to reflect, with help from her mentor-coach, on what happened and what s/he learned from the experience, and slowly build on it to begin to make the role. It would be distracting to go into the range of possible adaptations to behaviour that s/he might try out. It is a massive range, as any discerning reader who has thought about or experienced this position in a large school will easily be able to imagine. One instance might help the non-educationist reader. S/he might try to shift the balance of response to problems presented from sanctions to rewards, or, better still, to move away from imposing decisions towards what might be learned by the protagonists in situations referred to him or her.

> The role of the leader is not to be 'Head of Answers' but to lead the learning.
> (Pask, 2003)

Role and culture

No one who has thought carefully about their role will imagine that such shifts can be made quickly, for they occur – if at all – in the context of a culture (see the previous chapter). Just as culture takes significant periods of time to change, so also does role. What is really exciting to recognize, however, is that culture change and role development are like chicken and egg. Culture shift permits role development. Role development generates culture shift. Together they are powerful forces for behaviour change.

Finding, making and taking the role in mentoring-coaching

In the mentoring-coaching relationship there are three quite distinct roles to be found, made and taken. The first two are the role of mentor-coach and that of client. They profoundly influence the dynamic within the relationship. The third role in this context is held by the client, who has two roles in focus: client, and employee in the work place from which s/he has come. What the preceding paragraphs have addressed is the role of employee that a client needs help in clarifying. Addressing this need can be a more complicated business than it need be if there is no clarity around the roles of mentor-coach and client.

Defining the concept of mentor-coach may help but is not the same as finding the role

The onus in this relationship is first upon the mentor-coach to find, make and take his or her role. In the definition of mentoring-coaching used in this book it is suggested that a mentor-coach is a person who helps another think things through – 'Who I am, *my role* and so on'. Much that passes for coaching fails to produce any impact because this stage of thinking has been missed out. In order to help another person with this thinking the mentor-coach must also confront the questions 'Who I am, my role, moral purpose and so on' for themselves. So the question presenting itself here is 'What is the role of mentor-coach?' Note, this is not the same as the question as to the definition of the terms – that's the easy part. The challenge once again is to help the concept travel as well as the term.

The answer to the question cannot be presented in writing. The first half of this book has defined the concept, described the process, explained the skills and subskills, and even indicated some possible lines of questioning. The second part has explored to a limited degree some of the underlying theories and themes within mentoring-coaching. None of this has much meaning, however, until the mentor-coach has entered into the dynamic process of reflection and action that leads to the evolution of the uniquely personal role of mentor-coach for each person who wants to engage in this work. It is not sufficient to understand what is written in any book or even to have a substantial range of skills in this field.

The role must become part of the lived experience. It has to be found, made and taken by each person as they embark on and continue in this work. Although the role cannot be presented in writing, there are some helpful things that can be said.

Role cannot simply be assumed

The first observation is that anyone new to the role and concept of mentor-coach will find that their clients will include many who expect to be directed – to have someone else do their thinking for them. It can be very seductive to be asked to give advice, guidance and direction. To yield to the seduction will totally compromise the finding of the role by the person in it. What will happen is that the mentor-coach will find a role – or rather a function – thrust upon them, or assume one by default. Outside forces will have dictated it. The term 'outside force(s)' does not necessarily refer to the client. All that the client is doing is to make an assumption. It is most likely that s/he has no particular conception of the role – merely (and this is fairly common) an unthought-out assumption.

The second observation is that although role is quite a different concept from the dynamic of the mentoring-coaching relationship, the definition of the term 'mentor-coach', or a rational understanding of the process, clarity about these things will be very helpful. Nevertheless, they are only prerequisites of the process of finding, making and taking the role. It is the person of the mentor-coach that will have most impact on how the role is found, made (or shaped) and taken. Each person who enters a mentoring-coaching relationship must engage in the process in the way already described. A critical starting point will be self-awareness competency (see Chapter 10). The outcome (a continually evolving one) will be unique in every case – as each human being is unique. This is why mentor-coaches in training are asked to go away after two days and try out a few times what they have learnt, before returning for day 3 and day 4. They are, in effect, asked to go out and begin to find and develop their role. Further training aims to help them make or shape that role. Continual practice linked to self-critical reflection is required for the role then to be taken and retaken time and time again.

The role of client

The role of mentor-coach is one of two roles that need to be found. The second is that of client.

As indicated earlier, coaching often fails to have a sustainable impact where it is not preceded by mentoring. Conversely, mentoring-coaching works exceptionally well in the context where the client is engaged in a dynamic way first of all in thinking through who s/he is, his/her role, moral purpose, context and so on, particularly his/her role as client first of all. Finding that role and reflecting on it as a lived experience within the mentoring-coaching encounter is an essential precondition to finding his/her role as teacher, support assistant, head of department etc through the mentoring-coaching process.

The notion of the person-in-role as employee is analysed earlier in this chapter. What is written there about that aspect of role applies equally to the role of client. The client needs to reflect on what sort of behaviours are appropriate for them as a person within this mini-system of the mentoring-coaching relationship and seek to try them out and reflect upon them. By engaging in this way s/he will find the role that is unique to them and will grow in confidence as s/he makes it for him/herself by further relevant behaviours and eventually be engaged in that continuous dynamic that has been called taking the role.

This demanding process is not made any easier by some of the assumptions to be found in much of the literature and a great deal of common practice that is called variously 'mentoring' and 'coaching'. Several writers on the subject of coaching – including some who fail to discern a distinction between the two terms mentor and coach – describe how many people who present themselves for coaching expect that they will be working with an expert in their field who will be able to give them good advice. They often come expecting, in other words, to be told or shown what to do and how to do it. Some writers call this 'directive coaching'. There is a claim by one source (Bacon and Spears, 2003) that the majority of new clients come with that expectation and that this is what they actively desire. However, the same source indicates that they often express disappointment after they have received it! The writers have no experience of delivering 'directive coaching' (whatever it is), though many people have come with that sort of expectation.

Advice, guidance and direction actively deny the client a role

Such an expectation suggests that any role that the client might have is purely passive. That is to say that the client will not have to do too much thinking and their main behaviour will be to listen. So the impact of this view of what the client is likely to experience is to get in the way of any notion that there is a role for him/her to find, make and take. The experience reflected in this book, generated by the philosophy and methodology already explored in some depth, is that a client who comes expecting to be guided, advised or directed does not go away disappointed as a result of not receiving it. Even after one session, in which they are helped to begin the thinking process for themselves, including beginning to think about both of the roles they have, they go away feeling more in control of their situation.

The clear implication the reader is invited to take away is that once the mentor-coach has begun to find, make and take their role, the client will be invited and stimulated to do the same within the mentoring-coaching relationship. Having begun to find it in that one-to-one context s/he will want to do the same in the work situation. Why? Because finding, making and taking one's role is a deeply satisfying process for any human being to experience.

Questions for the reader to reflect on

- How clear to you now is the distinction between the terms job description, person specification and role?
- Try to define role in your own terms.
- Think of people you know who hold identical job descriptions and ponder those features of their behaviour that might distinguish between the roles they take.
- How many roles do you have? Think of some of them and reflect on how people who hold similar positions in a system or mini-system to your own take a different role from the one you take, for example, as son, daughter, father, mother, club member, consumer, employee and so on.
- How have you acquired the role(s) you have? Do you consciously reflect on and try to influence the role? What do you do to try to influence it? How easy is it to influence your role?
- Do you talk to anyone about any of your roles? For example, as the adult child of an ageing and demanding parent, does anyone help you reflect on and try to shape your role?
- What do you perceive as some of the forces that could get in the way of someone finding the role of mentor-coach? How seductive might some of these forces be for you as a person?
- When you consider the question of who you are, what else besides your name and perhaps the job you do comes to mind?
- How helpful might it be to you in finding, making and taking your role as a possible mentor-coach to achieve clarity about the concept of a mentor-coach?
- Similarly, if you are reading this book as someone who could benefit from being mentor-coached, how helpful might it be to you in finding your role to have clarity about the mentoring-coaching concept?
- If you are simply being guided, directed or advised, is there much of a role for you? Is there anything for you to find, make and take?
- Whether as a possible mentor-coach or client, have you reached a point in your work life where you are conscious of what is described here as a role that is unique to you? How important is a unique role for you?
- If you are not conscious of having a unique role, what steps could you begin to take, and what support might you find helpful, to embark on the process of finding it?

18 Child, parent or adult?

The process by which a person finds, makes and takes his/her role is strongly influenced by their dominant psychological disposition and, in particular, their stage of ego maturity. The focus in this chapter is on how readily a mentor-coach and a client can behave in an adult manner. The word adult is used in a particular way and not necessarily to contrast pejoratively other ways of behaving. Most people have it in them to assume any of the three dispositions listed in the title of the chapter. In mentoring-coaching the aim of the dynamic is to facilitate the adult disposition in all three of the roles distinguished in the previous chapter.

In his almost revolutionary work on the study of human consciousness Freud (1933 cited in references as 2002) outlined a conceptual framework that involved thinking about the human psyche as having three main components: the ego, the id and what came to be called the superego. In essence, the ego is the core of the psyche which, although it is at work both consciously and unconsciously, is at the centre of the character of the persona. It determines the kind of person one is and at a deep level influences one's behaviour.

Influenced, as he was almost bound to be at the turn of the 19th and 20th centuries, by Marx and Engels and by Darwinian theory, Freud came to the belief that just as everything that could be thought of as thesis had its antithesis, so also does the ego. Although it is a simplification, it helps to think of the antithesis of the ego as one's 'dark side'. Thus the ego may be thought of as that part of the psyche that gives rise to aspirations and behaviours that might be typically human. By contrast, one's dark side might generate aspirations and behaviours that are opposite to what might be considered human in a positive sense. He called it the 'id' – literally meaning 'thing' in Latin.

The capacity of the psyche to recognize the id and its power, and thus to develop the capacity to manage it and even to harness the energy it might generate through the conscious development and application of rules and values, came to be labelled the superego. In some senses, in terms of the Hegelian philosophy upon which Marxism was founded, the superego might be thought of as the synthesis of the ego and the id, but in a sophisticated way.

In this chapter it is the ego that is in focus.

Freud did not see the ego as something static. It has the capacity to grow as the human body grows, or rather it is capable of maturing, but not on the same plane as the body matures, nor necessarily at the same pace. So whereas the body of someone who is, say, about 20 years of age could be said to have matured or grown to physical adulthood, it would be perfectly possible for that person's ego to have matured at a different rate. S/he could have an ego that was still immature (in childhood) or was that of a mature person twice her age.

Human transactions

Building on Freud's seminal work and on work that became the precursor of the study of brain imaging, Berne (1961) developed a theory about how people and their ego interact with and relate to others. The theory focuses on how people communicate with each other, and, in particular, how they communicate verbally. A more academic study than this might explore in some depth the relationship between language and the persona – indeed the psyche – but it is sufficient to say here that the communication Berne referred to is not only the stuff of relationships but is also the expression of one's personality. His study and the theory surrounding it concerns the verbal transactions between individuals and has become known as Transactional Analysis.

The essence of the theory is that when people speak to one another, particularly face to face, the opening words may set the stage for the way in which they will relate to one another. He called this opening the 'transaction stimulus'. The way in which the other person responds is called the 'transaction response'. The nature of both the stimulus and the response, but especially the response, will depend upon the state of the ego – in relationship with another person it may help to think of it as the alter ego – literally the other ego. What Berne referred to as the state of the ego can be thought of as the level of ego-maturity.

He outlined three levels of ego development: child, parent, adult. These are terms that differ to some degree from the way in which they are commonly used in conversation.

Child

By the ego state of 'child' Berne (1961) meant the state in which our *feelings* have overall control of the way in which we react to other people or to situations. Reason is largely set aside. Our relationships with others when we are in that state are characterized by a form of dependence – we are looking to the other person to make us feel positive, secure, happy and often seek their approval. We draw our power less from internal sources and more from those around us – our parents, their status, our possessions, perhaps other powerful people we know. These are common characteristics of the physical young child. Many people mature physically but retain the ego disposition of the child as the dominant characteristic of how they relate to others, whether they initiate the stimulus (i.e. are the 'stimulus agent' in Berne's terminology) or are responding to it (the 'respondent').

This level of ego maturity is natural in the young child because of the physical dependency of the child, and is reinforced by the way in which the child's parents treat him/her. Equally, a parent can have an impact on the development of the ego by how s/he treats the child. Thus, rather than simply confirming the dependency of childhood, a parent can begin to stimulate different ways of approaching relationships and the situations in which they occur and upon which they impact. This stimulus can promote the development of either of the other two ego states – parent or adult.

In Berne's work the child ego state is ruled by the *felt* concept of life. While most of us experience all three states throughout our lives to some degree, most people progress from the child state as their predominant disposition as they go through adolescence. A small percentage of people fail to make persistent progress from this state and go through their lives with an undeveloped ego. For them such things as responsibility and authority lie with others or even a single other.

Parent

Reaching the parent state is progress of a sort. It represents what we most easily carry forward from the child state, indeed, from childhood itself. It is a kind of product of conditioning from a massive quantity of stimuli in childhood. In particular, it represents the voice inside us of our own parents, of mythological figures, including those in fairy stories, and of others who have influenced us. Our brain – according to research in the 1950s on which Berne drew – stores away the record of most of the things that happen to us and the feelings we associate with them. From these we learn another set of dispositions that will display themselves (often when we are quite unaware of them) in expressions of authority or instruction that put us in the position of power and authority, not just over ourselves but, typically, over others. Sometimes one can see the early stages of this ego state emerging when children are at play and one or more of them enter into a role of a grown-up.

This state is easy to spot in others through language and behaviour they adopt. Typically it will include offering unsolicited advice, giving instruction, laying the law down – wanting to make and impose rules and so on. The parent in us wants to be in control, not just of our own lives but also of the lives of others. Interestingly, people whose predominant ego disposition is that of parent will fairly readily default to that of child when the going gets tough and they are unable to gain the control they covet over others. Thus, it is not uncommon in organizations that are structured in an overtly hierarchical manner for people within the organization to come a bit unstuck when trying to exercise power. When this happens, they look to another person whom they perceive to be more powerful to relieve them of their difficulty and want him/her to take over in a way that will restore their equilibrium for them. This happens a great deal in some schools, for example, where some teachers will try to impose their will on children and, when they fail in those efforts, expect someone to do it for them.

In essence the parent state is one that involves a taught concept of life. In other words, life is what we have been taught as children – in both kinds of child state.

It is important to emphasize here that we are all ready to operate at either the level of child or parent throughout our lives, especially when things get tough. As with the competencies discussed earlier in Chapter 10, we all default under pressure from time to time, depending on how secure we are in those competencies or, in this case, in our level of ego maturity. Freudian psychologists would argue that it is in this field, ego maturity, that the key lies as to how far we default in other matters.

Adult

Although we acquire very early in childhood what becomes for a good part of our lives our predominant ego state, we do also have the capacity to develop the third level from very early days. Psychological studies indicate that our capacity to build a level of ego maturity that Berne labels 'adult' can be detected as early as the tenth month in this world. It can be regarded as the 'thought' concept of life and is the key to our ability to impact on and move forward from the other two states.

The adult state is one in which we think consciously about our relationships and our communication with others. We are thus able to develop our responsibility for ourselves and our own actions. We can also begin to exercise conscious control over our feelings and behaviours, can question what we have been taught and develop an authority that rests on our own thinking.

A considerable number of people find it very difficult to operate at this level of ego maturity in a sustained way, particularly in crises or under pressure. Thus someone who functions at the child or parent level most of the time will find it very difficult to change. Indeed, as they advance in years, it will become more difficult to change without habits of thinking that facilitate self-challenge and deliberate and structured reflection. Some writers on the subject of emotional intelligence claim, for example, that if EI is not developing strongly by the time a person reaches 60, they might as well give up!

Levels of consciousness

What may also have struck the reader by this point is how these levels of ego maturity relate to levels of consciousness. The child level is operating almost consistently below the level of consciousness. It might not be helpful to introduce the notion of the sub-conscious in a technical sense here, but the truth is that children are not especially conscious that they are acting like children; they just are! More importantly, however, is the fact that adults who are engaging in the felt concept of life as the predominant disposition are frequently unaware that they are doing so and are likely greatly to resent anyone who tries to point it out to them.

Similarly, people who are actually parents are often not very aware of how they treat their children in terms of their own ego maturity and are, for example, caught unawares as their children reach adolescence by the fact that coming on strong in parent style goes down like a lead balloon! It is interesting how many adults describe adolescence as a really tricky age – meaning more than the effects of that unique cocktail of hormones coursing through their children's bloodstream. What is not taken account of is that parents who rely on the 'parent disposition' in the terms of this chapter are themselves part of the problem of adolescence. Just as in secondary schools the way some teachers treat teenagers generates much of the difficulty they as teachers experience.

The parent level may lie closer to the surface of consciousness or awareness, but it catches its owner out too often for us to be able to say that it is normally above the surface. What we can say is that in our normal role as parents we can hear ourselves as we speak saying things that we know are at the 'parent' level, and we know as soon as we have spoken that we would have preferred to communicate in a different and more effective way. However, we are only conscious to that degree because we have begun to work at the level of 'adult' – the level at which we engage in thought, which by definition is on the surface of consciousness.

Being capable of regularly living at the adult level – the thought concept of life – does not mean that we will not frequently dip back into the other two levels. It does mean however that we can critique our own behaviour and communication by stepping back into adult mode. Having done so, we can consciously decide to try to respond differently next time and gradually develop adult habits of communication and behaviour. We won't always succeed – pressures and crises may still catch us out, but with help we can make good progress.

Interim summary

The three stages of ego maturity then – child, parent and adult – can be considered respectively as the felt, taught and thought concepts of life. The thought concept is the only concept/stage in which our behaviour is consistently consciously managed.

'Crossed' transactions

It has probably become obvious to the reader by now what the connection is between transactional analysis and mentoring-coaching. Before expanding on its relevance to this book, it is worth pointing out that, technically, transactional analysis itself is the means of analysing transactions – communication – between people to discover from the language used what the nature of the ego state is from the person sending the stimulus. In turn, that analysis can also indicate the ego state of the respondent. It can be particularly helpful in unblocking some of the frustrations of failed communication between individuals – failure caused directly by the nature of the language in use. By language is meant here not just words but all those other ways we communicate – tone, pace of speaking, volume and all forms of body language.

It must be noted, however, that a critical consideration is whether the stimulus and response are complementary. When a stimulus agent initiates a verbal transaction from, for instance, the ego state of parent, the transaction has potential to be successful in his/her terms if the respondent replies in child mode. That is what a parent expects. Indeed, it might be equally accurate to say that that is what the parent ego state *needs*. Similarly, if the agent initiates a transaction in child mode, the response needed is as from a parent. If the appropriate mode of response is not forthcoming, the transaction will be ineffective.

The repeated ineffectiveness of transactions in a relationship become so frustrating – to both parties in each of our examples – that the relationship itself is likely to begin to break down. It will certainly be less than satisfying or fulfilling for the two people concerned.

An example

In the science of transactional analysis exchanges of this kind, where the stimulus prompts a response from an uncomplementary mode, the transaction is said to be 'crossed'. An example might help. Imagine a particular organization, for example a school, in which the leader appears frequently to be in 'parent' mode when dealing with his staff. He gives lots of instructions, often without explanation, and sometimes with a clear hint of negative consequences of non-compliance. They are supported by tone and body language that is more than assertive, though sometimes ameliorated with a smile. Many of his staff try in their general relationships with each other to work on an adult-to-adult basis. If, in response to his parent stimulus, they respond in adult mode, perhaps seeking some explanation or even asking for clarification, they are very likely to meet an explosion beginning with something like, 'How dare you question my authority!'

In this example, the initiator of the transaction is expecting/needing only a response as from the child state. If his staff try to respond in parent mode themselves, there could be even worse trouble, for he would perceive it not simply as a question to his authority, but could decide they were trying to usurp it. Note also that when the parent stimulus draws forth a response from the 'wrong' mode, he defaults to child state, verging on and sometimes actually going into tantrums.

The example offered here may seem a little extreme but most readers will have come across instances of a similar kind. What it illustrates very clearly is that the stimulus agent in any transaction sets the rules for what follows. The respondent can only respond and the response must not be crossed or there will be trouble. A similar problem, though possibly less acute, will occur if the stimulus is in child mode. The respondent is expected to reply in parent state. If s/he responds in child mode there is competition – for support, reassurance, comfort and so on that cannot be supplied.

In each case it might seem that a response in adult state is the most appropriate. It would in many ways be the most respectful state from which to respond and it does have the best chance of working, but often fails to do so. The circumstances under which an adult response will work are when a parent or child stimulus has been offered from someone who is often able to (and may consciously want to) operate in adult state, but has defaulted.

Upon discovering theories like transactional analysis people try to switch to operating more in adult mode in their personal and professional relationships. With help this can work, but it is never easy and sometimes is fruitless. It is often fruitless where a long-standing relationship, particularly within a family, has become deeply ingrained with either the child or parent mode of stimulus. In the fairly extreme example offered here the possibility of change in the professional relationships involved is extremely small without help from the outside.

The message is, however, positive. It is that once people understand the dynamic this chapter describes, the issue is out in the open, or on the surface, and no matter how difficult it might be to alter the dynamic, change is possible. In addition, people constantly waiting for the stimulus agent – who operate in say parent mode – can take the initiative and become a stimulus agent in adult mode.

Some readers may want to explore this theory in more depth and can do so online or perhaps through reading the work of Stewart and Joines (1987). Our purpose now is to link this theory to mentoring-coaching.

Transactional analysis and mentoring-coaching

The previous chapter referred to three roles to be found, made and taken: mentor-coach, client and the client in the workplace (community, club or family etc.).

In the early stages of their work as mentor-coach many people find the tendency to guide, advise, suggest and so on, and thus to take responsibility for the situation of the client, very difficult to resist. One possible reason for this may be that new situations and relationships put them under pressure which causes them to regress in terms of ego maturity. This is most likely to be to the parent state, where telling and controlling are strong instincts. Interestingly, there are occasions when a client may come actually seeking someone to tell them what to do and in effect take control for them. This is very likely to be the case if the relationship is not a voluntary one – has been imposed by a superior authority – or has come about in order to remedy a deficit. In this instance the 'child' is looking to the 'parent' to get him/her out of the difficulty and to remedy the deficit for him/her.

If a client comes asking for such treatment, it is from the ego state of child, but this may not be the predominant disposition of that person. It could be that the beginning of a relationship of a kind s/he has not known before has generated pressure to default. It may, therefore, seem as though the respondent has to go into parent mode, but it will actually be counter-productive to do so. What will be very important to note is that sometimes a person in the role of client persistently asks to be guided, advised or told what to do and how to do it. This will even be supported by statements such as 'I know that you are a real expert in my field' or 'You have so much more experience than I have' (seeking to please the 'parent' and seduce them into supplying the child's need). When this happens, it is because the client is habitually operating in child mode and finding it very difficult to progress beyond it, even though they are also likely to operate on many occasions in parent state. Most likely it will indicate that the client easily eschews the adult mode without being aware of the fact.

Inexperienced mentor-coaches sometimes say, 'Surely, if a person keeps on asking you for advice and guidance, you have to provide it'. These are the very circumstances under which it would be least helpful to do so.

Adult-to-adult mode

To begin with, colluding with such requests causes the mentor-coach immediately to abandon their role and purpose – of helping another person *think things through*. Indeed, it actively absolves the other person of the need or responsibility to think things through. It thus cements that person further into the state of child, or child and parent. Mentor-coaches need to know what is happening here, and be able to deal with it in an 'adult' way. Before exploring *how* to deal with it (which will take the reader into applying TA thinking to the role of client), it is important to stress that operating as a mentor-coach is not simply to offer transaction stimuli from the ego state of adult, but to operate in adult-to-adult mode. This, in turn, requires in some instances the use of skills of a high order.

The definition of mentoring-coaching on which this book is based is that 'a mentor-coach is one who helps me think things through: who I am; my role; moral purpose; the context in which I work; the issues I face and so on'. The adult ego state applies to the *thought* concept of life. There is profound congruence here. Mentoring-coaching only happens when the transactions involved are on an adult-to-adult basis. The mentor-coach must find, make and take the role that enables them to generate such a relationship. In turn, finding, making and taking a role is to work in adult mode and the 'making' part involves helping others to respond in the same mode.

So how might a mentor-coach deal with persistent requests for advice and guidance? Readers might want to pause here and consider that question for themselves and write their thoughts in the empty text box that follows.

What the reader has written will reflect the way in which s/he has connected the perception of transactional analysis to the roles of mentor-coach and client.

If the thinking through of things begins with 'Who I am', a client who persists in the child or parent states has a need to deal with his/her essential being before s/he can go on to address the other subjects for thinking listed in the definition. To generate such thinking the mentor-coach will need to find a point at which to say something like, 'I've noticed that you are very keen to have my opinion/advice a lot of the time. Where's that coming from?' (Note the tentative nature of this intervention. A careful judgement needs to be made 'on the hoof' as to whether to follow the first bit with the word 'why', as in 'Why is that?' Various formulations are possible, including 'Why do you think that is?' or 'What might be causing that?' The tentative nature of the question is essential if the client is not to feel threatened by the invitation to come away from the comfort of their habitual ego state(s).)

It is important to be aware that any overt talk about transactional analysis can only occur easily with another person in adult mode. With anyone else the focus on this construct has to be developed very gradually. Under no circumstance would it be helpful to ask something like, 'Do you realize that you operate persistently in child mode and that this is a key to your problems?'!!

To ask 'why do you think that is?' is to suspend the discussion of the substance under discussion (say, how to deal with a difficult person in her team) and to try to surface a deeper matter. Note also that what is suggested is a question, not a short exposition of the theory of transactional analysis! From previous chapters the reader will know the importance of, indeed, the total dependence of the whole mentoring-coaching process on questioning. Here it is needed as the only way in which an intelligent adult can be helped to surface awareness and understanding of such matters as their habitual ego state. Progress from child and parent towards adult can depend substantially on accessing help – and the help is in developing a *thought* concept of life, and the communication habits that go with it.

For the client to find, make and take their role as client, it is necessary for the mentor-coach to do so and then to ensure that the transactions that occur are adult to adult.

Continuing to develop ego maturity

Once the pattern is established in the mentoring-coaching relationship of two people working together to think things through, not only will considerable progress be made in addressing issues but the client (and the mentor-coach) will make further progress in making the ego state of adult habitual.

The idea of offering a short exposition of transactional analysis theory was dismissed earlier as a way of surfacing the dependency of the client upon advice and guidance. It is not to be dismissed altogether. There is a place for this kind of contribution in the context we are discussing. It must be made clear, however, that expositions are not part of the process of mentoring-coaching. Nevertheless, the whole of life and learning cannot and must not be governed exclusively by the disciplines of mentoring-coaching. There are circumstances under which it might be helpful explicitly to come out of that very specific relationship to offer explanations, exposition, even training, in any number of skill or knowledge areas that might be useful to the client and pertinent to the issue being addressed. It should be offered with caution, however, for the last thing the mentor-coach should do is slip easily into the role of expert/guru. To continue our earlier example may help.

A member of the team being led by the person described previously might find it helpful at some point to consider why her leader might be behaving in what seems such an oppressive manner, and why rational behaviour appears to have no impact upon the situation. This consideration should as far as possible be generated from open questions by the mentor-coach (such as 'Are there any theories you have about why he behaves like that?'), but there may be a place for reference to theory or to a particular piece of reading that may throw light on it. A repeated caution is necessary, however: the mentor-coach must either come explicitly out of role or, better still, agree to search together for possible theories and explanations. A mentor-coach who turns into a guru/expert at the drop of a hat, will need to reconsider his/her own ego state.

Finally, there is little to add on how the ego state of the client will influence his/her ability to find, make and take their role at work or elsewhere. The influences and patterns discussed earlier apply to *that* situation just as they do to the mentoring-coaching interaction. It should be sufficient to understand that first-hand experience of an in-depth adult-to-adult transaction in mentoring-coaching will strengthen the ability of the client to transact communication in their workplace according to similar principles. This will be much more strongly the case if the nature of the dynamic and its underlying principles have been made explicit during the process.

Once a client experiences sustained adult-to-adult transactions in the mentoring-coaching relationship, s/he will want to seek out ways of generating more such transactions in their working (and personal) relationships? Why? Because – as with finding, making and taking the role – adult-to-adult transactions are deeply satisfying processes for human beings to experience.

Questions for the reader to reflect on

- Whom do you encounter who seems to exhibit behaviours, more specifically ways of communicating – that might reflect the 'child' ego state? Think about what they say and do.

- If the person you thought of in answer to the first question was a biological child, try to think in the same way of a biological adult who does the same things.
- It should be easier to apply the same thinking to someone you know who frequently appears to reflect the 'parent' state. What is it that this person says and does that makes you identify them as in parent state? Does this person sometimes seem to default to the child state? Under what circumstances does this appear to happen, and what is it that they do on those occasions?
- Think of two occasions on which you have defaulted – first to child, and secondly to adult. What caused you to do so, that is, what triggered it? What exactly did you say and do on those two occasions?
- To what extent do you consider that your communication with others is consistently on an adult-to-adult basis? What evidence could you cite for this assessment of yourself?
- With whom do you frequently find communication quite frustrating? Does this theory help in any way to throw light on that relationship? How might you use any insights gained from this chapter to approach that relationship in new ways?
- Does this theory offer any explanation about the ease or difficulty you experience in finding, making and taking your role – at home, in social life, at work?
- Try to work out how you might convey this theory in your own words in a succinct way.
- Look again at what you wrote (or thought of writing) in the blank text box provided on p. 206. Do you need to reconsider it? What was the rationale behind what you wrote?
- In what way has this chapter helped you to assess the ease with which you are able to find, make and take the role of mentor-coach?
- Are you now confident of your ability to help a client find, make and take her roles, even in the face of varying levels of ego maturity?
- What thoughts do you have about the possibility that mentoring-coaching may help both mentor-coach and client to (drawing on the words of the title of the book by Carl Rogers, 1961) become more of a person?

19 Building capacity on success

Mentoring and coaching that focus too much on identifying problems and blocks, especially if combined with an overly directive approach driven by performance management, can be less than liberating, threatening and even damaging to people's capacity to develop positively and meaningfully. The informed mentor-coach can safeguard against such dangers by drawing selectively on more success-affirming and energizing approaches based in positive psychology. Appreciative Inquiry, a field pioneered by David Cooperrider and his associates, offers a radical alternative to deficit models of change (Cooperrider and Whitney, 2005).

The four stages of Appreciative Inquiry (Discovery, Dream, Design, Destiny) chime well with the principles of mentoring-coaching presented in this book. Their consistent application and integration in the practice of mentoring-coaching can both enhance the effectiveness of the mentor-coach and help motivate and encourage clients to appreciate, draw upon and build on their success and strengths, rather than highlighting their failures, shortcomings or weaknesses. Of key importance in this process is the ability of the mentor-coach to ask unconditionally positive questions.

Affirming and building on success

Throughout this book emphasis has been laid upon the positive, holistic nature of mentoring-coaching – the relationship and the process. It is not a pathological or deficit model. You do not have a mentor-coach only if you have 'problems'. Nor do you have to be sick to get better. Clutterbuck (1985) contends that everyone needs a mentor-coach [at least sometimes!]. We reiterate that thinking things through is for everyone and that it is likely that the quality of everyone's thinking will improve with the help of a skilled and appreciative mentor-coach who attends by listening empathically and questioning dialogically.

The prior experience that clients bring to the process will range from sustained success at a high level to a constant struggle, at least initially, against seemingly intractable challenges. At all points in that range a judicious appreciation of what is and a determination to build on strengths and successes will provide both the foundation and impetus for thinking through both the elements defined as central to the first half of the mentoring-coaching model *and* the action that needs to be taken to make progress towards the 'ideal, unencumbered future' in the coaching stages of the model. Appreciation of what is, and building on strengths and successes (which everyone has) are also two key characteristics of Appreciative Inquiry.

What is Appreciative Inquiry?

As with other notions proposed in this book, definitions may be helpful. For example, the dictionary indicates of the word 'appreciate': 'to form an estimate of worth, quality or amount; to be sensitive to; to esteem adequately or highly; to raise in value'. It goes on to imply meanings such as 'to value; recognize the best in people or the world around us; affirm past and present strengths, successes and potentials; to perceive those things that give life (health, vitality, excellence to living systems); to increase in value'. Synonyms might be 'value, prize, esteem and honour'.

Inquiry is defined as 'to explore and discover; to ask questions; to gather data; to amass evidence; to be open to seeing new potentials and possibilities.' Synonyms might be discover, search systematically, explore and study.

It will be clear from this point on that the words themselves, when used together, are very carefully chosen to indicate the character and dynamic of the process they are used to label.

Attending and inquiring appreciatively

Henry (2003) relates how, when conducting research in 1980 into organizational behaviour with the Cleveland Clinic, David Cooperrider, lead creator of Appreciative Inquiry, observed that:

> when the interviews focused on . . . problems . . . his subjects' energy decreased and they felt demoralized. When the interviews focused on what was working, they exhibited increased energy and enthusiasm for their work. Cooperrider also noticed the same impact on those

conducting the interviews. When the focus was on problems, the result of the inquiry was a vicious circle spiralling downward. When the focus was on what was working and what was valuable, the result was a virtuous circle spiralling upward.

Cooperrider and Whitney (2005) reiterate the importance of the positive in the AI approach:

> What we have found is that the more positive the question we ask in our work the more long lasting and successful the change effort . . . We are more effective the longer we can retain the spirit of inquiry of the everlasting beginner. The major thing we do that makes the difference is to craft and seed, in better and more catalytic ways, the unconditional positive question.

The 4-D cycle of Appreciative Inquiry

Over several years Cooperrider and his associates have developed and revised an explicit cycle comprising four stages for understanding and implementing Appreciative Inquiry. The congruence between mentoring (Discovery) and coaching stages (Dream, Design, Destiny) of the model presented and the AI cycle is striking.

- *Discovery*: Through dialogue involving systematic inquiry the client is helped to identify within a particular focus the elements that they find challenging, interesting and energizing and to which they can commit.
- *Dream*: The client is encouraged to project positive elements of the identified existing situation into a positive vision or dream of how the future ideally might look.
- *Design*: The client thinks through and designs a strategy to achieve the articulated vision or dream.
- *Destiny*: The client focuses on implementing the vision, and, importantly, sustaining and developing the energy, hope, enthusiasm and positive relationships underpinning the design. Originally, this stage was called *Delivery*, but Cooperrider and his associates progressively perceived this description to be too limiting and renamed it to reflect the dynamic energy, spirit and increasing sense of ethical commitment and engagement it generates.

Constructing and reconstructing social reality

As humans, we socially construct our everyday reality, and man is the architect of his own destiny. Crucially, if we can construct reality, we can also *re*construct it. This is why a client can suddenly experience an exhilarating sense of liberation and empowerment as s/he discovers the possibility of a new and preferred 'state' to which s/he can commit with conviction and energy. It is in this sense that Cooperrider and Whitney (2005) argue that Appreciative Inquiry is not so much about new knowledge as about new knowing. They claim:

> Indeed people frequently talk, as they move through the pedagogy of life-giving Discovery, Dream, and Design, that something suddenly hits home: that interpretation matters – that the manner in which they/we read the world filters to the level of our imaginations, our relationships, and ultimately to the direction and meaning of our action. We create the organisational worlds we live in.

This emphasis on the dream, design and destiny leading to creating an alternative *outside the box* accords well with Zohar and Marshall's (2000) distinction between emotional and spiritual intelligence examined in Chapter 10. We are not doomed as humans merely to cope tactically with situations, we can reconstruct and transform them strategically towards what we particularly want. There are also links here to the issues explored earlier in Chapter 11 on dialogue, in Chapter 13 on images of the mind and in Chapter 14 on chains of meaning.

Mentoring-coaching presents a positive and affirmative growth model in today's climate. Like Appreciative Inquiry it is action oriented but focuses determinedly on people, issues and feasible outcomes generated by them with the support of others, rather than on problems requiring quick-fix solutions. Some might view such approaches as 'unrealistic', 'wishful thinking' or 'pink and fluffy'. However, White (1996) explains that while more traditional practices such as monitoring and troubleshooting have their proper place, approaches concentrating continually and over a long period of time on 'correcting problems' can lead to a very negative culture: 'Don't get me wrong. I'm not advocating mindless happy talk. . . . We can't ignore problems – we just need to approach them from the other side'. This 'other side' is what Appreciative Inquiry refers to as the 'positive change core' – all the positive potential that can be brought to light through systematic inquiry as a basis for creating and realizing new visions. This is precisely what mentoring-coaching is designed to surface as a vital source for helping the client succeed.

The crucial importance of enabling language

Language is of key importance in generating positive awareness, potential and actions. It is largely through our specific choice and use of verbal and non-verbal communication that our social construction of reality occurs. Whenever possible, it is important to avoid negative, de-energizing statements and questions and to help the participant towards acknowledging, analysing, celebrating positive aspects of themselves, their role, the context and their interface. By attending carefully, appreciatively and encouragingly, using positive and supportive verbal and non-verbal language and tone, and disciplined non-collusive, non-judgmental responses, it is possible to help build, (re)energize and bolster the self-confidence of the client.

> What distinguishes AI . . . is that every carefully crafted question is positive. Knowing and changing are a simultaneous event. The thrill of discovering becomes the thrill of creating. (Cooperrider and Whitney, 1999: 140)

When in 1928 Charles Inge wrote of Monsieur Coué (cited in Partington, 1992), he captured succinctly what has since become the essentially positive and optimistic spirit of both mentoring-coaching as presented in this book and Appreciative Inquiry:

> This very remarkable man
> Commends the most practical plan:
> You can do what you want
> If you don't think you can't,
> So don't think you can't; think you can.

If our language is negative, our thinking and perspective are negative and will focus on what's wrong and why we *can't* do something. Positive language expresses possibility and potential to achieve – what we *can* do, not what we can't! Mentoring-coaching and Appreciative Inquiry are constantly seeking opportunities and possibilities for positive growth and development in individuals. This is not to deny that at any time there may be problems or blocks in the way of positive thought and action. But neither mentoring-coaching nor Appreciative Inquiry would accept such situations as either insuperable or unalterable. They work *with* the client to search out and mark the positive aspects and potential of a situation, rather than becoming mired by seeing it as a problem. By topping up rather than draining further their human battery, the mentor-coach can help the client envision an alternative scenario and commit to framing and initiating appropriate alternative actions.

The power of positive questioning

In Chapters 3 and 4 describing Stages 1 and 2 of the model of mentor-coaching it was suggested that although it is not possible to provide a definite taxonomy of questions to be asked, certain examples could illustrate the spirit of the questioning required at each stage. So, for example, the question, 'What has pleased you most over the last . . . months?' offers an orientation towards the positive focus that would be most helpful to the client.

The art and practice of crafting unconditionally positive questions that strengthen the client's capacity to apprehend, anticipate and heighten positive potential are of crucial importance in mentoring-coaching informed by Appreciative Inquiry. For example, rather than asking what is wrong with a client's team, the AI-aware mentor-coach would invite her/him to think about the *strengths* of individual members of the team and a time when they worked to achieve something that the client valued! This might involve questions such as:

- Describe a high point experience in your senior leadership team – a time when you were most engaged or excited!
- Without being modest, what is it that you most value about yourself and your contribution to the team?
- What do you most value about the team and its contribution to the organization?
- What do you think are the core factors that give life to the team?
- If you had three wishes to heighten the vitality and health of the team, what would they be? (from Cooperrider et al., 1999: 11–2).

Integrating mentoring-coaching and Appreciative Inquiry

Appreciative Inquiry as a distinct discipline can be applied to work with organizations as well as with individuals. Hence, up to this point reference has been made to 'client' and 'consultant'. The congruence between the principles and methodology of mentoring-coaching on the one hand and Appreciative Inquiry on the other will by now be clear to the reader of this book. There is a similar congruence with the notion of Process Consultation as expounded by Schein (1999) in which context Appreciative Inquiry is now often used. While process consultation is more commonly applied to organizations, mentoring-coaching is focused, at least initially, on the individual.

A wide and varied range of dispositions are presented by people who engage to work with the help of a mentor-coach. For many there is a positive history of success and development of which they are consciously aware and that has generated confidence and a positive disposition. Conversely, some come with a sense of success constantly eluding them, and they may even have been persuaded or directed, perhaps against their will, to seek to work with a mentor-coach. For people across this spectrum appreciative mentoring-coaching has great potential. It has particular potential for the second group in generating a paradigm shift.

Used in this way *inquiry* can help the client identify, articulate and become more explicitly aware of – that is, *appreciate* – the positive and successful elements in their personal life and work. These are often things which they tend to understate, take for granted, or forget when they find themselves confronted by issues they cannot immediately come to terms with, or problems they cannot solve. Mentoring-coaching enables one to work in precisely such ways. The mentor-coach can use the spirit of Appreciative Inquiry selectively to refocus and draw on this positive energy source in attempting to help the client redress any imbalance in her/his perceptions, motivation, aspirations and outlook.

The nature of change

Cooperrider and Whitney (1999: 8) highlight what they consider a mistaken conception of change, namely that we first do an analysis, then we decide on change. They argue:

> inquiry and change are not truly separate moments, but are simultaneous. Inquiry is intervention. The seeds of change – that is, the things people think and talk about, the things people discover and learn, and the things that inform dialogues and inspire images of the future – are implicit in the very first questions we ask. The questions we ask set the stage for what we 'find' and what we discover (the data) becomes the linguistic material, the stories, out of which the future is conceived, conversed about and constructed.

This describes admirably the sense of 'change' that evolves in a mentoring-coaching dialogue. The role of the mentor-coach is to enable the client acknowledge, analyse and rearrange experiences, thoughts, feelings and values. And by ensuring that successes and achievements are highlighted the mentor-coach helps the client tap a key source of energy for change.

Harman (1990) welcomes the positive nature of AI questions which he sees as part of a much needed 'participatory science', 'a new yoga of inquiry', explaining that 'yoga' comes from the Sanskrit root 'yug', meaning 'link' or 'bond'. Thus, as mentor-coach, one needs to help the client make the memory link with someone or something positive by concentrating systematic 'inquiry' on their 'appreciable' aspects. Importantly, a key tenet of Appreciative Inquiry is that whatever you want more of already exists in you or your organization. Consequently, a key role of the appreciative mentor-coach is through inquiry to help the client identify, surface and incorporate success into their thinking and proposals.

Some imperatives for the AI-informed mentor-coach

Dos

- Note carefully and store any successes narrated by the client.
- Be alert to opportunities to highlight, draw out, build on and extend positive aspects of the client's context and issues.
- Observe carefully the client's non-verbal language which can often convey what they are feeling/meaning more accurately than words alone.
- Take every opportunity to encourage the client to acknowledge, appreciate and savour their 'successes', however defined by them!
- Manage carefully your own verbal and non-verbal responses.
- Focus on the person and issues. AI is solution focused, not problem focused.
- Keep the tone, the language, the body language 'upbeat', wherever possible.
- Take care to probe, refine and heighten awareness of how positive achievements were realized and how they can help motivate and generate further positive thinking and actions.

The reader will remember that these are precepts that emerge very strongly in the first half of this book, where the behaviours required of the mentor-coach are described more fully. Some of them are repeated here to illustrate the significant overlap between mentoring-coaching and Appreciative Inquiry. Exactly the same can be said of the examples of behaviours to avoid, listed below.

Don'ts

- Avoid trying to ignore or 'talk away' problems presented by the client as this can appear to be naïve or patronising to him/her and call into question the mentor-coach's credibility.
- Beware assuming that the client's analysis of and response to his/her situation is always accurate.
- Take care not to sympathize or collude with the client (see Chapters 12 and 15), particularly if s/he is feeling anxious, in low spirits or disempowered. Rather, call on relevant examples of her/his success.

- Don't miss any opportunity to encourage the client to build his or her sense of self-worth, self-esteem and capability. (This must be authentic and avoid being patronizing. It is best done by inviting positive judgement by the client and is characterized by non-possessive warmth.)

Thinking positively to help develop successful mentoring-coaching cultures

This has enormous implications for creating and nurturing mentoring-coaching cultures of the kind referred to in Chapter 16. Cooperrider and Whitney (1999) see organizations first and foremost as 'centres of human relatedness. Relationships thrive where there are appreciative ears [and eyes] – when people listen for [and see] the best in one another, when they share their dreams and ultimate concerns in affirming ways, and when they are connected in full view to create not just a new world, but better worlds. AI, we hope it is being said, is more than a simple 4-D cycle of Discovery, Dream, Design and Destiny; what is being introduced is something deeper at the core.' Precisely the same point applies to what we understand as *really* effective mentoring-coaching and its outcomes. Effective mentor-coaches believe in and strive to help clients co-construct these kinds of transformation. By the judicious use of Appreciative Inquiry in working positively with clients through the different stages of the mentoring-coaching process they can help them happen.

Working appreciatively and inquiringly helps both mentor-coach *and* client to harmonize the requirements of their role, and to become a fuller and more fulfilled person. For both parties, it heightens and refines our awareness of what impacts most positively on people we work with and how we draw on this awareness to help us deal more effectively with the issues that mentor-coach and client literally *con*-front.

Issues for the reader to reflect on

- Recall an occasion when someone really believed in you and saw your strength and let you know it. How did this affect you and your development? How are you feeling as you recall this experience? (What you are almost certainly experiencing is a 'dynamic state that emboldens change' (Henry, 2003). Henry goes on to explain that the process of accessing this state – 'locating the energy for change' – is what Appreciative Inquiry is all about.)
- Now think of an occasion when you adopted such an approach in

working with another. What was the outcome? How do you know – what was the evidence? How might your body language have reflected your intentions? How did the other person respond? Can you think of any ways in which you could have enhanced your role in this process? How might this have made the outcome even better?

- Recall a situation where you were not 'appreciative'. What did you say? How did the other person respond? With hindsight, how would you now adapt your specific behaviours in terms of AI in such a situation? What would you hope to achieve? What criteria might help you evaluate your success as an appreciative mentor-coach

- We have emphasized how imperative it is that the mentor-coach *attends* to the client. How are *attending* and the principles of Appreciative Inquiry complementary?

- How do you see AI in relation to empathy, sympathy and identification as discussed earlier? Why and how does the mentor-coach need to emphasize discipline in this domain.

- How would you respond to the suggestion that such an approach is unrealistic?

- Bearing in mind the questions used above in the discovery phase of building a high-performing senior leadership team, formulate some of the questions you might ask in the other stages of the 4-D model.

- How might you find out about the extent to which you actually incorporate AI principles into your mentoring-coaching practice?

- In what ways might *you* use Appreciative Inquiry to enhance specific mentoring-coaching competencies?

20 Mentoring-coaching as learning

Mentoring-coaching is essentially a learning process. The principles on which it is based are common to some of the richer models of learning to be found in recent writing, particularly experiential learning. The learning that takes place in the mentoring-coaching interaction is, first and foremost, the learning of the client, but there is also a very important degree of learning for the mentor-coach. In this chapter consideration is given to the question of who needs to learn and whether individuals and organizations can learn most effectively through processes that are framed by precisely those principles that underpin the model of mentoring-coaching that this book is about. Essentially, the mentoring-coaching process is about thinking – helping each other think. It is fundamentally, therefore, about learning and it will be argued that all effective learning depends on the application of the philosophy and, to a considerable degree, the methodology expounded in this book.

Who needs to learn? What exactly is learning? Is learning the same as education? Is mentoring-coaching really just for people who work in education services, or for people involved in formal aspects of learning? These are questions that are worth *thinking through*.

What is distinctive about being human?

One of the features that it could be argued distinguishes the human species from others with whom we cohabit the earth is the ability consciously to learn. The word 'consciously' is important. It would be arrogant in the extreme to claim that the human species is the only one able to learn. Many creatures appear to be able to adapt their behaviour in response to a variety of stimuli, and may even do so from a state that could be described as conscious. A variety of writers, perhaps most notably Umberto Maturana and Francisco Varela (1987), have described the evolutionary processes that numerous species have passed through in the history of their adaptation in response to 'perturbation in their environment'. This adaptation or response to perturbation (cause of disturbance) could be called a form of learning. The detection of a perturbation could be labelled cognition.

The development of consciousness in human beings has reached a stage where we can not only learn, we can decide to learn, choose what to learn and even how to learn. We can also discern whether or not, and to what extent, learning is taking place and we can reflect not only upon learning that we have experienced but upon the process itself – a sort of meta-learning. These characteristics of human capability may well be distinctive of our unique nature. This is not a book about anthropology or biology, nor about neuroscience. For a detailed consideration of the scientific background to these issues the reader is referred to the writings of Maturana and Varela (1987), and to Antonio Damasio's excellent discourse, *The Feeling of What Happens* (2000). It is sufficient here to state the contention that learning lies somewhere close to the heart of what it means to be human.

Alongside the notion of learning lies the notion of thinking.

Who needs to learn?

The answer to the question 'Who needs to learn?' is almost certainly 'Everyone'. It is a capacity and probably also a need that all human beings have. What precisely is learning? There are many ways of approaching this question. Reference has already been made to the work of Maturana and Varela (1987) whose thesis is that, on a biological level learning is a response to or adaptation in the face of a perturbation in the environment. The perturbation has first to be sensed by the organism and a behaviour has to be evolved that will enable its continued survival. In turn, this may over time cause the organism to adapt itself structurally. This process is referred to as autopoiesis – remaking oneself. On a simple level it would make sense to talk about the ability to adapt to change.

Some definitions of learning

Writing that has been prompted by recent research and practice in neuroscience points to learning as 'a process of developing new neural pathways that when sufficiently practised become "hard wired"; what we call "knowing" and "experience". This process applies not only to "facts" but also to behaviour' (National College for School Leadership, 2005.) This is a helpful perspective.

Its focus is primarily behavioural. The argument is that connections in the brain are made when something is learned, but that these connections need to be consciously and deliberately practised before the appropriate behaviour becomes 'natural'.

Doing is knowing; knowing is doing. (Maturana and Varela, 1987)

To progress our understanding of the subject of learning beyond the behavioural it may be helpful to consider some recent writing on the nature of learning. Three sources may be illustrative. It is not unusual to read or hear of learning that takes place at a number of *levels*. West-Burnham (2004) refers, for example, to *shallow, deep* and *profound* learning. Shallow learning might be information or theoretical knowledge that has been acquired that has not been practised to a significant degree and may be understood only super-ficially, while something that has been practised thoughtfully and to some degree reflected upon might count as deep learning. The distinction between deep and profound learning is slightly problematic because the two words are synonymous. Profound learning, however, would link information, theory and practice (several times over) through systematic and structured reflection (often with the help of feedback from others). The tangible outcome of these processes would be changed behaviour that was embedded or natural to the individual in question.

Attached to the notion of profound learning is coherence – the way in which new learning is related to prior learning that helps one to make sense of it in the light of experience.

Much of what West-Burnham calls profound learning is similar in many ways to the self-directed learning and change about which Boyatzis writes in Goleman et al. (2002).

Some models of learning

Two other writers' work is worth considering here. Both are part of a com-munity of thinking on this subject at the Institute of Education, University of London. Watkins (2001, 2002, 2004 and 2005) writes in several publications of learning taking place at three levels. The first is learning by being taught. This is a relatively passive process where the learner is seen as a vessel (at one time empty) that is filled from the outside with information and possibly ideas and even skills. The test of its effectiveness is commonly the ability to perform the skill, or to re-present the information and ideas with reasonable clarity, most often under traditional examination conditions.

The second level is about the ability to make meaning from or to understand what has been taught or experienced. (Watkins calls this 'individual sense making'.) It involves thinking in a more active way and will include critique and analysis. Although this is a richer form of learning, it is, as its label suggests, carried out mostly in an individual way, on a private basis.

The third level in this structure of learning (which is seen to a degree as hierarchical) is defined as 'creating and sharing knowledge by doing things together with others'. Here learning is seen among other things as a social process with symbiotic connections to the concept of language and language interchange. It draws upon shared critique and reflection. It involves shared experience and collective as well as individual review. To frame the process Watkins uses the learning cycle that Dennison and Kirk (1990) adapted from Kolb (1984) – an essentially iterative cycle with four stages: Do, Review, Learn, Apply.

The third writer who sheds some light on this and, importantly in this context, seeks to relate models of learning to the subjects of mentoring and mentor-coaching (note the use of separate terms) is Carnell (2006). She labels the three levels or rather three learning models: Instruction, Construction and Co-construction. These models are similar in substance to the levels that Watkins also writes about. What is important in the context of this book is the claim that Carnell makes 'that if richer models of learning are adopted (such as construction and co-construction) and if the learning is made explicit, the processes of mentoring and coaching will be more effective'.

Linking learning with mentoring-coaching

While Carnell is linking three processes – mentoring, coaching and learning – this book argues that mentoring-coaching is a single continuous process that is defined with sharp clarity. This chapter is therefore considering only two processes – mentoring-coaching and learning. Yet the contention Carnell makes about rich models of learning applies strongly here – only more so. Mentoring-coaching is a process in which two people with clearly defined roles think things through together. It is a classic instance of the model that Carnell calls co-constructionist and that Watkins defines as 'creating and sharing knowledge by doing things together with others' – in this case with just one other, a mentor-coach. The thing they are doing together is thinking things through – things about being, relating and doing. Both the model and the learning are made explicit.

The reader who turns back to the chapter describing the model and defining the terms will notice that this model of mentoring-coaching is derived directly from Kolb's (1984) Learning Cycle. It is in other words a Cycle of Learning. The learning is made explicit by the application of the skills explained and illustrated in the first half of the book:

- listening
- questioning (for information and for understanding)
- attending closely to the person and present context of the learner (client)
- paraphrasing
- summarizing (to clarify and also to fix, temporarily, learning that has so far taken place)
- hypothesizing
- testing to confirm or disconfirm
- envisioning the future
- prompting wide-ranging creative thinking
- action planning
- micro-planning, as necessary.

These are all eminently tangible ways of co-constructing knowledge and making it explicit. Like Kolb, and Dennison and Kirk, the model of mentoring-coaching is also iterative, that is, it takes one back to a fresh starting place from which the model can be applied all over again.

> We shall not cease from exploration
> And the end of all our exploring
> Will be to arrive where we started
> And know the place for the first time. (T. S. Eliot, 'Little Gidding')

Dominant discourse in learning

If one were to witness a highly successful learning encounter of any sort anywhere, the person leading, managing or facilitating it would almost certainly be doing many of the things already listed. S/he would also be helping the learner(s) do those things too. Sadly, research suggests that in the majority of places one might *hope* to find learning at its most effective (schools, colleges and universities) the dominant discourse is *telling* and *being taught*. These are seen as weak forms of learning. This is also true in many instances of both mentoring and coaching – usually considered separate activities, though poorly defined – the dominant activity is telling, that is, the mentor or coach tells the client what s/he needs to know, what to do, how to do it and so on. The client asks the questions and the mentor or coach gives the answers. Some learning occurs but it is often insecure. Control and power both lie with the mentor-coach. Interestingly, the dominant discourse around what should be happening in our schools often emphasizes the power and control of the teacher and ignores the need to transfer these steadily to the learner from the very beginning of the relationship.

By contrast, mentoring-coaching, as defined in this book, is an example of a rich model of learning. At its most basic it offers a constructionist approach to learning and when working well is co-constructionist.

Elsewhere in this book reference has been made to double loop learning. Both Watkins and Carnell refer, as does this chapter, to meta-learning. The two concepts have much in common.

Making learning explicit

Carnell (2006) writes of the importance of the learning being made explicit. She refers to a model where the learning agenda is made explicit at the start. In the model of mentoring-coaching under consideration here this *may* occur from the start of the second iteration of the cycle – though this may not necessarily always be the case. A client may not know what s/he wants to learn or even what issues to explore. As explained in Chapters 3 and 4, a client may even come with one issue in the forefront of their mind but decide partway through that something different, perhaps more fundamental, needs to be explored. What is vital, however, is the contention that the learning should be made explicit *as it occurs*. By the end of the first iteration of the cycle the mentor-coach should have helped at several points – perhaps at the end of each stage – to sum up the learning that has taken place. This summing up is most effective when the client does it – with whatever help the mentor-coach needs to offer.

What users of this model have discovered, however, is that the learning is often at its most powerful when reflection is facilitated by the mentor-coach on the action that has been taken as an outcome of the first cycle. Learning at this point often includes surprises – things the client not only did not come intending to learn, expecting or even hoping to learn, but had not even considered possible to learn. This may include things about him/herself and about others to whom s/he has to relate. In particular, s/he may learn about skills and potential s/he didn't know s/he had, about possibilities in the workplace and about opportunities worth developing. S/he may also learn some things about him/herself as a person that s/he either didn't know or knew, but had forgotten. In addition, s/he may find creativity that s/he either didn't know or had forgotten that s/he had.

Meta-learning

Perhaps the most valuable outcome for a client is meta-learning. The link with double loop learning stems from the belief that the work of a mentor-coach is not just about helping a person think through how to move from where s/he is to where s/he needs/wants to be, but to become familiar with *the process by which that 'thinking through' was framed or guided*. There is a strong commitment here to empowering and enabling the client so that s/he becomes increasingly independent from the mentor-coach. This means becoming competent and eventually confident in using the model, framework and skills, especially formulating questions, as a set of tools for their own thinking and reflection so that s/he can make progress with issues on his/her own whether they are similar or different in kind from those that s/he has focused on with her/his mentor-coach. How can this be brought about?

Should the model be made explicit?

Facilitators on courses designed to develop skills and understanding in this model are often asked whether it is good practice to show the client the six stage model. Often course participants have in mind explaining the model to their client before the first interaction begins. Experience suggests that such practice has some potential to be distracting.

It has been indicated in Chapter 2 that when using this model a mentor-coach might (maybe should) indicate that s/he will be framing the interaction in a particular model so as to give a sense that there is a direction and a structure to help them both make a constructive learning journey that is often quite complex. It can also be helpful to indicate a willingness to share the model – perhaps after the client has experienced it. Clearly a judgement is called for. Whenever a client asks to see the model and have a short explanation of how it works, it should not be refused. The mentor-coach should provide whatever explanation is needed to help the client have control and feel stronger. In practice most are happy to know that they have the security of a structure and are willing to wait for the exposition till they have experienced it. Like the courses provided for mentor-coaches the process itself is experiential.

Nevertheless, unless the client comes to understand the framework and the process (and included in the word 'understand' is the notion of having a 'feel' for the process) the learning will remain single loop. To become double loop the learning must include learning about the model – how it works and why it comprises each of the six stages as well as what each stage includes – and a sense of its applicability as a process to other issues that they may encounter. Is this what the reader is to understand by the term 'meta-learning'?

One possibility is that a client might be encouraged to read Part One of this book. Indeed, the writers intend the book for both mentor-coaches and clients.

Making meta-learning explicit

Meta-learning goes a stage further. Carnell (2006) helpfully talks of mentoring and coaching encounters as learning conversations in the constructionist and co-constructionist senses. In those contexts the dialogue that occurs includes reflection not only on what has been learned and the processes that were facilitated by the mentor or coach but also on the parts of the process that were particularly helpful to the client, why that was so and how it impinged upon the way that the client learns best. It is vital to note, however, that this is not a static matter and is categorically not simply so that the learner – mentor-coach or client – can stick to modes and methods of learning that make them feel most safe. These should merely be starting points.

It is likely, in fact, that the model advanced in this book will have already taken the client beyond his/her customary patterns of learning and the encounter is likely to have included some reflections on this fact. For instance, it is by no means uncommon for a client never to have been asked before to engage in envisioning the future and its potential through drawing a picture. Frequently, both on courses and in fieldwork, the facilitator or mentor-coach faces some resistance to the request to draw a picture. Doubts are raised by the participant/client as to whether s/he can do it, how helpful it will be, whether it is likely to open up possibilities and so on. Assuming s/he can be gently persuaded to engage in the activity, it is very likely that reluctance will be followed by surprise as to how helpful it was as part of the learning process. The awakening of a latent creativity is often palpable. It is always valuable, and particularly with those who work in schools, to consider whether such an approach could have other applications.

Extending learning behaviours

Readers who regard themselves as visual learners will not be surprised by the previous paragraph. That illustrates the key point. The technique invites the learner who does not see him/herself as a visual learner to step beyond his/her habitual learning behaviours. The critical point about reflection upon how you normally learn is that it permits thinking about how your learning behaviours might be extended. This is a legitimate topic in the mentoring-coaching relationship. Only when you can reflect upon how learning occurs to the point that enables you to consider expanding the range of learning behaviours can it truly be claimed that meta-learning is taking place. In truth, if 'knowing is doing and doing is knowing' you have perhaps to move beyond considering extending your learning behaviours to actually trying new approaches and practising them until they too become 'hard-wired'. In particular, the model of mentoring-coaching empowers and enables the client both to learn and to learn more about how to learn. When it goes according to plan, the process performs this function cogently for both parties to the relationship.

Who's doing the learning?

In many models of mentoring or coaching it is the client who is expected to do the learning. The mentor or coach dispenses the wisdom or expertize that is to be learned and the balance of talk is often in his/her favour, that is, s/he does most of it. This corresponds to the notion of learning as 'being taught'. In those models the mentor or coach is assumed to have or know answers. In this model the mentor-coach is thinking things through *with* the client.

In constructionist models of learning the learner does the majority of talking but it is still possible for the learning to be one-sided. Mentoring-coaching overtly espouses the co-constructionist model of learning with *both* parties engaged actively in dialogue – a search for meaning. Even so, the task of the mentor-coach as facilitator is to help formulate relevant and helpful questions. It is categorically not to give answers. So it involves listening, with enabling prompts and probes as the client tries out a variety of responses until clarity emerges for him/her. The most valuable help a mentor-coach can give is help in framing questions. This can only come from a disposition by the mentor-coach that is one of genuine inquiry – *of learning*. Once the client has developed a significant degree of skill in evolving questions, s/he is well on the way to becoming an autonomous learner. (The word autonomous is used rather than independent as the potentially social nature of learning in the richest models has high value.)

Lest it not be absolutely clear by now, it is worth summarizing so far some of the responses to the questions that opened this chapter:

- All human beings learn – it's part of their nature.
- Learning is the way we respond to our environment and to activity in it that we encounter.
- It means developing new behaviours that can become our natural reaction.
- It's about our personal management of change, including our management of ourselves.
- Learning is far more than what is traditionally thought of as education.
- Mentoring-coaching involves rich forms of learning.

Learning organizations

It follows from these principles that the concept of mentoring-coaching holds great potential for all individuals and for most organizations. It is now being applied widely in education, especially in London, and as far afield as South-East Asia and Australia. It has evident potential for organizations across the public service sector, but will only become part of the culture of such organizations if someone near to the top of their leadership structure has a vision of them as *learning organizations*.

There is a strong stream of literature on organizational learning, perhaps most clearly exemplified by Argyris and Schon (1996). Most of it addresses the private and, particularly, commercial sectors. Whereas public sector organizations are likely to survive (because of twin support from public policy and funding) whether or not they engage in organizational learning, private companies of all shapes and sizes depend for their very survival on their ability to adapt to rapid and often radical change and, therefore, how effectively they are able to learn.

Organizations and companies are among other things collections of individuals. The *learning* character of a company is totally dependent on whether the individuals in it are learners and whether learning is a predominant disposition. The practice and culture of mentoring-coaching can, when consistently applied, guarantee such a disposition, almost regardless of the environment. This is not to say that every activity in life and work should be approached in the mode needed for this model to operate. It *is* to say that when something needs thinking through – when learning is needed – the principles and methodology of the model set out in this book will do a great part of the business. This is more explicitly the case in all aspects of education.

If learning matters, mentoring-coaching matters too.

Feedback

A postscript on the subject of feedback may be important before leaving for the time being this aspect of mentoring-coaching.

In much of the writing on the two issues of mentoring and coaching feedback is a point in focus. Usually it is seen as something the mentor or coach *gives* to the client. In other words feedback is seen as coming from an external source. The original notion of feedback does not accord with this perception. The early use of the term was to convey the concept of a system (most notably a sound production system) that produced an output that it could not itself manage. This would lead, for example, to a high-pitched whistling noise emerging from a speaker through an overperforming amplifier. The system itself produced the feedback.

To give a concrete and simple example, the common notion of feedback might be expressed when a parent tells a child that s/he will have tummy ache from eating too much of a particular food. What is happening is that the parent makes a judgement and *tells* it to the child. In essence, however, it's the tummy ache itself that is the feedback. The feedback is effective when the child has been helped not only to understand the connections between the pain and its cause but also to evolve behaviours that will produce a different outcome. The learning involved is most effective when the child is able to articulate this for him/herself and acquire self-managing abilities applicable to similar future situations. In other words, feedback involves very little, if any, *telling* and is entirely about a person processing his/her experience to the point where there is clarity. Because this process occurs through language, the help of another person in gaining this clarity can be very valuable.

Whenever this view is advanced in public, it is likely that someone will say that this is impracticable because it takes time. One might respond by saying that it is not worth wasting *any* time on learning that is not effective, and that while teaching takes place *in* time, learning takes place *over* time. The same train of thought may need to be pursued with regard to the subject of mentoring-coaching as a whole.

The question at issue here is the place of feedback in mentoring-coaching. Feedback is central to mentoring-coaching. It may, however, be sensible for a mentor-coach to think more in terms of *reflecting back*. So when a client needs some judgement on his or her thinking or upon their actions, to help them decide further action, the mentor-coach has the responsibility to help the client replay the actions or events in question. This replay would be aided by prompts to ensure the whole of the event has been explored, followed by probing questions to help the client evaluate not only the event itself but also their behaviours and most importantly, their intentions.

The mentor-coach articulates no judgement – negative or positive. S/he acts in a way that helps the client to frame his/her thoughts about the actions in question and to form a judgement about them in his/her own words – words that express for him/her the meaning or significance of the events/actions that are, as a result of the process, in clear focus. When there is clarity in the mind (and words) of the client with regard both to the events and their meaning/ significance, feedback has been achieved. It is a matter of clarity in the mind of the originator of the actions. This clarity is most effectively achieved by help in thinking the events through and then framing the language that expresses their impact and value. Feedback, in this sense, is at the heart of learning.

Questions for the reader to reflect on

- What do *you* mean by 'learning'?
- How helpful to you is the idea of 'meta-learning'?
- How aware are you of the ways in which, and the conditions under which, you learn best?
- What might you need to do to extend your own range of learning behaviours? How might you begin to do this? What kind of learning activity might offer you a manageable challenge?
- Is there clarity in your mind about the distinctions between 'instructionist', 'constructionist', and 'co-constructionist' models of learning? How helpful might these models be in supporting your own learning and the learning of others?
- How close for you is the relationship between knowing and doing?
- Why does learning need to be made explicit?
- How helpful is it to think of learning as 'wiring' in the brain, and of deep learning as something 'hard-wired'?
- What part does learning play in the organization you work in? In your thinking about this what models of learning have prominence?
- To what degree would you say that your organization is characterized by learning dispositions?
- To what extent does mentoring-coaching seem to you to be almost synonymous with learning?
- What is your current understanding of the term 'feedback'? How has this chapter helped you to reflect on the giving and receiving of feedback?
- How easy is it for you to identify clearly the learning that takes place within the mentoring-coaching relationship by, on the one hand, the client and, on the other, by the mentor-coach?
- What especially are the things that the mentor-coach might learn?
- If mentoring-coaching is primarily a form of learning and conscious learning is a distinguishing characteristic of being human, what value would you want to place on this model and its practice in a range of contexts?

21 Mentoring-coaching in leading-managing

Mentoring-coaching is a very powerful way of leading. It enables the leader to build long-term capacity and is thus highly sustainable. It is a critical part of systems thinking, and is a very robust tool for professionals who are system leaders. Yet, as noted in earlier chapters, it can appear counter-cultural. In spite of the loud rhetoric around the issue of shared or distributed leadership, much of the reality is that insufficient patience is expended on system and capacity building. Credit goes too often to those who claim to be able to fix things quickly. Heroic or charismatic leadership attracts public acclaim even though it can be argued that such styles create dependency through external rather than intrinsic motivation and even undermine capacity. Mentoring-coaching does none of those things. It is entirely about helping people in all walks of life become clear about the contribution they can make, and how and where they can most effectively make it. There is a wealth of research to support this claim – from professions and work contexts across the board and from social and personal contexts. This chapter explores these thoughts and shows how leadership at all levels can become a less stressful, more purposeful and fulfilling activity.

What are leadership and management?

In the last ten years there has been a shift in the popular focus on how all kinds of organizations work. This has included more careful definition of how they are *led* – as distinct from how they are *managed*. For the purpose of this chapter a point of distinction might be that management is 'doing things right' while leadership is 'doing the right things' (Bennis and Nanus, 1985). It could be expressed in terms of management being operational and leadership being strategic. This book is not primarily about leadership and/or management. The assumption is made that both leadership and management are essential to the effective and purposeful functioning of any organization. To neglect either is to court disaster.

There are, however, very different ways of both managing and leading. It is not the distinction between the two terms that is the focus of this chapter, but rather the concepts that together they might represent and how mentoring-coaching offers profound ways of making respectful, as distinct from instrumental, approaches to leadership and management highly effective. A cautionary note is offered at the start. The concept of leading that aligns most powerfully with mentoring-coaching is much less likely to propel its practitioners to public prominence than heroic, charismatic or even successful autocratic leaders. Indeed, in some sectors most acclaim is given to the leader/manager apparently able to perform quick fixes and fast turn-arounds. This is not to say that there is no place for rescue types of action by leaders. Though they often have only a short-term effect, they are sometimes necessary – *but never sufficient.*

Everyone as leader/manager

An underlying presupposition of what is written here is that all human beings have leadership and management capability to some degree. It is certainly the case that 'doing the right things' and 'doing things right' are aspirations that might characterize every aspect of human activity, not just those that relate to the work context. From the earliest stage of life outside the womb humans are developing these concepts and learning to behave accordingly. Both notions encapsulate something highly significant in the evolution of human consciousness. The reader is invited, therefore, to think of leadership and management in very broad terms, though it may help focus on mentoring-coaching implications if they are discussed in slightly formal terms – as in the leadership of an organization.

What follows however is not couched in narrow terms. For by the word 'organizations' is meant groups, both large and small, of human beings working and/or living together for explicitly shared purposes; it might include a commercial company of any size or scale, a hospital, a school, a police service, a college or university, a local authority, a bank (local or national), a department store, a village, a local community, or a section or department within any of these – and many other such working groups. It might also include a family or group of friends or relatives as well as a club or society. Within education it may mean a class, or a working group of three or four staff or students (or both) or even a pair. In other words, we are thinking here about humans working or living together.

Leadership/management is not a 'steady state'

No assumption is made about leadership/management roles being fixed, monolithic or steady state. Within any organization everyone can have some kind of leadership role and no one will always operate through leadership functions. Everyone will sometimes be led, even the person paid the highest salary and having the most public prominence. (This is an essential condition if everyone is sometimes to lead, even though some people's leadership may seem to operate on seemingly prosaic functions.) It is simply assumed that leadership goes with insight – the person who has, by dint of regular experience or systematic thinking, the most insight in a particular context will be best placed to offer a lead on how most effectively to do something and to argue the importance of its being done.

Even though a leader in whatever context may have a particular view – from experience, systematic thinking or other form of insight – about what needs to be done and how, this cannot be evolved in isolation. This is because of another characteristic of leadership, namely the ability to get those who are being led to join their own efforts to the venture or aspects of the venture that is the object of the organization. Leadership has also been described as doing things through others. If this description holds true a leader needs insights – sometimes called 'vision' – to be shared by the team members s/he is leading.

Sharing vision as an example of leadership

Sharing vision is often treated as no more than telling people what are the right things to do, or circulating a document that states it. This method of supposedly sharing vision is merely a means of *telling* people, whom it would be more proper to call 'followers', what it is the leader expects of them. It can be helpful to know what a leader expects of those s/he leads – indeed, it is a prerequisite of effective leadership at a basic level. This is not, however, *sharing vision*. A vision is not shared by *telling or writing*.

A vision is shared if it represents in some way those who are said to share it. This is not to say that it is something democratic in a strict sense. It means rather that the team members can identify links to things of value that matter to them, and can see how the abilities they have can be harnessed to the vision and also how they can make their contribution to its implementation. Generating a vision – a critical aspect of the work of leaders – involves careful joint consideration of what matters to team members, what it is that they place value upon and what it is that they can contribute to the enterprise. Generating a vision is a multifaceted activity involving all the team. One person can *devise* a vision, and this is a possible way of *creating a vision* but it can so easily remain the professional territory of a single person where others feel alien. The word *'generating'* has been chosen because a truly shared vision can only come about through a *generative* process – where the ownership is shared and where team members genuinely feel that they *possess it.*

Generating a shared vision is a particularly important example of the crucial work of a leader – hence its selection as the first concrete example of what is meant by the title of this chapter. It will be clear to the reader from the content of the previous two paragraphs that generating a shared vision requires leaders and their teams to engage in a significant degree of thinking, and that the outcome of that thinking implies very strongly a sharing of *responsibility* – the title given to the pivotal stage of the model of mentoring-coaching that this book expounds (see Chapter 5). Further, the stage that follows – labelled *Future* – is directly about *vision* and how vision might become reality. What is being argued here is that there is a constant and close connection between the business of generating and implementing a shared vision – a central part of leadership – and the stages of the mentoring-coaching model. The activity that needs to go on between leaders and their teams is *thinking things through together.*

In summary, no shared vision can emerge in any context unless something happens that is very like the activity this book seeks to promote – *mentoring-coaching.* Shared vision has no point unless it goes on to include the management part, that is, putting into action whatever is necessary to bring the vision to reality – *coaching.* What is contended is that mentoring in this definition equates to the work of leadership and coaching equates to the work of management.

So, to express it as shown in Figure 21.1 might help:

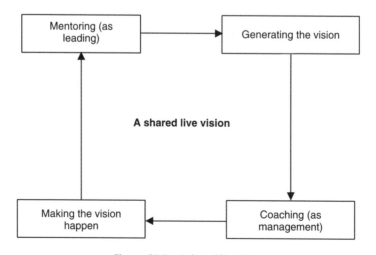

Figure 21.1 A shared live vision

The word 'live' has been introduced into Figure 21.1 to indicate that no vision is ever static. Further, it is more likely that a shared vision will be 'alive' than one that has simply been devised by a single person and set down on paper. Like all powerful models representing human activity the model of the Shared Live Vision is iterative and cyclical, so that as the vision is made to happen, it is evaluated and reviewed, using the processes set out in the first part of this book and the stages of the mentoring-coaching model.

The reader's attention is drawn to the fact that, although this figure separates the terms mentoring and coaching, it does so only to the degree that leadership and management are separated. It has been suggested that neglecting either leadership or management is to court disaster. Similarly the whole thrust of this book implies strongly that disaster is also courted by neglecting either mentoring or coaching, as is argued in the final chapter. That is why it is seen as a single two-part process. The point here (so as not to pre-empt the next chapter) is to suggest that leadership and management could be taken as a two-part process that can best be carried out by a parallel two-part process of mentoring-coaching.

Further important work of leaders

Generating a shared vision is by no means the only important work of leaders/ managers. It has already been argued that creating and managing culture is similarly important (and indeed that this activity overlaps with the generation and implementation of shared vision). Hand in hand with both of these are the vital issues of clarifying and guarding the organization's values, articulating aims, perhaps making clear the philosophy underpinning the values, developing the climate in which team members work on a day-to-day basis, holding team members to account and developing team members as well as the organisation itself. This is by no means an exhaustive list of the work of leaders.

'Doing *to?*'

The reader is invited to note, however, that the language used in the previous paragraph was selected to signify that this is work that leaders do, and that they do it to the organization and to the team members within it. The reason for putting it in this way is that this is how it is generally seen. Contrasted with this traditional view is the mentoring-coaching methodology where, instead of leaders doing it *to* their organizations and teams, they do it *with* others and *help others to do it* for themselves. How this can happen may by now be clear to the reader, but it is worth reiterating in some way. An example may help.

An example: holding people accountable

According to Hay McBer (1998), one of the distinguishing characteristics of a highly effective leader is that s/he consistently holds team members to account to the point of 'confronting poor performance'. Many leaders/managers find this difficult to do without 'going over the top' and eroding the confidence and competence of their staff. As a result – due to the emotional factors involved – it is often neglected for fear of getting it wrong, doing more harm than good. Somewhere between being brutal on the one hand and ducking the issue altogether on the other, there is a point to be found that avoids the dangers without avoiding the issue. Indeed, there is a way of doing this that not only minimizes the dangers but also maximizes the benefits. That way is through the processes and skills of mentoring-coaching.

It should be noted that reference to mentoring-coaching here is not to a formal process carried out on specific occasions but to the structure and nature of a working relationship and the skills and behaviours (competencies) that characterize it. In this context (confronting poor performance) it might work something like this:

Subject Leader (SL): When we decided to rewrite the scheme of work for KS2, you agreed to draft the section for Year 5. How did that go?

Team Member (TM): Well, I finished it on time.

SL: How pleased were you with what was achieved?

TM: Well I finished it in time for the team meeting.

SL: So how helpful was it to the team?

TM: (after a pause) Quite helpful, I think.

SL: Say some more about that.

TM: (after a further pause) Well, they didn't seem to like my ideas all that much.

SL: Why do you think that was?

TM: I'm not sure, but they said that what I proposed was not very clear.

SL: In what way?

TM: They said I hadn't set it out in the format agreed for schemes of work.

SL: Had you?

TM: Well, I suppose not . . .

SL: So, did the way you set it out seem better to you?

TM: Not specially, but I had got most things in there somewhere.

SL: Most things?

TM: Well, I'd got most things in, but I hadn't proposed clear learning objectives.

SL: How did that affect what you'd done?

TM: Mary said that she couldn't see the point of some things that I thought were quite important because the objectives hadn't been proposed.

SL: How far does that matter?

TM: Well, if people couldn't see the point of what I've submitted, it's a bit of a waste of time – mine and theirs.

SL: So, what do you need to do next?

The conversation moves on in the same way to look at action that needs to be taken to recover the situation and to avoid similar difficulties in future.

A similar conversation was held by one of the authors of this book with a teacher following observation of a 'relatively poor' technology lesson with a group of Year 8 students (12–13 year olds). The teacher was invited to make a general comment on the effectiveness of the lesson. The leader (as mentor-coach) asked the teacher to share (with prompts) the story of the lesson – what had actually happened. The prompts were in the form of questions. When a narrative that accorded reasonably with the perception of both parties had been shared, the observer asked about the learning intentions and the plan the teacher had made to give effect to them. This produced an agreement that the learning intentions were appropriate, but as she explained the plan the teacher began to question whether it was adequate in certain respects. The observer limited himself to asking clarifying questions. The teacher eventually stated a number of things she felt she could do to make her planning more appropriate.

It had occurred to the observer that one weakness of the lesson was that some of the more able children had stopped learning ten minutes before the lesson ended:

Observer (O): Did you want the brighter children to help others during that time? (They had agreed that what had happened at this point was that these children got up and went round the room chatting to friends.)

Teacher (T): No. I wanted them to move on to some slightly more challenging task.

O: Had you included this in your plan?

T: Yes. Look! Here are my notes on it.

O: You refer in your notes to some additional work-sheets for them. Forgive me, but I didn't see those work-sheets.

T: No. That's because I left them in my bag at the start of the lesson and forgot about them!

The conversation ended with the observer inviting the teacher to sum up the things she would want – as a result of the experience and the shared analysis – to do differently in future. She confirmed them in a note of the meeting later that week.

There was no particular note of threat in either of these two conversations, though lines of management can express an inherent power imbalance that may infer threat and effective leader/managers need to be aware of this. The main point, however, is that in both instances the leader/manager takes time to hear the story and asks questions to gain information and generate understanding – both for him/herself and for his/her team member. In each case some point of focus is uncovered by dialogue that enables the team member to discern for him/herself a critical point in the process where a different action might have produced a better result.

A time-consuming activity?

The cost of mentoring-coaching in terms of time is relatively small but not totally insignificant. The benefits are on two levels.

The first is that future projects/lessons are likely to turn out better in the hands of the two team members than in the instances narrated. On the same level the team members have *themselves* developed some insight into how to perform better in similar circumstances and thus have developed their professional competence.

Perhaps more significantly, and hence at a deeper level, they have actively engaged in a thinking process that can be applied across a much wider range of their professional activity. They may need help with this process on one or two further occasions before it becomes a habit (or *hard wired* as it was described in the previous chapter), but once it does so they will become self-starters in terms not only of the quality of their work and their ability to critique it, but also in terms of their broader self-development.

A discerning reader will be able to see how similar aspects of the work of leaders/managers – including those others listed nine paragraphs back – may be transformed from things leaders/managers do to others into things that team members can be helped to learn how to do for themselves. Why is this so important?

Many conversations of the writers with leaders and managers, and various research studies provide evidence of the stress to which leaders and managers are constantly subjected. There are many accounts, too, of burn-out experienced by people in this role – sometimes after only a relatively short period. In some professions this is apparently so commonplace that there is a growing shortage of people willing to take such responsibility. For example, there is a looming crisis in headteacher recruitment.

One cause of such stress and burn-out is that leaders/managers find that they cannot cope with all the things they are expected to do – often *to others*. This includes not only the tasks themselves but also the resentment they perceive from others when things get difficult. They also cite the sheer quantity of tasks – many of them mundane, that almost anyone in the organization could do – that are heaped on them hour by hour. This heap of tasks is not put upon them malevolently. It is generated by the culture of dependency that grows from the expectation that the leader/manager will sort everything out that goes wrong, that leaders are 'heads of answers' rather than 'leaders of learning'. It doesn't have to be that way.

Leadership that empowers and enables

Once a leader establishes that and signals that s/he will help others to sort things out (largely by helping them to think things through and identify the action *they* need to take) the burden on the leader/manager begins to diminish. This is not the only benefit. The team members themselves begin to feel both empowered and enabled and as a result find their work more fulfilling, their self-esteem more resilient and their sense of self-worth more robust.

The discussion has centred so far on the parallels that can be made between mentoring-coaching and leading/managing (or should it be *leading-managing*?) It might be helpful to focus for a short while on certain behaviours or patterns of behaviour that leaders and managers need to display. The word 'display' has a particular force. It is not the same as 'employ'. To display a behaviour is *to be seen by others* – in this case by those being led – to employ it. The difference is crucial. Leadership is a highly visible activity.

Mentoring-coaching skills in the leadership role

What is being argued here is that leaders and managers may need to display the whole of the mentoring-coaching cycle in a number of different circumstances, both with whole teams and with individuals – for example, when generating a shared vision or helping someone with a longer-term personal development plan. It would attract ridicule to suggest that leaders and managers ought, or would be able, to employ that process/model as their standard approach to most of their actions on a day-to-day basis. Instead, it is argued that in organizations (schools, teams, sections, departments, branches, families etc.) where a significant number of members are familiar with the principles and practices of what is called mentoring-coaching, leaders who use the key skills and subskills on a day-to-day basis have a more sustainable and profound impact.

By this stage the reader may welcome being reminded that the two critical skills are listening and questioning.

Listening liberates leaders and led

In his book *Leadership and Liberation* Sean Ruth (2005) argues forcibly that listening is the fundamental practice of leadership – implying strongly that leaders who listen assiduously liberate both themselves and their team members. This can seem like a truism, for leaders who manifestly don't listen often encounter deep and unnecessary turbulence. Worse still, they bring that turbulence upon those around them. Most readers will have observed such circumstances (and maybe suffered some of the unnecessary turbulence!) and may, therefore, think that what has just been stated is blindingly obvious. What is not so obvious is that there are levels of listening – from staying quiet just long enough to spot the moment to make one's point to deep and sustained attention to the other person and to the intention behind their words. It is this latter behaviour that leaders need to practice. When team members have been listened to by their leader/manager in this way they stay listened to.

Many leaders behave as though they do not have sufficient time to do this. When they make time for it, they usually find they make a bigger impact – *simply by listening* – than they could with many speeches or hours of writing.

Questioning also liberates leaders

Questioning is the twin of listening in the toolkit of leaders. Many leaders seem to see themselves as 'Head of Answers'. This is a very stressful and hugely demanding role to have. To purport to be 'Head of Answers' is also deeply dishonest (which is part of the stress, for it cannot be sustained). It is not, however, simply that anything other than listening and questioning creates stress and is dishonest that comprises an argument in their favour. It is that genuine questioning is also liberating both for leaders and team members. 'Genuine' is inserted here because it is necessary to exclude that category of question that invites the other person to come up with the answer that the questioner is holding in his/her head. Those are just silly games – usually played to accrue personalized power for the supposed questioner. To be positive about the idea of genuine questioning is to focus on questions that will help the other person communicate their intention, develop and articulate meaning, and evolve shared understanding.

As is argued elsewhere in this book, questions are the drivers of learning. If the culture of the learning organization is to develop, rather than be led by a 'Head of Answers', teams need a lead learner. That person will distinguish him/herself by the quality of questions s/he asks, and by the inward and outward listening that follows the questions.

There are two obvious benefits accruing from this kind of leadership behaviour. The first is the thinking that team members are invited to share with the leader. The second is the habit of formulating skilled questions that they can ask themselves and each other as well as their leader.

When team members start to engage in this kind of questioning with other members of the organization (leaders and managers included), learning will take place and will accelerate in pace over time throughout the team. [There is no intention here to say anything about something that is called Accelerated Learning since neither writer has any experience of it on which to base comment.] There is one sure way to accelerate learning, namely to help learners (team members in all organizations) to advance their skill in formulating questions, and to develop questioning as a lifelong habit.

Mentoring-coaching and sustainability

Before closing this chapter it is worth referring to what have become known as leadership styles, as researched by Hay McBer. In his paper, 'Leadership That Gets Results', Goleman (2000) quotes correlations between six different leadership styles and long-term high standards. His disquisition is relatively undeveloped (with regard, for example, to how each style can most effectively be deployed) but the correlations he quotes give rise to the view that the style he calls coaching has a very high correlation with sustainable high levels of effectiveness. (Readers should try to distinguish between correlation and causation. There is a subtle but important difference. The focus on what is meant by coaching is what is important here, as it is one half of what this book has been about.)

The critical parts of *coaching* are the evaluation and analysis – the talk – in which it is vital that the understanding of the client is displayed and reinforced. The opportunity to practise what has been learned is also essential. So:

Coaching = Practice + Talk

Or, broken down still further, it might be expressed thus:

Coaching = Demonstration (by the coach) + Talk + (Practice + Talk – primarily by the client)

The distinguishing feature of the encounter is the talk, particularly the talk by the client. When leaders structure their leadership interventions in this way they build capacity in their organization. Further, although it can take time it has the greatest and longest term impact of all leadership behaviours upon the standards of performance by their team members and by their organization.

Coaching, stress and compassion

In a recent paper, Boyatzis, Smith and Blaize (2006), propose that coaching presents an opportunity in the work of leadership that involves consideration of the issues of stress and compassion. They argue that, through the experience of working in this way, the stress of leadership is alleviated through the compassion that coaching inevitably generates. The analysis advanced is neuroscientific and the evidence adduced is an account of the chemicals at work in the brain when this kind of activity is occurring, and how they counteract the chemicals produced by stress. The current book is not intended to be scientific in the same sense and readers can access the detail through the bibliography.

It was argued earlier that both stress and distress in a variety of situations is alleviated to a considerable degree by being coached. At this point the claim is made that through compassion (one might prefer to focus on *empathy*) coaching alleviates the stress of *the coach* – particularly the stress that the coach experiences from other aspects of leading/managing. This is an important part of what this book refers to as *humane* approaches to leadership.

In an earlier chapter it was suggested that a mentor-coach might not usually be the line manager of the client. The reason offered for this statement was that issues of accountability can get in the way of the relationship needed in mentoring-coaching. Considered in the way described in this chapter, accountability is much less likely to do so – indeed, it may actually enhance that relationship. When this is the case, one might argue that it is very appropriate for the mentor-coach to be the team member's line manager. It might even be better to put it the other way round and say that the most effective leaders or line managers work on a consistent basis with their team members in the mode of mentor-coach.

Some issues for the reader to reflect on

- How do you define the terms leadership and management? What distinctions do you make between the two? Does one of those terms label your role more accurately than the other?
- Think of the people you work with. Try to find for each of them an aspect of the work of the organisation that involves leadership – no matter how big or small. Have you been able to include everyone? Is there anyone who always leads and never is led?
- To what extent can leadership be a shared activity?
- What does distributed leadership look like and what might its connection be to mentoring-coaching as a leadership approach?
  Is your organization guided by a clear vision? If so, whose vision is it?

How was it evolved? If not, what would be the way in which you would like to see it developed?

- What, in your opinion, are the most important sorts of things that leaders do?
- What styles of leadership have you experienced in people who have led you? Which gave you most confidence in the leader? When you lead, what is (are) the dominant style(s)? What makes something you do into a 'style'?
- How difficult is it to hold team members to account in an appropriate manner? Can neutrally toned and carefully structured questions do the job?
- How, in your view, can/do leaders most effectively empower and enable team members? What are the precise skills needed to do this?
- Is there a sort of paradox in the idea that listening liberates both those who lead and those who are led? Can questioning be viewed similarly?
- How far does it seem to you that unthinking leadership behaviours, including pace setting, can lead to burn-out? Can this be effectively countered by a mentoring-coaching approach for much of the time?
- What is the critical component in mentoring-coaching? How do listening and questioning come into it?
- It was argued earlier that stress and distress can be alleviated by being mentor-coached. Is it realistic to think that the stress of leadership can be alleviated through being a mentor-coach? What place might compassion have in this dynamic?

22 The crucial hyphen

The literature of mentoring and coaching is rife with definitions of both, based often on the claims and counterclaims that seek to highlight particular features of either and to downplay the merits of the other. More recently coaching has been very much in the ascendancy and mentoring has waned somewhat in popularity. Some models of coaching regularly begin with the question, 'What is your problem?' assuming that there *is* a problem and that the client already knows what it is!

The authors view the above as unfortunate and plainly mistaken and argue that effective coaching cannot begin until the clarifying mentoring phase, as defined in this book, has been undertaken. In the model of mentoring-coaching set out here mentoring and coaching are seen as distinctive but complementary and mutually indispensable phases of an integrated helping process that is focused throughout on the individual client. This said, the mentor-coach can also gain great benefits from the process.

As this book reaches its conclusion it is important to return to the subject of uniqueness – the uniqueness of each person, of each person's situation, of the relationship between mentor-coach and client, of each mentoring-coaching encounter and also of the concept and model that are expounded and advocated in this book.

The uniqueness of concept, model and process is represented and to an important degree generated by the way that mentoring and coaching are linked, rather than as – in the view of many writers – set in opposition to one another. This uniqueness and the relationship of mentoring and coaching are both bound by the hyphen.

Clutterbuck and Megginson (2005) analyse the turf war claims of mentoring and coaching and demonstrate 'how practitioners in both fields have tried to claim the facilitative end of the developmental spectrum for themselves, while denigrating the other by placing it at the directive end'. They conclude:

> And so the lesson for proponents of both mentoring and coaching has to be that devaluing one approach at the expense of the other simply reduces the credibility of both.

The purpose of this book is to provide both a sound rationale and a proven practical guide for an integrated approach to mentoring-coaching. Hence the hyphen!

Vision alone is daydreaming.
Action alone is merely passing the time of day.
Vision and action together can change the world. (Barker)

In the model of mentoring-coaching presented here, mentoring focuses on gaining understanding by the client, of the context and the point(s) of focus emerging from careful analysis of the interface between the individual, the context and their role. Mentoring is the overarching concept, assembling accurately the picture of present 'reality' and any tensions/points of focus as perceived by the client. But there would be little point in the exercise if the process were to stop there. The point is not merely to analyse the present situation, but to change it! Coaching helps the client identify, plan and effect the changes which s/he perceives to be necessary to realize the vision identified for the client's future. Mentoring-coaching entails moving from framing and understanding the present to reframing and implementing the preferred future alternative through carefully reflected action. Mentoring is the essential prerequisite to coaching and must be followed by it to avoid 'analysis paralysis'. Mentoring and coaching belong together. To engage in one without the other is futile. Hence the hyphen!

Stage 3 of the model is of crucial importance. The mentor-coach's insistence on the client's taking ownership and responsibility for what s/he has identified as the aspect of his/her situation that both needs to change and can be changed. This helps seal the commitment to taking whatever actions are necessary. It is also pivotal in marking the client's readiness and commitment to consider action designed to effect change – a resolve that may well be put to the test again at Stage 6 as the reality of carrying through intentions and decisions is brought closer through micro-coaching. In this sense Stages 3 and 6 can be seen as bridges from thinking to action. But they are definitely not bridges for burning! Very often clients will need to return to explore and refine further aspects of their context before crossing back again into the coaching action zone. Hence the hyphen!

There will be occasions when the whole process of mentoring-coaching will progress smoothly and straightforwardly through the various stages of the model. However, in the authors' experience such occasions are rare. Rather, the role of the mentor-coach is often analogous to that of the moviemaker – panning out to capture the big picture/context and frame the overall scene/context (mentoring), then focusing in to highlight particular features/issues (coaching), and finally pinpointing and 'exploding' key details (micro-coaching). This process, moving at the speed of thought and feeling, often requires zooming in-out-and-in-again to ensure that the dynamic relationship of present reality, preferred vision and action are held together objectively, appreciatively and constructively to support the client. Hence the hyphen!

The arrows linking the various stages of the model with each other and, individually and severally, with the use of evidence at the heart of the model represent not only the linkage, but also the continuity and coherence of the model. Collectively the hyphen and arrows symbolize the dynamic processes both of mentoring-coaching and the need to acknowledge the complex and by no means always straightforward nature of genuine personal change and development in people. Hence the hyphen!

Some guru mentors and coaches still attempt, explicitly or covertly, to provide *their* 'solutions' to *their* diagnoses of clients' 'problems'. But such approaches fail to respect the individual and can so easily and dangerously bypass the person at the centre of the process and leave the client feeling more *in*adequate and *dis*empowered. We need to understand in detail both the person and the context before we can help the individual client formulate and carry out a uniquely detailed plan of action that is both feasible and acceptable to her/him. Hence the hyphen!

Meeting successfully the challenge of moving fluidly within and between the mentoring-coaching phases to facilitate this dynamic helping process can also provide enormous professional satisfaction and development for the mentor-coach. S/he needs to attend carefully to the client's responses to be able to sense her readiness to move on or need to return to a particular stage/phase – not to intervene, suggest, manipulate, tell or direct to save time, but rather to work empathetically, responsively and flexibly across both phases of the model at the client's pace and at the point s/he has currently reached. This requires of the mentor-coach a special combination of mental acuity and emotional and ethical attunement with the client. Hence the hyphen!

The model is heuristic – designed to help the client learn and progress through inquiry and discovery, and with increasing self-confidence and autonomy through both the mentoring and coaching phases of the process. But the journey is complex, so the model is designed to acknowledge and address the potential fallibility of the mentor-coach. For whatever reasons and however skilled one might be, one can sometimes get things wrong. If that happens, the model provides both a means of orientation – to allow for a check in which phase or stage one is – and where the focus needs to be at any time. It also provides the flexibility to get there swiftly, smoothly and without harm or embarrassment to self or the client. Hence the hyphen!

The process has integrity based on deep respect for individuals. It is, therefore, neither manipulative nor compliance-oriented. Rather, it is about helping *both* parties to the interaction to become more fully human and to enhance the contributions they make to their work and their social relationships. Mentoring-coaching is a complex developmental continuum along which one moves, often tentatively, forwards and backwards because of the challenging dynamic involved in preparing for and effecting meaningful personal change. The mentoring and coaching phases of the model are designed to help both partners orient themselves in moving through the stages of their developmental journeys as reflective practitioners. For all the above reasons mentoring and coaching are presented here as symbiotically linked, mutually indispensable, complementary parts of a continuous, holistic and integrated process. Hence the hyphen!

Some questions for the reader to reflect upon

- How would you respond to the contention that the main difference between mentoring and coaching is the spelling?
- Summarize in your own words the importance of the hyphen in the model of mentoring-coaching set out in this book!
- Would it change the nature of the model if one substituted 'and' in place of the hyphen? If you think it would, consider how!

References

NOTE: At several points in the text, statements by the authors have been quoted. Where the precise source of the text is not identified, the reader is to understand that the reference is to materials devised for mentoring-coaching training purposes. They give single indications of some of the thinking that is developed on the training programmes.

Argyris, C. and Schon, D. (1996) *Organizational Learning*. Boston, MA: Addison-Wesley.

Ash, E. and Quarry, P. (1995). *Listening*. Melbourne: Ash Quarry Productions.

Bacon, T. R. and Spears, K. I. (2003) *Adaptive Mentor-coach-coaching*. Mountain View, CA: Davies Black.

Bateson, G. (1972) *Steps to an Ecology of Mind*. London: Chandler.

Bennis, W. G. and Nanus, B. (1985) *Leaders*. New York: Harper & Row.

Berne, E. (1961) *Transactional Analysis in Psychotherapy*. New York: Grove Press.

Bottery, M. (2004) *The Challenges of Educational Leadership*. London: SAGE.

Boyatzis, R. E., Smith, M. L. and Blaize, N. (2006) 'Developing sustainable leaders through mentor-coach-coaching and compassion', *Academy of Management Learning and Education*, 5(1): 8–20.

Carnell, E. (2006) 'Mentor-coaching, mentor-coach-coaching and learning: examining the connections', *Professional Development Today*, 9(2).

Clutterbuck, D. (2001) *Everyone Needs a Mentor-coach*. London: Chartered Institute of Personnel and Development.

Cooperrider, D. L. and Whitney, D. (1999) Appreciative Inquiry: A positive revolution in change. In Holman, P., Devane, T. (eds), *The Change handbook: Group methods for shaping the future*. San Francisco, CA: Berrett-Koehler Publishers, Inc.

Cooperrider, D. L. and Whitney, D. (2005) *A Positive Revolution in Change: Appreciative Inquiry*. San Francisco, CA: Barrett-Koehler.

Damasio, A. (2000) *The Feeling of What Happens*. London: Vintage.

Deming, W. E. (1982) *Out of the Crisis*. Cambridge: Cambridge University Press.

Egan, G. (1992) *Adding Value*. Pacific Grove, CA: Brooks/Cole.

Egan, G. (2002) *The Skilled Helper*. Pacific Grove, CA: Brooks/Cole.

Freud, S. (2002) *Meta-psychology*. London: Penguin.

Fullan, M. (2001) *Leading in a Culture of Change*. San Francisco, CA: Jossey-Bass.

Fullan, M. (2005) *Leadership and Sustainability*. London: SAGE.

Gobillot, E. (2006) *The Connected Leader*. London: Kogan Page.

Goleman, D. (1996) *Emotional Intelligence*. London: Bloomsbury.

Goleman, D. (1998) *Working with Emotional Intelligence*. London: Bloomsbury.

Goleman, D., Boyatzis, R. and McKee, A. (2002) *The New Leaders*. London: Little Brow.

Harman, W. W. (1990) 'Shifting context for executive behavior: signs of change and re-evaluation', in S. Srivastva, D. L. Cooperrider (eds) *Appreciative Management and Leadership: The Power of Positive Thought and Action in Organization*. San Francisco, CA: Jossey-Bass.

Hay McBer (1998) *Leadership Programme for Serving Headteachers, programme notes*.

Henry, R. (2003) 'Leadership at every level: appreciative inquiry in education', *New Horizons for Learning*. Available at: http://www.newhorizons.org/trans/henry.htm.

Heron, J. (1996) *Co-operative Inquiry*. London: SAGE.

Hutton, J. (1997) Re-imagining the organisation of an institution: Managing Human Service Institutions in: *Integrity and Change: Mental health in the Marketplace*. Eileen Smith (Ed) Routledge.

Hutton, J. (2000) Working with the concept of Organisation in the mind (unpublished – available from the Grubb Institute, London. info@grubb.org.uk).

Hyakawa, S. I. (1949) *Language in Thought and Action*. Melbourne: Harcourt Australia.

Josephson, M. (2001) *You Don't Have to Be Sick to Get Better*. Los Angeles: Josephson Institute.

Joy, B. K. (2006) *Mentoring-coaching*. London: University of London.

Kolb, D. (1984) *Experiential Learning*. New York: Simon and Schuster.

Ledoux, J. (1998) *The Emotional Brain*. London: Wiedenfeld and Nicholson.

McClelland, D. (1973) 'Testing for competence rather than intelligence', American Psychologist, 28: 1–14.

Maslow, A. (1968/1999) *Towards a Psychology of Being*. New York: Wiley.

Maturana, H. and Varela, F. (1987) *The Tree of Knowledge: The Biological Roots of Human Understanding*. London: Shambhala.

Onions, C. T. (1983) *The Shorter Oxford Dictionary* (3rd edition). Oxford University Press.

Osbourn, S. M. and Harris, G. G. (1975) *Assertive Training for Women*. Springfield, IL: CA: Charles C. Thomas.

Osterman, K. and Kottkamp, R. (1994) 'Rethinking professional development', in N. Bennett, R. Glatter and R. Levacic (eds) *Improving Education Management Through Research and Consultancy*. London: SAGE.

Partington, A. (ed) (1992) *The Oxford Dictionary of Quotations* (4th edition) Chatham: BCA and Oxford University Press.

Reed, B. (2000) An Exploration of Role (unpublished – available from the Grubb Institute, London. info@grubb.org.uk).

Reed, B. (1999) Organisational Transformation in *Leading, Managing, Ministering – Challenging questions for Church and Society.* John Nelson (ed) Canterbury Press.

Rogers, C. R. (1961) *On Becoming a Person.* London: Constable.

Rogers, C. R. (1975) 'Empathic: an unappreciated way of being', *The Counselling Psychologist,* 5(2).

Ruth, S. (2005) *Leadership and Liberation.* Hove: Brunner-Routledge.

Schein, E. (1999) *Process Consultation Re-visited.* Boston, MA: Addison-Wesley.

Senge, P. (1990/1998) *The Fifth Discipline.* London: Random House.

Senge, P., Cambron-McCabe, N., Lucas, T., Smith, B., Dutton, J. and Kleiner, A. (2000) *Schools That Learn.* London: Nicholas Brealy.

Stewart, I. (1989) *Transactional Analysis Counselling in Action.* London: SAGE.

Vygotsky, L. (1978) *Mind in Society.* Cambridge, MA: Harvard University Press.

Watkins, C. (2001) Learning about Learning enhances performance. National School Improvement Network. *Research Matters* (13) Institute of Education, University of London.

Watkins, C. (2002) *Effective Learning.* London: Institute of Education.

Watkins, C. (2004) *Classrooms as Learning Communities.* London: Institute of Education.

Watkins, C. (2005) *Classrooms as Learning Communities.* Milton Park: Routledge.

White, T. W. (1996) 'Working in interesting times', *Vital Speeches of the Day,* LXII(15): 472–4.

Whitney, D. and Trosten-Bloom, A. (2003) The Power of Appreciative Inquiry: a Practical guide to positive change. San Francisco, CA: Berret-Koehler Publishers, Inc.

Yankelovich, D. (1999) *The Magic of Dialogue: Transforming Conflict into Cooperation.* London: Nicholas Brealy.

Zohar, D. and Marshall, I. (2000) *Spiritual Intelligence: The Ultimate Intelligence?* London: Bloomsbury.

Index

Locators shown in *italics* refer to figures.